The Postcolonial Careers of Santha Rama Rau

NEXT WAVE: NEW DIRECTIONS IN WOMEN'S STUDIES

A series edited by Inderpal Grewal, Caren Kaplan, and Robyn Wiegman

The Postcolonial Careers
of Santha Rama Rau

ANTOINETTE BURTON

Duke University Press ⚜ Durham and London 2007

© 2007 Duke University Press

All rights reserved

Printed in the United States of America

on acid-free paper ∞

Designed by Katy Clove

Typeset in Fournier by Keystone Typesetting, Inc.

Library of Congress Cataloging-in-Publication Data

appear on the last printed page of this book.

For Patricia Ryan
in memoriam
1937–2007

beautiful
loving
brave

Contents

List of Illustrations

A gallery of illustrations is located between pages 108 and 109.

ACKNOWLEDGMENTS

As this project drew to a close I found myself overwhelmed by a sense of indebtedness to the myriad people who have helped to shape what it has become. Audiences at the "Crosstown Traffic" conference at Warwick, the University of Wisconsin-Madison, the University of Chicago, the University of Illinois, the American Historical Association, the Organization of American Historians, Duke University, SUNY Stonybrook, Columbia, and NYU offered spirited feedback and often provocative suggestions for revision—all of which I have endeavored to incorporate. I am especially grateful to Lou Roberts, Leora Auslander, Anu Rao, Lila Abu-Lughod, Susan Thorne, and Kathleen Wilson for organizing such stimulating venues in which to think through the analytical challenges of cosmopolitanism. Tony Ballantyne, Gerry Forbes, Barbara Ramusack, George Robb, Laura Mayhall, Herman Bennett, and Minnie Sinha have long been among my most faithful and critical readers; without them, my conviction about my ability to do justice to Santha Rama Rau's storied careers would have flagged long ago. Tony's knowledge, enthusiasm, and friendship have been especially wonderful, deepening even with distance. George read chapters and, even more importantly, embellished my research with his inveterate love of kitsch, whether of the Victorian or the Cold War kind. Various chapters and parts of chapters have also benefited greatly from the care and attention of Dane Kennedy, Jed Esty, Durba Ghosh, Clarence Walker, Adam Geary, Steve Johnstone, Philippa Levine, Brenda Gayle Plummer, Parama Roy, Sally Singh, Rebecca Walkowitz,

Farina Mir, Srirupa Prasad, Michael Fisher, Becky Conekin, Saadia Toor, Andrew Thompson, Kristin Hoganson, Erik McDuffie, Lauren Goodlad, Tamara Chaplin, Jean Allman, Harry Liebersohn, Dorothee Schneider, Shefali Chandra, Damion Thomas, Clare Crowston, Marilyn Booth, David Roediger, Poshek Fu, Kathy Oberdeck, Jamie Warren, Rebecca McNulty Schreiber, Debbie Hughes, and Danielle Kinsey. Together with Kate Bullard, Rebecca, Danielle, and Debbie have all provided valuable assistance with the research for this project, for which I thank them.

Archivists at the Houghton Library at Harvard and the Howard Gotlieb Archival Research Center at Boston University were helpful and accommodating. I am grateful for their professionalism and their acts of kindness large and small. The two readers at Duke University Press were spot on in their comments and queries; the introduction and epilogue bear more than mere traces of their influence. Miriam Angress continues to be an exemplary editor: thoughtful, supportive, efficient, and genuinely invested in me and in Santha Rama Rau's stories. I count her among my most crucial readers. Augusto Espiritu and Fanon Wilkins have been coconspirators in radical history and resisting empires; in so doing, they have left their marks on this project in ways perhaps only they can see, but which are profound nonetheless. Thanks in part to them, a version of chapter 1 appeared in the spring 2006 special issue of *Radical History Review* ("New Imperialisms"). To Ania Loomba I owe a very great debt indeed. Her critical engagement with the book and the questions it tries to grapple with has been characteristically intelligent, impassioned, and trenchant. This is a much better book for her having read it.

Funds from the University Scholars program and the Bruce C. and Catherine A. Bastian endowment—both at the University of Illinois—have made travel and research possible. Without the love and labor of Holly Hastings and especially Mina, it's hard to imagine how this book would ever have been conceived, let alone completed. To Mina especially I owe a debt that can never be repaid for her love and friendship as well as her dedication to me and mine. My mother accompanied me on a research trip to Boston, and she and my father remain as interested in my work as ever. Monica and David faithfully turned up to hear me in NYC; Jennifer Morgan loves me through thick and thin, for which I am extraordinarily grateful. Vicki has been and remains a gem, pure and simple. Dana Rabin is a touchstone like no other. The intellect, principle, and loving friendship of Kathy Oberdeck makes so very many things possible. Paul, Nick, and Olivia never fail to remind me of the limits of career and the joys of the pool, the park, and the swing set. I hope they know that they reside, individually and together, at the very heart of everything I am and hope to be.

As many of my friends and family who have lived through the researching and writing of this book with me can testify, I have been at once astonished and humbled by the generosity of Santha Rama Rau in helping me to recapture the contours of her life. From the moment I first contacted her she has answered my questions, given me all manner of helpful leads on material relating to her life, and graciously listened to me as I have attempted to match my training as a historian with a critical appreciation of her varied careers. She read several chapters of this book and offered correctives and suggestions with tremendous grace and good humor. Needless to say, it's been a privilege and a pleasure to get to know her, and an honor to be associated with her work. I offer this book to her with gratitude and even greater affection.

 My work is not art. —Santha Rama Rau

The East as a Postcolonial Career

When we talk of Asia, remember that India, not because of any ambition of hers, but because of the force of circumstances, because of geography, because of history and because of so many other things, inevitably has to play a very important role in Asia. And not only that; India becomes a kind of meeting ground for various trends and forces, a meeting ground between what might roughly be called the East and the West. — Jawaharlal Nehru, "India's Foreign Policy"

What is the fate of the historians' informant? — Gayatri Chakravorty Spivak, *A Critique of Postcolonial Reason*

Santha Rama Rau (b. 1923) was one of the best-known South Asian writers in postwar America. The author of half a dozen books between 1945 and 1970 (travelogues, novels, a memoir, and a Time-Life cookbook as well as a Broadway play), she was a regular contributor to *The New Yorker*, the *New York Times*, and a range of periodicals from *Holiday* magazine to *McCall's* to *Reader's Digest*.[1] Her books were routinely advertised and reviewed in a variety of print culture outlets from Hartford to Kansas City to Shreveport and beyond—venues in which she was typically celebrated as the embodiment of "East Meets West."[2] She was an occasional radio personality and television guest, a recurrent figure on the New York social scene, and a public defender of "the American image abroad."[3] She was, arguably, one of the most popular translators of India—in both its late Raj and its postcolonial incarnations

—to an aspiring middle-class, white U.S. public not only aware of its new role on the world stage but increasingly alive to its responsibilities as the inheritor of the geopolitical power and cultural capital of the former British empire. Though her politics was made at a different historical moment, like the figure of Arundhati Roy in the late-twentieth-century West, Rama Rau enjoyed wide circulation in and, as significantly, "critical promotion" by, the mass media, producing narratives of "the Orient" for an appetitive, consumerist public during an extended moment of American neo-imperial hegemony.[4]

Today, Santha Rama Rau scarcely registers as even a minor diasporic writer, let alone as a major postcolonial figure, whether in India or in the United States. Most people to whom I mentioned her while working on this project had never heard of her. Those who had (mainly South Asians of a certain generation) viewed her as a negligible talent and expressed surprise that I thought she merited any sustained critical attention. What little academic criticism there is on her tends to evaluate her writing as literature, rather than focusing on the trajectory of her career as an authority on India, its role in Asia, and its significance in the postcolonial world.[5] As for Santha Rama Rau herself, she is aware of and bemused by the fate of her public image. As she told me rather self-mockingly in an interview in 2004, she was once introduced to a woman at a cocktail party who said to her, "Santha Rama Rau? Didn't you used to be famous?"[6] Understanding the phenomenon of Rama Rau's career in the marketplace of transnational political culture and historicizing her as a precursor to later generations of postcolonial experts on India and "the East" are, together, the major concerns of this book.

The minor celebrity that Rama Rau's career provided her in the first few decades of postwar America stemmed in part from the opportunities that her elite family background afforded. Raised in India and Britain with stints in prewar South Africa and postwar Tokyo, she was the daughter of nationalist parents with well-established transnational reputations dating from the interwar years. Her father, Benegal Rama Rau, had been a member of the Round Table Conference and served as the first Indian ambassador to the United States after 1945, while her mother, Dhanvanthi Rama Rau, was an ardent advocate of birth control whose feminist commitments and activities spanned two continents.[7] The Rama Raus senior represent just one of several generations of highly mobile elites that include Rabindranath Tagore, Mohandas K. Gandhi, and Jawaharlal Nehru: Indian nationalists whose relationships to the British imperial center as well as to America, Europe, Africa, and Asia remind us of the often neglected, contrapuntal geographies of travel in the pre-postcolonial world.[8] Santha Rama Rau's intimacy with these traditions, together with her parents' personal and professional connections, gave her an entrée into the upper echelons of American political culture where, especially during the Kennedy years, the cult of celebrity intersected with and was in turn shaped by the diplomatic world of the Washington embassy scene and the United Nations in ways that historians are just beginning to appreciate.[9]

Breaking with a century-old tradition of higher education in Britain for the children of nationalist elites, Rama Rau was the first diplomatic daughter to be sent to college in the United States. She was also the first Indian woman to graduate from Wellesley College (1944), to be followed more famously by Vijay Lakshmi Pandit's daughter (and Nehru's niece), Nayantara Sahgal, who finished three years later.[10] These affiliations created a corridor of influence between Boston and Washington that Rama Rau was to traverse throughout much of her adult life, and which helped cement her reputation as a diasporic Indian writer in America. Although she enjoyed national recognition in her day, and while she traveled back and forth to India on a yearly basis for almost fifty years after graduating from Wellesley, at the height of her career Santha Rama Rau's "America" was effectively New York City and environs, which has served more or less as her permanent home since the early 1950s. Once her uncle, Sir Benegal Narsing Rau, was appointed as Indian delegate to the Security Council in 1950, Santha Rama Rau became privy to its "countless sessions and debates" as well as to the well-heeled social world that swirled around them, first on Long Island, where the UN was temporarily headquartered, and later in Manhattan, where she made some of the most important literary connections of her career, including with Harold Ross of *The New Yorker*.[11]

Santha Rama Rau's relationship with and marriage to Faubion Bowers, who had been an aide to General MacArthur in Tokyo and who traveled in many of the same postwar diplomatic circles as her family, also benefited the career as a journalist and travel writer that she cultivated from the late 1940s onward. Bowers was an expert on Asian arts and theater, and it was the convergence of his interests with hers that took them to Southeast Asia, Africa, and Russia in the first decades of the Cold War.[12] Although enabled by her family of birth and her choice of partner, the modicum of fame Santha Rama Rau achieved resulted mainly from her success at being recognized as an authority on India on the eve of independence. As the titles of two of her most popular books (*Home to India* [1945] and *This Is India* [1954]) suggest, she entered the American scene as an India expert—someone with impeccable credentials by virtue of her pedigree and her personal experiences.[13] Regardless of the forms it took, Rama Rau's writing offered American readers an insider's view of Indian cultures, traditions, and histories in an effort to counter what she viewed as serious misrepresentations of India in the public mind. As I argue in the ensuing pages, Santha Rama Rau modeled a Cold War cosmopolitanism that was at once grounded in her Indian experiences, inflected by her American careers, and shaped by gendered apprehensions of "the East" that her work both embodied and challenged.

Those postcolonial careers were, in turn, rooted in vigorous criticism of images of India in the Cold War culture of the globally ambitious United States. Although she did not use the word "orientalism"—after all, Edward Said's book of the same name was first published in 1978—Santha Rama Rau elaborated a taxonomy of common misapprehensions about India that anticipated the critical purchase of that now famous term. In *This Is India* (1954), for example, she characterized Western images of India that associated it only with the "primitive" and the "miserable" as "the Mother India school" of thinking—referring to the American reformer Katherine Mayo's book *Mother India*, which caused an international sensation in India, Britain, and America when it was published in 1927 because of the way it pathologized Indian society, particularly with respect to its treatment of women.[14] Several years later, in a series of lectures she gave across the United States to promote her autobiography, *Gifts of Passage* (1961), Santha Rama Rau expanded this critique, telling audiences that the extant literature on India written by Westerners fell into four broad categories: The Lean Bronzed Horseman School; The Sensitive People of a Foreign Culture School; The Earth and Mystery School; and The Mystical Mysterious Orient School.[15] Without naming names, she indicted a whole cadre of Western writers on both sides of the Atlantic who had carved out a niche for themselves since the interwar period by orientalizing India for Western consumption. These would have included a raft of 1950s writers—including Gardner Fox, whose *Woman of Kali* was advertised with copy that read "in her temple of exotic love the fate of an empire was decided"—as well as interwar writers like Edison Marshall, whose *Love Stories of India* sold in 1945 for the pulp fiction price of twenty-five cents.[16] As Dorothy B. Jones noted in her 1955 study of images of India and China in American film, portrayals of India after independence were less focused on failed attempts at rebellion against the British than their pre-1947 predecessors; this was due at least in part to the influence of Ram Bagi, who began to select Indian-made films like *Light of Asia* for American release in 1949.[17] As she also notes, the themes of primitive tribesmen, affable or treacherous rajahs, and stalwart Bengal soldiers persisted both on screen and off in the Cold War popular imagination.[18]

In the pages that follow, readers will get a glimpse of how densely populated the cultural landscapes of the postwar United States were by images of India—through popular venues like *Reader's Digest* to middlebrow magazines like *Holiday* to the photographs of Jackie Kennedy's 1962 trip to India (which arguably mediated "high" and "low" apprehensions of the "East" to the American public). Despite the rare challenge to stereotypical views, the dominant character of Indian representations was orientalist. And it was the preponderance of these images that Rama Rau sought to refute by representing India as a site of multiple cultural influences, as the home of lively aesthetic and culinary practices both ancient and modern, and, above all, as an appealing tourist destination.[19] Whether she was likening Jaipur to Paris or Bombay to Manhattan (calling the latter "the New York of the Orient"), Rama Rau strove to rescue India from the condescension of Cold War commentators by materializing its complexities and by putting it on the same cultural plane as Euro-America.[20] If in the process she consolidated her own reputation as a "citizen of the world," she did so by rendering India more majestic than miserable, more modern than primitive, more cosmopolitan than provincial. As we will see, for Santha Rama Rau, this meant that India was not just emblematic of the power and possibility of Asia in the new world order; it was also, both literally and figuratively, representative of "the new world of Asia" *tout court*.[21]

How do we account for the fact that an Indian woman was able to fashion a career as a semi-professional authority on India in a culture saturated with what Christina Klein has called "Cold War orientalism"?[22] We could begin by conceding that simply by entering the public sphere as an Indian woman, Santha Rama Rau was subject to fetishization as an emblem of the Orient herself: that whether she was speaking of India or not, she was always already speaking "as India," with all the gendered connotations (primitiveness, exoticism, sexual availability) which that locative position entailed. It is easy enough to read American press coverage of her in light of this "problematic visibility," as Nandini Bhatta-charya has termed the fate of the Indian woman in public, both histori-cally and now.[23] As recent work on the subject suggests, the history of American orientalism is a long and complex phenomenon, and in empha-sizing the orientalist character of Rama Rau's Cold War profile I don't want to suggest that she in any sense originated the role of twentieth-century female "oriental" cosmopolitan—a figure embodied by Anna May Wong in the interwar years and by Han Suyin in the same period as Rama Rau.[24] But Santha Rama Rau was certainly one of the more promi-nent postwar incarnations of oriental and orientalist "mystique." From the appearance of her first book, *Home to India*, published by Harper in 1945, Rama Rau was championed as a writer with "a Western mind . . . [and] an Indian heart."[25] This characterization drew on decades of British colonial discourse about the colonizer / mind / masculine-native / body / feminine split as a rationale for imperial power, redeploying it to oriental-ize the figure of the Indian woman in historically new but eminently familiar ways. The ornamentalizing effects of this particular brand of American orientalism are also evident in the images of her that appeared in advertisements for and reviews of her books in the *New York Times*, in the poses she struck for fashion outlets like *Flair*, and in the lush and exoticized visuals that accompanied her work for *Holiday* magazine— images over which she exerted some but not total control, and which give a whole new meaning to the phrase "arm-chair orientalism."[26] Although her class status protected her to some degree from the associations with disrespectability that might have attached to her as a single Indian woman traveling the world, even elite connections such as hers were not necessarily a failsafe against the gendered dangers of "reputation" (an analog of career) in 1950s America. Thus despite her trenchant critique of the "Mystical Mysterious Orient School" of Indian literature, early photographs of Rama Rau often framed her from the neck up, semi-shrouded in a headscarf—at least until she embraced that signature coiffure of the period, the beehive hairdo.[27]

Orientalism certainly offers a powerful interpretive possibility for appreciating how and why Santha Rama Rau was able to do the ideological work she did in Cold War America. But in the end it is a far too limited frame through which to view her. For narratives about her career operated in and through another equally powerful postwar cultural discourse: that of cosmopolitanism. Although the journalists reviewing her books never defined the term, they riffed on the cosmopolitan ideal of universalist, worldly disinterest, casting her work as a combination of detachment from and identification with "local" culture that fulfilled the fantasy of Kantian global community for a newly postcolonial world.[28] It is important to note that in doing so, they sheared cosmopolitanism of some of its negative meaning, including its derogatory associations with merchants and Jews—this in a postwar world filled with millions of people on the move who were not considered cosmopolitan in any sense, positive or negative: partition refugees, concentration camp survivors, and all manner of displaced persons across the globe.[29] In any event, "cosmopolitan" was a term applied to Santha Rama Rau and her work across American print culture in the 1940s and 1950s. Sometimes accompanied by the term "tolerant" (and in one instance, "precocious"), it was a consistent feature of evaluations of her work from *Home to India* through *My Russian Journey* (1959).[30] The progressive, emancipatory logic of some recent theoretical engagements with the concept might lead us to expect a tension between critics' embrace of Rama Rau's cosmopolitan credentials and their eagerness to underscore her orientalist appeal.[31] Not only did the two discourses complement each other; the cosmopolitanism attributed to Rama Rau depended, rhetorically and structurally, on the very East-West nexus her career was said to represent ("where the twain meet," as one newspaper headline proclaimed).[32] Rama Rau was a career cosmopolitan, in other words, because she was, technically at any rate, a career orientalist: that is, a producer not just of knowledge about India but about the East for the West.[33] As I detail in chapter 1, Rama Rau's 1950 book *East of Home* (published by Harper, as was *Home to India*) used India as a vantage point from which to survey Asia and to stage the story of her own education in pan-Asian sentiment and solidarity—a series of maneuvers that consolidated her reputation as a cosmopolitan writer authorized to interpret "new voices from the Far East," including but not limited to those from the Indian subcontinent.[34]

As with all celebrities, even of the minor variety, Santha Rama Rau's career was not self-made. It depended on "the power of media to disseminate visibility and publicity," which in her case included not just the press but the tentacled publicity machine of Harper, her first publisher and to whom she remained loyal for over two decades.[35] As is clear from Santha Rama Rau's correspondence, her editor there, Elizabeth Lawrence, tried to shape the young author into what she perceived as a marketable mold, especially at the start of Rama Rau's career, when she was asking for guidance about how to "thread together . . . all the odd bits of information and comment . . . that is necessary for a book." Lawrence's advice, which was to emphasize the "woman angle," helped shape what *East of Home* was to become, by Santha Rama Rau's own admission.[36] As for the American media, it was a force she was canny enough to recognize and to try to control, with some success.[37] So, for example, an undated interview with her reported the following reflection on Westerners' accounts of India: " 'Humor. That's what's missing; the Indian sense of humor.' She inhaled her very un-Indian Winston. 'Bengal Lancers indeed!' [she exclaimed]."[38]

To be sure, Rama Rau did not script herself as the cigarette-smoking Indian woman, but smoke she did, and in public, thereby destabilizing some of the gendered stereotypes her image was, perhaps, drafted to evoke. And despite the fact that she relied on representatives from William Morris (one of the major talent agencies of the day) to promote her, Rama Rau was very much her own agent when it came to shaping the ideological contours of her writing career. In *East of Home* she staged her pan-Asianism as a conversion experience: one predicated on a turn away from the old British empire toward the new American empire—an empire which was invested at an accelerated rate in specific postcolonial outcomes in and for "the Orient" during the high noon of her career. As chapter 1 details, Rama Rau's identification with the realities of postwar American power was in many respects a bid for a new kind of transnational identity. What she offered was a form of Cold War cosmopolitanism that realized the Nehruvian vision of India as a leader in the socalled Third World and defined the parameters of acceptable anti-colonial nationalism. In the process, Rama Rau made visible a variety of semi-imperialisms both within Asia (India over Japan, India over China) and beyond it (India over Africa).[39] These were new, or at least newly prominent, hierarchies of status and value whose origins lay in the ideological legacies and superstructural remnants of the British empire, but whose points of reference were, in the heyday of Rama Rau's career, the socalled Third World and only secondarily "the West."

In many ways, Rama Rau anticipated what Neloufer de Mel has identified as "lateral cosmopolitanism." By this de Mel means a subcontinental perspective that swings north from Colombo to Delhi and Lahore, rather than taking Europe as its lodestar or its pivot.[40] In this sense, it operates in marked contrast to the hierarchical Kantian version, where vectors of influence emanate from imperial centers and radiate outward toward "alternative" modernities. It is also akin to what Françoise Lionnet and Shu-mei Shih have called "minor transnationalism," in that both aim to rethink the verticality of cosmopolitan cultural visions and global/izing analyses especially.[41] As articulated by Santha Rama Rau, cosmopolitanism was a horizontal vision that echoed the commitments to Asian solidarity enunciated by Nehru in the years leading up to the Bandung Conference of 1955, where the doctrine of non-alignment began its official career on the world stage, albeit belatedly in terms of the cross-nationalist practices that had been going on between and among anti-colonialists since at least the 1920s.[42] For some postcolonial critics writing today, the radical potential of this lateralism is undercut by the fact that Santha Rama Rau wrote mainly in the United States, for a Western audience, rather than from India and for India.[43] Indeed, references to her work are scarce on the ground in Indian print culture, at least compared to the thickness of coverage her writing received in American mass media.[44] One telling exception was *JANA: The News Magazine of Resurgent Asia and Africa*, which was published in a comparatively "off-center" Asian locale,

Colombo.[45] The where of Rama Rau's postcolonial was, in other words, the where of much postcoloniality, historically speaking: perennially (if not permanently) out of India. And yet as we will also see in chapter 1, the sweep of her eye, the geographical orientation of her criticism, was—like her brand of cosmopolitanism itself—a break with Eurocentric models, even as it pivoted on an often unspoken American axis. As her early travel writings illustrate, Santha Rama Rau used her reputation as an Indian expert to promote Nehru's vision of India as a "third force," producing knowledge about the historical and cultural meanings of an Asia-centered Indian perspective for consumption in the West and, more pointedly, for postwar American readers.[46]

The question of audience to which I have alluded above is of course crucial, since if Rama Rau had only been writing for Indians and other "others" she would not have been understood as cosmopolitan in the same way, if at all. Indeed, in many respects her claims to postcolonial cosmopolitanism were directly proportional to her deracination from India itself—a critical point to which I will return below. Living in America and pitching to an American public had undeniably constitutive effects on the directions her work would take and, by extension, on her career in the world of American letters. As her writings from the 1950s testify, her "cosmopolitan" approach to Asia bore the imprint of her American experiences and, increasingly, her American sympathies as well. By the end of *East of Home,* and after a few short but formative years as a diasporic subject in America, the knowledge she was producing about the Orient was as in tune with Washington's foreign policy as with Delhi's. This reorientation had to do in part with the influence of Faubion Bowers, whose expertise in the languages and the arts of Asia—and whose earlier career in the American military—clearly shaped her political education.[47] But it also reflected the transformation Rama Rau underwent as she pursued her career as a translator of India and the East to America and Americans. In those first heady days after the publication of *Home to India,* Rama Rau had told Hal Boyle of the *Wichita Beacon* that "our job—those of us lucky to have lived in these two countries—is to interpret them to one another. If we can make ourselves—the Indians—real people to the Americans, we shall have done more than our politicians have been able to do."[48] This is not to say that her efforts at translation or her political perspectives were overwhelmingly embraced. That was certainly not the case in a venue like the *New York Times,* where all her books were reviewed and which functioned as one point of intersection between political / diplomatic culture and the world of American letters. There she was alternately patronized as a sentimental woman writer and castigated as a mouthpiece for Nehru.[49] Nor was she exempt from being satirized for her modicum of success as an Indian in America. In her compatriot Ved Mehta's blistering account of her in *The New Yorker* in 1962, she comes off as a no-talent writer who panders to the American market, whether literary or Hollywood.[50] These are interpretive spins which suggest that, however much the press tried to contain her through the rubric of cosmopolitanism, Santha Rama Rau was as threatening as she was, finally, unintelligible to the status quo, which did not, and perhaps could not, recognize the complexity of her position as a diasporic figure in America, preferring to read her as an Indian "national" expert on India. For Mehta, who aspired to be a less strictly popular but nonetheless sought-after India expert, there was apparently not room for more than one on the Cold War American scene — evidence, in turn, of a minor celebrity competition that, in the end, reminds us of the seduction of the nation for would-be cosmopolitans and their audiences in the postwar period.[51]

In the end, Rama Rau's determination to present India to Americans by opposing reductive orientalist images with complex and often politically unsettling alternatives made her cosmopolitan vision idiosyncratic if not unique in Cold War America. In this context, making "the East" intelligible in the United States was nothing less than a herculean task. Santha Rama Rau's career took off well before the 1965 U.S. Immigration Act, which changed patterns of migration from South Asia to the United States and delivered Indians to the neighborhoods, classrooms, playgrounds, and offices of Americans at a historically unprecedented rate.[52] This is not to say that there were not Indians, and even prominent ones, in local and national life before the 1960s, though their numbers — only a few thousand in New York City, for example — are an inverse indicator of their cultural capital and political significance, not least because so many were affiliated with the United Nations.[53] As recent scholarship on the Indian diaspora in America has demonstrated, Indians were considered a model minority well before the term had accrued the national political valences it came to have in the context of affirmative action and multicultural educational policy.[54] Still, India remained a largely unknown quantity during the height of Rama Rau's writing career. As Harold Isaacs's 1958 study, *Scratches in our Minds: American Visions of China and India,* revealed, as late as 1942, only 60 percent of Americans interviewed were able to locate India or China on a map. The events of World War II went some way toward changing that, though as his study also documents, classically orientalist images (of heathen peoples, teeming cities, and "Mongol hordes") rushed in to fill the void.[55] So did experts of all kinds, making the American public sphere overcrowded with India-wallahs and "oriental" pundits (diplomats, policy makers, missionaries, travelers, and fiction writers) jockeying for power and influence in official and unofficial circles alike.[56] Rama Rau was well aware of this, and her celebrity as a singular—in the sense of both exceptional and highly individuated—Indian woman set her dramatically apart not just from the growing numbers of Indians in American life but also from one of the dominant images of South Asia in Cold War America: that of the starving Indian masses crippled by devastating and persistent famine. Santha Rama Rau was as aware of the market power of the "oriental" celebrity as she was of the comparatively subordinate position of India in the U.S. imaginary vis-à-vis Japan and especially China. As she told Hal Boyle, what India needed was "another 'Pearl Buck' to make Americans as interested in India as . . . they are in China."[57]

Rama Rau's career interest in "the East," and the competitive intra-Asian identity politics through which it came to be articulated, was, then, inexorably shaped by the exigencies of the Cold War as they played out in the U.S. public sphere. Clearly Nehru's non-alignment policy, together with the United States' shifting relationships with India and Pakistan, was instrumental to how her career developed and was in turn perceived. Her career trajectory was also influenced by the United States' relationship with Britain and the decolonizing British empire—a relationship which developed in the context of Cold War landscapes, of course, but which had deeper roots in and specific ramifications for the project of translating India and Indians in U.S. culture. In many respects, the conjuncture of orientalism and cosmopolitanism which the American media saw in, and of course attributed to, Santha Rama Rau was a result of the Kipling effect: that is, the long shadow that the Raj and its literature cast on American belles-lettres in the mid-twentieth century and beyond. In many respects it would be more accurate to call the postwar media "Anglo-American," in order to capture the transatlantic sympathies of organs of opinion like the *New York Times* and *The New Yorker* as well as the presumptive whiteness of the audiences they targeted and the cultures of influence they trafficked in. For even if we acknowledge Eric P. Kaufman's recent argument that the race- and class-specific coherence of the American establishment had been in crisis since the 1920s, the Anglophilic tastes and impulses of political and cultural elites persisted well into John F. Kennedy's presidency and beyond—in ways that shaped the terms through which Santha Rama Rau was managed, and sought to manage her career, in public discourse.[58]

Santha Rama Rau's accomplishments as a writer were often evaluated against the standards of the English canon. Reporting for the *Herald Tribune* in 1945, Ernestine Evans called *Home to India* "an Indian comedy of manners" and dubbed Rama Rau someone who was "as faithful to her English past as she is plighted to her Indian nationality."[59] Well before her very public association with E. M. Forster's novel *A Passage to India*, her fiction was compared favorably with his for its embrace of "simple human contact" as the solution to the world's ills.[60] And well beyond the early stage of her career, Rama Rau's cachet depended on her affiliations with English life and literature—in part because even in the age of Indian independence, American cultural understandings of India were still refracted through the lens of the Raj. As such, they mirrored and helped to popularize American foreign policy attitudes toward India that had existed since before the war, when it was commonly recognized that American interest in India was derivative of "British relations with India."[61] This could be ascribed to American nationalist identification with Indian anti-colonial struggles, though the reluctance of Roosevelt's administration to do anything but turn a blind eye to Indian National Congress activities against the British in the 1940s undoubtedly complicates this interpretation. The explanation for Americans' tendency to see India through British eyes lies as much in ideas about shared Anglo-American cultural and racial affinity as it does in high politics, unless of course we imagine, in keeping with the thrust of much recent diplomatic history, that "political culture" is precisely the dynamic space between those interdependent domains. For our purposes, the drama of Santha Rama Rau's career is to be found in the ways she was positioned, and tried to position herself, as an expert on a former Anglophone empire in order to be understood and appreciated by an emergent one. To paraphrase Saadia Toor, her career demonstrates how access to things English, and the ability to traffic in them, was crucial to the intelligibility of an Indian *qua* *Indian* in middle- and upper-middle-class circles, given the hold that "culture" in an Arnoldian sense still had on the postwar American reading public.[62]

As with Asia, Rama Rau's relationship to Britain in the age of nascent American empire was by no means self-evident. Chapter 2 explores those moments in her career when Santha Rama Rau actively cultivated identification with high English literary tradition, as when she undertook the writing of a stage play of E. M. Forster's *A Passage to India*, which was produced on Broadway in 1962 and later served as the basis for David Lean's 1985 film version.[63] Rama Rau not only understood Forster's representations of India to be closest to her own; she defended them against a fiscal / critical New York theater establishment that sought to Americanize what she and Forster both thought were essentially the English modernist values of the original novel. In the course of promoting the play in the early 1960s, Rama Rau became a spokeswoman for Forster in America at what can be seen, retrospectively, as the height of her own career. She became his agent in the American media not only because she perceived her own career to be at stake but because she believed his reputation as the voice of a certain liberal philosophy of empire—as embodied by Forster's quotable quote, "Only connect"—to be in danger of misappropriation by American audiences looking to Britain as the once great, now fallen global imperial power.[64] Equally in danger of "Americanization," in her view, was the sexual plot of the play, which Broadway producers were determined to sex up, if not heterosexualize—a move that Rama Rau endeavored to protest, without effect. Even more significant are the ways in which Rama Rau, together with some of the critics who reviewed the play, tried to route the story of interracial desire at the heart of *A Passage to India* through both contemporary struggles over decolonization *and* domestic racial struggles in the

United States. Nor was this the first time Rama Rau had used her authority as a postcolonial cosmopolitan to interpret Cold War civil rights issues in the light of global race struggles. As chapter 1 elaborates, her reportage on Mau Mau for the *New York Times* and *The Reporter* in 1953–54 represents her attempts to translate, and effectively to domesticate, African nationalism for an American public while at the same time establishing a promontory, British-India–centered position on contemporary decolonizing impulses.[65] Rama Rau was, without putting too fine a point on it, a curiously quasi-colonial postcolonial cosmopolitan, especially when she took the "Third World" beyond India as the object of her gaze.[66]

In this context, Rama Rau became more than an expert on British India per se; she became a custodian of Anglo-imperial values from the vantage point of an "independent" and of course a highly privileged former colonial subject. It was a position she capitalized on to enunciate postcolonial ways of knowing about sex, race, and empire—ways of knowing whose authority derived ostensibly from her presumptively disinterested cosmopolitanism but were in fact refracted through the very particular experiences of being an Indian expatriate in Cold War America. It could be argued that Rama Rau used the exceptional status of India in the Anglo-American imagination (that "jewel in the crown") to speak to an audience rife with its own convictions about national exceptionalism. This line of argument is slightly more complex than explanations that root Indian-American comparisons in a "the world's two largest democracies" explanation, though the distinction is admittedly one of degree rather than kind. In any event, the real power of her cosmopolitanism depended on her custodial role vis-à-vis Asia and Africa, by which I mean the impression she cultivated that as a postcolonial herself, she had a "special relationship" with and hence a uniquely informed and authoritative perspective on the former and current colonial scenes. By the early 1960s, she had also begun to articulate that promontory perspective with respect to the embodiment of British high culture itself: E. M. Forster.

Santha Rama Rau's class position surely facilitated these kinds of appropriations. But her racial location—between black and white, and perhaps even between white and yellow—was as instrumental to the brand of career cosmopolitanism she was able to pull off in the marketplace of Cold War culture. Rama Rau rarely wrote about race per se, and when she did it was in the context of African nationalism or, rather more allusively, domestic American civil rights struggles.[67] When I asked, in the context of a wide-ranging interview with her, whether she had ever experienced racial prejudice in the United States, she told the story of her early days at Wellesley when she had wanted to take the train to Washington. Because she was aware of segregation, she asked one of her father's diplomatic friends if she needed to do anything special when making the train reservations; he told her no, that as the daughter of a diplomat she should have no trouble. She followed that memory with the observation that many people mistook her for "a very tanned Italian" and, because of her height, did not necessarily identify her as Indian (at least, presumably, when she was not wearing a sari).[68] This is in stark contrast to her experience of pre-war South Africa, where her memory of being restricted in movie theaters and other public spaces left an indelible imprint in her autobiography.[69]

Santha Rama Rau's capacity to pass for white in the U.S. context might be attributed to her Kashmiri background and its typically fair complexion —a well-known and much commented-on attribute in South Asian communities and in Indian fiction as well.[70] Though it might be going too far to say, à la George Lipsitz, that Santha Rama Rau had "a possessive investment in whiteness,"[71] it is clear that her liminal position in the racialized culturescapes of 1950s and 1960s America gave her a latitude which other postcolonials might not have enjoyed. This liminality, together with the critical reception of her as an England-identified, if not exactly Anglocentric, cosmopolitan, gave her unlooked for opportunities to represent an implicitly but no less powerfully Anglo-Saxon version of empire to those American publics who encountered *A Passage to India* on Broadway and the publicity whirl that accompanied it. Championing Forster's novel gave new impetus to Rama Rau's career as the 1950s drew to a close: she became the translator of a liberal, interwar, and highly particularistic English-imperial ethic to an American public interested in, if only vaguely aware of, the cultural legacies of the Pax Britannica. Taken together, her promotion of Forster's imperial vision, and the spaces of American enthusiasm for British India it allows us to see, suggest that the 1960s were a precursor to later forms of Raj nostalgia. These latter were largely visual forms (*The Jewel in the Crown* [the series], *The Far Pavilions*, of course Lean's *A Passage to India* itself) whose colonialist and racialist impulses have been subjected to critical scrutiny.[72] But they have tended to be understood as sui generis, to the extent that they have received much historical attention at all. An analysis of Santha Rama Rau's role in selling Forster in the American market enables us to historicize the 1980s craze for empire and to appreciate its genealogies, in all their racial, class, and gendered dimensions, in the not-so-distant past. As we will see, Rama Rau returned to the sightline of American readers in the mid-1980s with the opening of Lean's film—in part because she had sold the rights to the screenplay to him (and hence her name was associated with it), and in part because she so deplored what she viewed as the further corruption of Forster's message by Lean. That Rama Rau continued to be concerned about *A Passage to India*'s fate beyond the limited run of the Broadway play suggests how invested she also was in the long-term future of Forster's version of British India, together with its imperial / imperialist messages, well beyond his death and the confines of her own career.

I do not want to leave the impression that Rama Rau's various careers—as a traveler, as a dramaturge, and later as a cookbook writer—happened serially or, for that matter, in some kind of evolutionary fashion. Even when they are expertly managed, careers have lives of their own, and hers were of decidedly uneven development. She wrote about India throughout the 1950s, even as she gained a reputation as an expert on "the Far East" more broadly. Her stage version of *A Passage to India* was likely begun in the summer of 1955 and opened on Broadway almost seven years later after runs in Oxford and London. During this time she continued to travel extensively and write about her journeys in a number of periodical publications, some of which formed the basis for her books, including *My Russian Journey*.[73] She undertook the Time-Life book *The Cooking of India* while she was trying to complete her second novel, *The Adventuress* (1970), which was set in Tokyo, Manila, and Shanghai. If there was any continuous thread in her public career as a writer, however, it was a preoccupation with representing the complexities of what a historian who was her contemporary famously called "the wonder that was India."[74] The cookbook project provided her with a unique opportunity to do just that, insofar as the Time-Life series of which it was a part utilized the travelogue genre in the service of a larger cosmopolitan purpose: to highlight the cuisines of the world. Rama Rau's approach to *The Cooking of India* would draw on all her career skills as a writer—her talent for storytelling, her autobiographical tendencies, her disposition toward history, her eye for capturing the familiar in the foreign—in order to make a case for India as the home of a multicultural culinary heritage. The "India" that resulted may have been centrifugal by default (she was after all being paid to write under the rubric of a national cuisine), but it was centripetal by design. In addition to local and regional traditions, Rama Rau emphasized the many foreign influences that had gone into "the cooking of India." The net effect was an image of India that was not one but many cultures as a consequence of conquest, migration, and enduring linguistic and religious diversity.

The process of producing this layered account was a vexed one, as chapter 3 reconstructs through her correspondence with her Time-Life editors. While she sent them chapter drafts from India, they fought her on every point from New York, especially on the issue of whether Pakistan should be included as a separate chapter in the book—a fight she ultimately lost, to the detriment of the text as a whole. The archive of *The Cooking of India* allows us to see just exactly what was at stake in the moniker "cosmopolitan" for Santha Rama Rau as she entered the twilight of her publishing career. For with the appearance of the cookbook in 1969 and of *The Adventuress* a year later, Santha Rama Rau began to fade from public view. She continued to write for venues like *Reader's Digest* and the *New York Times* into the late 1980s, during which time she was occasionally enlisted as an expert on subjects pertaining to the first incarnations of Raj nostalgia in the United States.[75] But *The Adventuress* was not a critical success, and Santha Rama Rau ceased to be on the literati A-list as a new generation of Indian celebrities—mostly from the world of film—began to erupt into the American public sphere in the early 1970s. For this reason, and as chapter 3 demonstrates, *The Cooking of India* marks an endpoint, if not the endpoint, in the arc of her career. After over two decades of producing knowledge about India and the East, and of achieving a species of fame as a career expert in the postcolonial marketplace, Rama Rau used the cookbook to make the argument that India needed to be understood not just as an object of curiosity or even as a sovereign player in the postwar world but as a cosmopolitan subject in its own right:

one with organically cosmopolitan histories, traditions, and futures. For Santha Rama Rau this was the effect of local, national, and transnational influences—a series of dynamic processes that was evocative of Nehru's global vision of and for India, but which perhaps only an extranational subject like Santha Rama Rau could fully articulate.[76]

This is not to say that Rama Rau's eccentric locations provided her with a necessarily progressive, enlightened, or even emancipated space from which to apprehend India or translate it in the West. For on the one hand, as I hope this book makes clear, hers was not a fixed position but a perennially shifting ground, and India came into focus for her and through her in different ways in 1945, in the 1950s, and in the late 1960s, from New York, Tokyo, Moscow, Nairobi, and Bombay—to name just a few of the vantage points, temporal and geographical, available to her over the course of her career. On the other hand, her structural location was hardly ex-centric, rotating as it did around the fulcrum of American power, beginning with her sojourn in occupied Japan in 1947. In this sense she modeled what R. Radhakrishnan calls an "ex-orbitant" cosmopolitanism, albeit in a particularly gendered way.[77] What I would like to engage here is the possibility that by historicizing the career of cosmopolitanism through a postcolonial figure like Santha Rama Rau, we might arrive at a more nuanced understanding of its valences in the current conjuncture. The stakes of this genealogical project are especially high for "the Indian woman," who remains available for appropriation as an object of cosmopolitan desire, but who is rarely permitted to represent, either literally or figuratively, a cosmopolitan subject herself, replete with all its historical contradictions, orientalism among them. The work of Martha C. Nussbaum on SEWA (Self-Employed Women's Association) is especially apposite in this regard. In an effort to make her case for balancing human rights with "human capabilities" on a global scale, Nussbaum enlists the women of SEWA as a kind of pathetic basis for a new cosmopolitan human rights philosophy. In ways that echo and reproduce some of the tensions to be found in Santha Rama Rau's own career, Nussbaum encodes longstanding orientalist tropes at the heart of her analysis, unselfconsciously but nonetheless powerfully rooting her particular call for cosmopolitanism in "the Indian woman," who serves as the object of humanitarian interest and concern but whose own worldly visions are scarcely audible. As is now a well-established historical fact, these are longstanding traditions in Western feminism.[78] Given the role of that movement and its ideological practices in the modern history of liberal humanism, it is hardly surprising that they have helped to inform contemporary debates about the nature and possibility of cosmopolitanism itself.[79] As Timothy Brennan has suggested, this is especially true in the American context, where cosmopolitanism "has been refining itself for the better part of a century," in ways that accommodate older articulations to newer realities but not, as Nussbaum's case demonstrates, necessarily by interrogating the neocolonial hierarchies of status and value at the heart of its identitarian project.[80] Rigorously contextualizing specific instantiations of "the cosmopolitan self"—and attending as vigorously to its colonial genealogies and its rhetorical play in gendered fields of power—exerts a critical, corrective drag on its career as an inherently progressive or purely emancipatory impulse and, of course, helps to produce it as a contingent subject of history.

I am also interested in understanding Santha Rama Rau as an avatar of certain postcolonial ways of seeing and knowing: a precursor to the postcolonial expert whose authority—and career legitimacy—stems precisely from his or her apparent ex-centricity, and especially from his or her cosmopolitan relationship to both India and the West. I want to understand, in other words, what Rama Rau's story can tell us about the forms and functions of the postcolonial writer more generally in the current scene of political culture. In many respects this effort is a minor attempt to engage the history of what Russell Jacoby calls "the non-academic intellectual": that species of public interlocutor which he notes fell into steady decline precisely at the moment that Rama Rau was gaining a foothold in the popular American imagination.[81] If she can be counted among one of his "last intellectuals," her career also reorients his self-avowedly nativist account of the disappearance of such a cadre after the 1950s. More significantly for our purposes, her attempts to navigate the porous border between "popular professionalism" and the more academic variety once again anticipates those of a whole generation of postcolonial writers—writers whom one wonders if the likes of Jacoby would recognize as "intellectuals" (as opposed to Spivak's "native informants") at all. The most obvious turn to make here is toward fiction: to see Santha Rama Rau as the precursor to authors like Bharati Mukherjee and, more recently, Chitra Divakaruni—novelists whom Inderpal Grewal suggests need to be understood not simply as diasporic figures but as makers of the very parameters of the postcolonial imagination.[82] Indeed, in many respects the tenor of Mukherjee's 1980s fiction, especially where her embrace of American-style identitarian politics is concerned, is rendered much more intelligible if we understand Rama Rau's 1970 novel *The Adventuress*—with its Americo-centric politics and its faith in the capacity of U.S. soil to enable people's perpetual reinvention—as the back story to Mukherjee's eponymous novel *Jasmine*.[83] Equally important (and, given its volume, its range, and its capacity to bridge high and low cultures, even more influential) was Santha Rama Rau's travel writing and journalism: her work, in other words, as a postcolonial critic and intellectual. It is in this postcolonial domain—that of the Third World public intellectual / native informant—that Rama Rau serves as the most illuminating predecessor.

There will be some who will find impertinent my suggestion that the minor career of even an elite Indian woman in 1950s America might be linked to the histories of such monumental figures as Homi Bhabha, Gayatri Spivak, or Edward Said. This is perhaps an especially audacious comparison with the latter, whom Benita Parry has memorialized (and not in entirely flattering terms) as the quintessential "postcolonial cosmopolitan."[84] And yet, if only as a heuristic exercise, the comparison proves instructive. At first glance, the institutionalized mechanisms of Western social science—the publicity machine, if you will, of postcolonial reputations and careers in the Euro-American academy—hardly seem comparable with the U.S. mass media in postwar America. In terms of differences of scale, Rama Rau's "pop nativism" may have received more attention than, say, Bhabha, though less, of course, than Salman Rushdie —unless we adjust for the exponential growth of media outlets in the period between the 1960s and the late twentieth century, not to mention the overlap between academic and popular debates in the wake of the culture wars and Fox TV. In terms of scales of value, again, Rama Rau cannot and perhaps should not be placed in the same frame of analysis as the likes of Said and Spivak, who are admittedly among the intellectual giants of their time. Her "pidgin anthropology," to borrow from Marshall

Sahlins, cannot compare with the work that, by now, at least two generations of postcolonial critics have done to reimagine the relation of the East
to the West and of West to "the rest." Her minor celebrity, her minor
status, her minor career—the "minority" of which derives directly from
her (highly gendered) identification with mass culture—all act as brakes
on any facile articulation between Santha Rama Rau and the cadre of
postcolonial critics who have risen to prominence in the academy and
outside it, albeit notoriously, as representatives of the postmodern, linguistic, and cultural turns, in the last two decades.

And yet we have already seen how Rama Rau anticipated de Mel's
lateral cosmopolitanism, the Raj nostalgia of the 1980s, and even, in a
popular register, some of the objections that Said's *Orientalism* raised to
knowledge production about the East in the West—observations which,
not incidentally, made his now-famous career. Indeed, it is no mere
contrapuntal irony that the epigraph for *Orientalism* was Benjamin Dis-
raeli's celebrated phrase "the East is a career."[85] Broadly speaking, the
archive of *The Cooking of India* illustrates too how perspicacious Rama
Rau's interest in the culinary was in the late 1960s. As I touch on in
chapter 3, this was the exact moment during which the careers of Claude
Lévi-Strauss, Mary Daly, and McKim Marriott—some of the most distinguished anthropologists of their day who drew on the artifacts of Indian
and other non-Western foodways to synthesize their theories about culture and its formations—were very publicly made. This was also, generally speaking, the golden age of area studies in the United States, when
different forms of orientalist knowledge proliferated and were repudiated
in settings that linked them to very specific "North American styles of
thinking."[86] Last but not least, Santha Rama Rau fits many of the characteristics Brennan has associated with the "new cosmopolitans" of the
1980s. Writers like Rushdie, Mario Vargas Llosa, and Isabel Allende were
"propelled and defined by media and market," acting as "spokesmen [*sic*]
for a kind of perennial immigration, valorized by a rhetoric of wandering
and rife with allusions to the all-seeing eye of the nomadic sensibility."[87]
Brennan's argument is built on the premise that the 1980s generation was
a first, and as a critical mass they certainly were. If Santha Rama Rau's
career was a forerunner to the rise of "the cosmopolitan writer," it also
anticipated the commodification and institutionalization of the domain

that has been called "world literature" in an attempt by Western critics to fix the "nomadic" Third World writer for consumption in a global marketplace. In doing so, Santha Rama Rau's story dramatizes the historically contingent relationships between academic expertise and pop professionalism, signaling again the genealogy of that phenomenon long before the current conjuncture, as well as its roots in a Cold War political economy and the peculiar role of Indian elites in shaping its postcolonial character.

In this context it is tempting to ask: who, indeed, has been read by more people, Santha Rama Rau or Gayatri Spivak? Rama Rau or Bhabha?[88] I trust it is clear that I am not advocating that we "raise" Santha Rama Rau from relative obscurity so that she can now "count" in the pantheon of postcolonial critics. What I *am* suggesting is that her career be considered "coeval," to borrow Johannes Fabian's phrase, with the work of later postcolonial critics, as we begin to reflect on and ultimately to write the histories of postcoloniality in the shadow of globalization and its handmaiden, Euro-American imperial hegemony.[89] By this I do not mean to suggest that she anticipated everything that postcolonial studies was to do, but rather that she not be dismissed as an early incarnation simply because she operated in the realm of the popular.[90] Nor do I want to fetishize the celebrity character of the holy trinity of Said-Spivak-Bhabha—in part because to do is to obscure (again) the work of many other late-twentieth- and twenty-first-century postcolonial critics who operate from very different vantage points than Said and Co. While it is perhaps a stretch to see the latter as derivative of the Nehruvian vision Rama Rau articulated, however ex-centrically, they share its perspectives far more than the next generation of postcolonial critics in the academy (Amritjit Singh, Vijay Prashad, and Ania Loomba, for example)—for whom the descriptor postcolonialism "from below" (where "below" signifies as much the global south as it does the social "bottom") attests to a very particular politics of location. If the cleavage in both reception and celebrity between these two sets of postcolonial critics can be attributed to generational difference (and hence to historical contingency), it also raises questions about which postcolonials get to become public intellectuals and which remain "native informants"—a question that the multiple and variegated Cold War careers of Santha Rama Rau arguably throw into bold relief.[91]

Of course, it should be said that too much emphasis on Rama Rau's originary role is as dangerous to a full-blown history of postcolonialism's pasts as accounts that occlude her altogether. In many respects she is one in a long line of famous Indian personalities who used American soil to stake claims for India and Indian causes, including Pandita Ramabai in the 1880s and Swami Vivekananda in the 1890s—both major figures in South Asian and Indian diasporic history alike.[92] At the same time I want to hold on to rather than reject out of hand Santha Rama Rau's distinctively and undeniably minor status. I am well aware of how easy it would be, in the context of certain practices of women's and gender history, to recuperate, by recovering, Santha Rama Rau's biography for a progressive, emancipatory feminist narrative, as well as, in her case, for a similarly triumphalist diasporic one. This is precisely why I have not cleaved to the genre of biography but have insisted instead on the phenomenon of her career as the subject of my inquiry. As the work of Marilyn Booth has brilliantly shown, biography need not simply reconsolidate the historically fragmented subject into a coherent individualized whole, despite its historic tendency as a genre to do just that.[93] And yet even proponents of "the new biography" (Booth excepted) have called for the "resurrection" of the form and its subjects in order to intervene in the logic, and redirect the velocity, of "master narratives," most typically national ones.[94] I prefer to capitalize on Santha Rama Rau's minority status, and not just out of dissatisfaction with the redemptive character of such resurrectionist tendencies (especially among the champions of minor literature, as Gilles Deleuze and Félix Guattari demonstrate).[95] I do so in sympathy with David Lloyd's conviction that the location of "minor" writer registers "a negative critical position" which, in turn, rejects the very possibility of autonomous subjectivity that tends to animate the politics of the canon (i.e., "major" writers and their literatures).[96] I do so also because it is the structurally subordinate location of "the minor" *qua minor* that allows us to see the operations of dominant discourses and material power with an analytical precision that is, arguably, impossible from any other vantage point. Or, it allows us to view such operations not as cause / effect—as in, Santha Rama Rau had this impact on that attitude or policy—but to recognize them as more diffuse and therefore vulnerable to appropriation, as in a kind of "scattered hegemony" (to borrow from Karen Caplan and Inderpal Grewal), than their own self-representations permit.[97]

Such a negative critical position—like the one Santha Rama Rau occupied throughout her career in the political culture of Cold War America—is not intrinsically subversive. It does not necessarily furnish its inhabitants with the power to bring down dominant structures, though it is a kind of unhinged and hence unhinging position nonetheless, even if not consistently or programmatically so. Nor should it be conflated with subalternity per se. Indeed, as is the case with Rama Rau's career, such a position can and usually does entail some collaboration in the ideological work of hegemony, even and especially in the recesses of "national" political culture. Thus the attention I direct to Santha Rama Rau's "co-evalness" is less about deprovincializing her, or about reorienting the master narratives of either postwar America or the Indian diaspora, than it is about (re)establishing the angle of vision from which she worked, and through which we, now, can see the rifts and fissures, the unevenness, of cosmopolitan identity in the twin contexts of postcolonialism and Cold War American imperialism. In this sense, and again, I am in sympathy with the call to understand the phenomenon of "minor transnationalism" identified and theorized by Lionnet and Shih, though my emphasis is on Santha Rama Rau as a minor figure rather than as a representative of a minor cultural formation. In terms of her career cosmopolitanism I understand her too as a carrier of transnationalism "from above" and as a "coauthor of the global order" (to cite Ali Behdad and Susan Koshy respectively from that volume) rather than as an insurgent subject per se.[98] Above all, I historicize her as an example of the complex incarnation of the pressures that empire has the capacity to exercise on apprehensions of the relationship between nationalism, cosmopolitanism, and American identity among historically "minor" subjects.[99]

Despite even these rationales, the question of Rama Rau's minority can and undoubtedly will persist. Not surprisingly, they mark the career of this very book. One major university press to whom I submitted the manuscript turned it back without sending it out to reviewers because, according to the editor, he could never publish a book about a minor writer in this unstable market.[100] "Why this writer?" is a question that has, in other words, shadowed this project from its inception through its publication and no doubt beyond. Not only did many colleagues in South Asian history and studies express surprise that I saw fit to undertake a scholarly study of Santha Rama Rau but one of my readers for Duke reported the same reaction when s/he talked about the project. At a historical moment when biographies of men and women great and small are making a commercial as well as an academic comeback, the hesitation is equally fascinating, if also slightly vexing—in no small part because it would seem to ratify one of the central claims of the book: namely, that for all that minority and majority status are deeply historically contingent, even work that attempts to track those phenomena through a critical engagement with a figure like Santha Rama Rau is dangerous simply by association with the fate of "minority" (however that is adjudged) in the marketplace.

And yet there is also a postcolonial dimension to the problem of recognition that this book grapples with. For among the queries on offer in *The Postcolonial Careers of Santha Rama Rau* is what—or more precisely, when—is the time of the postcolonial?[101] If Santha Rama Rau seems out of joint (that is, both ahead of her time but also prematurely posthumous), what does that tell us about the temporalities of postcolonial recognition not just in the context of political culture but also in the postcolonial capitalist arena—of which academic knowledge production is a constitutive part? My aim here is emphatically not to reclaim Rama Rau as a mournful figure, even if that is one route to professional or commercial recognition. Nor is it to elegize her in the name of diasporic or feminist recovery politics. It is rather, to borrow from David Scott, to use her as a lever for prising open a series of "problem spaces," prime among them the terrain shared uneasily (and unevenly) by postcolonial criticism and globalization.[102] And it is here that the deracination of Santha Rama Rau—the out-of-Indianness of her cosmopolitan career— becomes most historically significant. For what is key is not just that as a postcolonial figure she capitalized on a locale that she in fact only sporadically inhabited, or even that her claims to cosmopolitan identity were effectively enabled by, if not grounded in, a postwar American imperial territorial imaginary. It is that her career expertise was always already predicated on a vision of *globality* that required a simultaneous embrace *and* disavowal of India in the very name of Cold War cosmopolitanism—a globality that was temporally coincident with rather than a latecomer to the moment of the postcolonial. In this sense, the time of the postcolonial and the time of globalization are not serial but coincident in historical terms. Rama Rau reminds us that like history itself, neither postcolonialism nor cosmopolitanism is innocent of the politics of globalization because each has been implicated, however differentially, in its emergence as a field of power from at least the middle of the twentieth century.

Significantly, it is the question of career and its transnational terrains that has dogged postcolonial scholars in an age of global identity politics—that is, in the recent fin de siècle. Assaults by Arif Dirlik and Aijaz Ahmad on the credentials of postcolonial critics have revolved around the hypocrisy of their careers, with a recurrent emphasis on their failure to live out their professional lives full time in the territorial spaces (the non-West) upon which they have built their reputations as social science experts.[103] The reception of Edward Said's autobiography, *Out of Place* (2000), is perhaps the most powerful example of this; for although the critical furor was focused on the location of his birthplace, the truth or fiction of his biography was considered crucial to the legitimacy of his *career* as both a pro-Palestinian public intellectual and as a postcolonial critic.[104] Postcolonial theorists hailing from South Asia have come in for some of the most searing criticism, to which they have responded with an equal degree of acrimony, and perhaps rightly so. The tenor of the debate is something of a sideshow to its significance for the problem which concerns me here: that is, how the cosmopolitanism of the postcolonial expert has come under fire for failing to actualize, in the end, the Kantian desideratum: the disinterested observer, the citizen of the world, and the "liberal universalism" that that entails.[105] For all their rancor (not to mention their myopia about their own cosmopolitan career locations), Dirlik and Ahmad point to the constitutive contradiction of a career cosmopolitanism that professes to be rootless and even promiscuous intellectually and ideologically, while its genealogies are routed, however circuitously, through South Asian and British colonial genealogies. As such, postcolonial cosmopolitanism is hardly "the view from nowhere." Its modern vantage points are historically intelligible through, if not largely derivative of, the career of British colonialism itself.[106]

There is no denying the multiple streams of influence, including the Vietnam War, graduate training in the United States, and the impact of various local and national political struggles in India and elsewhere beyond the West, which have shaped the career trajectories of many of the leading lights of postcolonial studies. This is exactly the problem that the volume *At Home in Diaspora* (a collection of autobiographical accounts by the likes of Gyan Prakash, Arjun Appadurai, and Dipesh Chakrabarty, organized by two South Asianists working from France) so frankly rehearses.[107] For it is the circulation of these biographies—all originating in South Asia, and virtually all men—not just in the world of letters but *as* the "global republic of letters" that remains at the heart of the kind of false universalism which the Kantian ideal of "cosmopolitanism"—in all its unmarked masculinity—threatens to conscript.[108] Recourse to such universalism is historically and politically intelligible, as Chakrabarty's recent scholarship has been at pains to demonstrate.[109] It also enacts certain lateral exclusions and violences that may not be immanent, yet are nonetheless part of the lived experience of others in the postcolonial world, especially if we take the most expansive and elastic measure of that geographical and imaginative ambit. Hence the culture of complaint surrounding the limits of postcolonial theory's translatability in/to other "former colonial" or "semi-colonial" venues (like China and Latin America).[110] Hence too the argument, made most cogently by Malini Johar Schueller, that postcolonial critics have been unable and moreover unwilling to deal with race as a category of analysis, one that is either entailed by or constitutive of the condition of postcoloniality itself.[111] There are, of course, important exceptions to her generalization, and they deserve our attention.[112] But at the center of Schueller's critique is the reflex she reads in figures like Bhabha, who has incorporated African American writers (like Toni Morrison) into the postcolonial canon without specifying how and under what conditions African Americans can or should be viewed as postcolonial rather than (or also) as persistently racialized subjects in the context of enduringly colonial regimes. If Bhabha's use of Morrison is not necessarily representative of postcolonial theory's problem with race, Schueller's critique is nonetheless germane to my argument about some of the maneuvers at the heart of Santha Rama Rau's career. For the presence of African Americans in postcolonial theory, and of race in postcolonial studies, operates in a register of semi-imperialism, especially where the postcolonial critic not only acts like the all-seeing, all-knowing custodian of national/transnational/world literatures but does so from the universalizing standpoint of the United States. Such a vantage point is not new to the fin de siècle; it can be traced through a variety of elite diasporic South Asian formations, of which the postcolonial careers of Santha Rama Rau represent just one iteration.

Although Schueller does not press this case as far as she might, she implies that intracolonial hierarchies of race and color—generated, I would add, both by the historical experiences of British colonialism and by forces outside it—help to explain the implicit if recurrent association between race and blackness in postcolonial criticism. Given the symbolic economies of blackness from whose influence no modern practice is automatically exempt, this is an equation that would appear to explain the disappearance, erasure, or, if you will, the relatively minor status of race as a category of analysis in postcolonial studies. Relationships between Indians and Africans, between black and brown have, of course, long histories and complex contemporary manifestations, as David Arnold's recent work on Gandhi's attitudes toward "Kaffirs" in South Africa and Rukmini Bhaya Nair's parenthetical confessions about the psychic "demons" of negritude provocatively suggest.[113] This is not to discount recent engagements with dalit-African solidarities, or the very real histories of Afro-Asian connection and "Afro-Orientalism" that scholars like Vijay Prashad, Bill Mullen, and Michael Gomez have made available.[114] Nor is it designed to reposition cosmopolitanism as something individuals "possess" but, rather, to remind us that postcolonial criticism of the kind deployed by Santha Rama Rau and Homi Bhabha alike has historically operated in racialized economies with Anglo-American antecedents and a decidedly Cold War / postcolonial U.S. accent.

To echo Neville Hoad, I want to suggest that far from transcending its time and place, postcolonial cosmopolitanism in all its varieties operates as a structure of feeling, "a web of relations" in and through all manner of worlds—deeply racialized as well as highly gendered worlds—and that the association of elite South Asians with the hegemonic whiteness of postcolonial America has become something of a naturalized phenomenon, even and especially when Africa and African Americans are invoked as signifiers of "otherness."[115] The "minority" of Santha Rama Rau then and now must be scrupulously evaluated against the various "other" minority communities that were coming into being as minorities during the very period in which she was writing. As a consequence, we must begin to work more systematically through the connections between cosmopolitanism's immediate postwar career and its long-term postcolonial effects if we are to appreciate which political strategies of affiliation and alliance work under conditions of postcoloniality, and which do not—if we are, in short, to keep visible the economies of race which late-twentieth-century American power invested in, made available to, and consistently naturalized even for progressive projects.

This does not, and should not, mean renouncing the histories of dominant elites, even individual ones; and it ought to be accompanied by more than a mere acknowledgment that a variety of people had and have cosmopolitan imaginaries, experiences, lives. As Pheng Cheah and Bruce Robbins have observed, cosmopolitan's "new cast of characters," especially those brought to our sightlines by the work of subaltern studies and others, gives new historical meanings to "a very old ideal," in ways that offer—precisely through the genealogies of specific and historically contingent figures—alternative accounts of national histories, if not necessarily alternative national histories per se.[116] But in the end, the contretemps over Santha Rama Rau's minority—"why this writer?"—is a red herring, directing our attention toward the migrant individual who is at once desired and disavowed by the market and away from her temporal and territorial context itself: in this case, the United States and the simultaneously postcolonial *and* global order it engineered. The comparative invisibility of the United States (not just as a superpower but as a figure in the postcolonial imagination) in postcolonial work is only just beginning to be fully reckoned with, in part as a result of the irrefutable evidence of contemporary American imperial-global design. If, however belatedly, the time to denaturalize American *nationalism* (a constitutive part of American imperialism in both its contemporary and its historical incarnations) is now, critical histories of work like Santha Rama Rau's offer one way of doing so, insofar as they document the impact of American nationalist discourses on historically postcolonial critics. As convictions about the tenability of American nationalist-universalist aspiration continue to unravel under the pressure of critical histories of the global, the ideological work of people like Rama Rau can and should come to be appreciated not merely as the remnants of pop culture orientalism or even as the reworkings of a Western tradition of cosmopolitanism but rather as a prehistory of the kind of postcolonial aspiration and ambition made possible by Cold War U.S. global hegemony. Needless to say, the postcolonial careers of gender—as an effect of, among other things, the political economy of value and the marketplace of transnational culture in a decolonizing and recolonizing world—in that prehistory are only just beginning to be appreciated.

In a vocational sense, the call to begin to historicize the postcolonial career of cosmopolitanism presupposes the mutually constitutive impact of politics and history, as well as a conviction about the work that history can do in and for critically engaged communities, whether of ordinary people, politicized elites, or academics.[117] It is, in turn, a salutary reminder of the multiple cultures made available by public discourse, as well as the imprint left on them by the collision of individuals with those historically contingent forms of hierarchy and value that go into making "celebrity," whether major or not.[118] The call to historicize the embodied careers of postcolonial cosmopolitanism is, in other words, one of many possible responses to Spivak's provocation, "what is the fate of historians' informant?" In keeping with my skepticism about redemptivist narratives, I propose this history of minor cosmopolitanism not in order to rescue postcolonial studies from the oblivion or comparative irrelevance we are told is its fate in the so-called new age of globalization, nor to explain away its failures by tracing the genealogy of some of its critical blind spots—nor even to embrace a triumphalist feminist reading of a spectacularly gendered figure. Rather, I offer Santha Rama Rau's career as an indisputably minor footnote in the story of Cold War orientalism in the conviction that, as with knowledge produced by any citationary apparatus, even and especially the history that is in the details requires recognition *as history*, followed by sustained attention and, ultimately, radical critique.

1

Cold War Cosmopolitanism

The Education of Santha Rama Rau in the

Age of Bandung, 1945–1960

We drove past the conference building and saw the flags of the twenty-nine participating nations of Asia and Africa billowing lazily in the weak wind; already the streets were packed with crowds and their black and yellow and brown faces looked eagerly at each passing car . . . to catch sight of some prime minister, a U Nu, a Chou En-lai, a Nehru . . . it was the first time in their downtrodden lives that they'd seen so many of their color, race and nationality arrayed in such aspects of power, their men keeping order, their Asia and their Africa in control of their destinies.—Richard Wright, *The Color Curtain*

When Santha Rama Rau burst onto the international literary scene in 1945 with her first book, *Home to India,* she was just twenty-two years old. Over half a dozen books and half a century later, she was anthologized in a Norton reader as a writer, a writing teacher, and the prototypical cosmopolitan of the twentieth century: "born in Madras, India . . . [she] lived all over the world, from England to South Africa to Japan, until she settled in the United States."[1] Rama Rau's transformation from fledgling author into the embodiment of the modern cosmopolitan ideal was largely a function of her elite status, her family connections, and the opportunities available to her as an educated Indian woman. The daughter of a diplomat-father and an activist-feminist mother, she had all the credentials of the classic cosmopolite, including a transnational childhood lived across the spaces of the British Raj and an equally mobile adulthood facilitated by marriage to an American and a career as a travel-writer. Though she did not recognize herself as exceptional, she conceded that her contemporaries might find her life "odd, peculiar, even a little mad . . . or exotic."[2] Exoticism was, of course, a fate to which many formerly colonial people who aspired to a cosmopolitan identity were subject in the decades following the breakup of the British empire. But Rama Rau's story does more than reveal the possibilities and limits of cosmopolitanism. Taken together, the books she produced in the wake of her travels in the 1950s articulate a shifting vision of global community: from an earlier, Eurocentric model—rooted in a British and imperial worldview—to a pan-Asian model—rooted in the realization of an emergent America-centered global hegemony. Like most if not all women's travelwriting, Rama Rau's work demonstrates how the sentimental journey of development articulated in the travelogue helps to shape a gendered narrative of political education—in this case, that of a privileged Indian woman in a newly, if unevenly, "postcolonial" world.[3] It also enables us to see with particular vividness the intersection of a historically specific form of cosmopolitanism with the realities of the late-twentieth-century world order as symbolized by the 1955 conference in Bandung— that historic gathering of non-aligned states that marked an attempt by "Third World" nations to declare independence from Cold War politics —and to appreciate the role of India, and Indians, as sites of translation between one Anglophone empire (Britain) and another (the United States).[4]

As we will see, Rama Rau was not always comfortable confronting this "reality" or discovering that she was, by virtue of being Indian at a particular world-historical juncture, expected by many she encountered to identify both with an all-Asia identity *and* an American-realpolitik view of the future. Specifying Rama Rau's unease as she encountered, lived, and tried to work through the shifting ground of cosmopolitanism in a decolonizing context reminds us of cosmopolitanism's spatial and temporal contingencies—a historical dimension which has been curiously neglected in recent debates about the utility of "cosmopolitics" in a putatively postnational world. Indeed, although there is general agreement that cosmopolitanism is "a very old ideal," there is little work that actually historicizes the long career of the concept, let alone its embodied subjectivities.[5] Its transnational appeal has been accompanied, in other words, by a presumption about its transhistorical character. To be sure, more democratic expressions of cosmopolitan identity—made visible by the self-conscious appropriation of a historically elite model for the subjects of diaspora, transnationalism, and "flexible citizenship"—are at the heart of a host of recent global research agendas.[6] But what Kumkum Sangari calls "the pressure of historical placement" weighs very lightly on many of the accounts of cosmopolitanism, whether narrative or analytical, that are being produced in the context of a globalizing academic culture.[7]

Perhaps less surprisingly, attention to the ideological and material work of gender in marking out cosmopolitan spaces and constituting cosmopolitan subjects has also been remarkably scant. Historians interested in international women's movements, especially in the early twentieth century, have made visible the cosmopolitan circuitry of transnational feminism in a global framework, drawing attention in the process to the unequal power relations between East and West which consistently undergirded the systems of political power created by this global feminist imaginary.[8] But cosmopolitanism in all its complexity, variety, contradiction, and instability has not been entertained as a category of historical analysis in this work, even though doing so might enable the deparochialization of women's and feminist history that Mrinalini Sinha, Donna Guy, and Angela Woollacott have called for.[9] Nor have those invested in reclaiming cosmopolitanism for public debate or postnational political projects been particularly attentive to its gendered character, either historically or now. This neglect has to do in part with the fact that the revival of interest in cosmopolitanism as an object of intellectual investigation has rehabilitated Kantian universalism as the originary moment of the cosmopolitan ideal—and with it, Enlightenment Europe as the originary site of cosmopolitan identities.[10] While some postcolonial engagements with Kant (most notably by Gayatri Spivak) have been informed by feminist concerns, the Kant revival has reanimated the question of universal values as if feminist critiques of this tradition had never bccn mounted.[11] Given the role of feminist theory and history in revealing the theoretical impossibility of a universal rights-bearer *except* as the unmarked white, male, middle-class Western subject over the past quarter of a century, the renaturalization of an implicitly masculinist universalism as the grounds from which all cosmopolitanisms proceed is as alarming as it is remarkable.[12]

This is not to say that women per se have been absent from these conversations, or that the world beyond the West has not left its imprint on "cosmopolitics" writ large. As the work of Martha C. Nussbaum has demonstrated, the stories of Third World women are the very grounds upon which claims about universal rights, civic participation, and transnational belonging can, apparently, still be made. Nussbaum has singled out Indian women for special consideration in her prodigious writing in defense of "cultural universalism" and "universal values."[13] Relying on interviews with and observations of the women of SEWA—the Ahmedabad-based Self-Employment for Women Association—in the 1990s, Nussbaum mobilizes the figure of the disenfranchised Indian woman to make her case for the necessity of balancing rights with "human capabilities" on a global, universal scale. Despite her determination to distance herself from traditions of both the colonial state and imperial feminism—which distinguished themselves historically for establishing Indian women as the subjects, both literal and figurative, upon which justifications for the civilizing mission were founded—Nussbaum ends up reinscribing "the Indian woman" as the pathetic basis of a newly invigorated call for a cosmopolitan human rights philosophy. And yet as troubling as this is, it is not the most significant problem that her work poses to the conjuncture of "women" and "cosmopolitanism." For Nussbaum, the women of SEWA are the subjects of cosmopolitan concern and intervention, rather than agents of cosmopolitanism themselves. This, despite the fact that SEWA's world-vision, far from being provincial, reflects and in many ways anticipates the very kind of visionary commitment to individual well-being, economic "flourishing," and universal principles of social justice that Nussbaum prescribes as the international ideal.[14] Significantly, Nussbaum does credit some Indians with a cosmopolitan vision: most notably, Jawaharlal Nehru and Rabindranath Tagore, both of whom she admires for struggling against the narrow interests of Indian nationalism and reaching instead for "the worldwide community of human beings."[15]

The extent to which Nehru and Tagore advocated cosmopolitanism as a strategy of *anti-colonial* nationalism is not of especial concern to Nussbaum. In the end, they are as ornamental as Vasanti and Jayamma, the "SEWA women" whom Nussbaum foregrounds in order to make her case for the capabilities approach to transnational justice. Quotes from Nehru and Tagore adorn the pages of Nussbaum's *Women and Human Development*, while an account of Tagore's novel, *The Home and the World*, does little more than launch her famous salvo on cosmopolitanism as the best, most desirable form of identity politics.[16] There, it is "the cosmopolitan stance" of the landlord Nikhil which inspires her admiration because it "asks us to give our first allegiance to what is morally good—and that which, being good, I can commend as such to all human beings."[17] If Nikhil—and by extension, Tagore himself—emerges as a kind of Indian Kant in this account, it is at the expense of a character in the story who is barely mentioned by Nussbaum: Nikhil's wife, Bimala. The object of Nikhil's nationalist/patriarchalist, reformist/humanitarian desires, Bimala herself is the vehicle for Tagore's critique of a nationalist cosmopolitanism gone awry.[18] As such, she is effectively evacuated from Nussbaum's narrative of the story: the absent-present Indian woman who enables cosmopolitanism, its critics, and even its late-twentieth-century resurrectionists but who is invisible at best, consistently instrumental at worst in Nussbaum's plea for an embrace of cosmopolitan values on the threshold of the new millennium.[19]

If these narrative strategies underscore Nussbaum's indebtedness (however unwitting or insouciant) to the historically freighted legacy of orientalist thinking, they also situate cosmopolitanism squarely in an orientalist tradition, in which India and Indians and especially Indian women serve as opportunities for humanitarian intervention (however updated) rather than as makers of cosmopolitan visions themselves. A recent and very promising exception to the Nussbaum view appears in the scholarship of Neloufer de Mel, whose book *Women and the Nation's Narrative* offers the paradigm of "lateral cosmopolitanism" to describe the ideological, cultural, and political work done by Sri Lankan women in the local and intraregional landscapes of twentieth-century South Asia.[20] In these contexts, the case of Santha Rama Rau opens up the possibility of a similar kind of counterhistory of cosmopolitanism, though not perhaps in a self-evident way. Locating Rama Rau as a cosmopolitan subject in her own right challenges a long tradition of subjugating Indian women and their knowledges to the "humanitarian" projects of Eurocentric politics and philosophy, of which Nussbaum's is just one contemporary incarnation.[21] The work that Rama Rau did to "cosmopolize" the variety of "natives" she encountered during her travels—and the record she left of their resistances—is also a challenge to the discourses of cosmopolitanism that continue to come down to us as simultaneously "European" *and* geopolitically disinterested. And yet in suggesting this I do not wish to reclaim formerly Eurocentric versions of cosmopolitanism as postcolonial "Indian" property ("natives" can be cosmopolitan too). What is historically significant and politically consequential about Rama Rau's work is that her performance of cosmopolitanism—its riff on the Kantian ideal of universalist, worldly disinterest—was the enactment of a very particular, highly contingent promontory perspective on both Asia and the decolonizing world more generally.[22] An inheritance of British colonialism and Indian nationalism both, Rama Rau's cosmopolitanism was also the effect of her identification with American geopolitical power and her desire to be seen as an extranational Indian expert in the first decades of the Cold War.

As we will see, Rama Rau was above all an uneasy cosmopolitan, in part because she came to realize that a peculiar brand of orientalism animated her aspiring cosmopolitan visions—a phenomenon she recognized with surprise, puzzlement, regret, and, finally, a very publicly staged political transformation. In the process, she mapped the progress of her particular postcolonial "education" for the benefit of the postwar readers in Britain and the United States especially: readers who had a growing appetite for what Christina Klein has called "Cold War orientalism."[23] Equally provocative is the pointedly gendered dis-ease Rama Rau experienced as she tried to negotiate the shifting role of "India for Indians" at once within the parameters of the cosmopolitanism she had inherited from a pre-postcolonial world *and* against the backdrop of a pan-Asianism with which she felt a deep and unanticipated sympathy. Nor, as we will see, did the "new world of Asia" represent the territorial limit of her Cold War cosmopolitanism. She viewed Africa, through the lens of Mau Mau, as an object lesson in the challenges of managing insurgent nationalism and "the race question" in the years leading up to the Bandung Conference. Reading Rama Rau as an emergent and uneasy cosmopolitan allows us to begin to historicize the cultural politics of nationalism in the age of Bandung. Rather than festishizing the Conference as an unequivocally liberatory or even inaugural event, made possible by the demise of European empires and the emergence of avowedly "nonaligned" postcolonial leaders on the world stage, we need to appreciate Bandung, its immediate prehistory, and its aftermath as an extended historical moment during which a set of semi-imperialisms (India over Japan, India over Africa, India as *prima inter pares* in Asia) also emerged. These semi-imperialisms were animated by postwar realignments, by the colonial legacies that helped to shape the ideological character and the political culture of new states (India prime among them), and by the exigencies of that quintessential Cold War figure: the postcolonial expert.[24]

Rama Rau's diasporic childhood and adolescence set the stage for the kind of Cold War cosmopolitan she became. Her father, Sir Benegal Rau, had been financial advisor to the Simon Commission and, later, secretary to the Round Table Conference.[25] As a result, the family lived in England for much of the 1930s, with the two children, Premila and Santha, attending a Quaker school in Surrey as boarders, and in South Africa, which is where they were when World War II broke out. Her mother, Dhanvanthi Rama Rau, was an equally prominent social reformer with a special interest in family planning. President of the All-India Women's Conference, she was willing to stand up to British feminists of the period over issues like child marriage and purdah in the interwar years.[26] The Rama Raus were fierce Gandhians and then Nehruvians, in deed as well as word: Santha's father served the postcolonial Indian state as the first Indian ambassador to Tokyo and then to Washington, career moves which were to shape his daughter's apprehensions of the global arena in life-changing ways. Rama Rau's mother, for her part, was a staunch defender of the Nehruvian vision, with its secular (meaning both nonreligious and worldly) commitments and its developmentalist agenda of social progress.[27] But she eschewed the companionate marriage model that had undergirded Indian nationalism (at least of the Congress variety) since the nineteenth century, refusing to accompany her husband on his diplomatic mission to Tokyo, for example, in order to carry on her work with the All India Women's Conference (AIWC) on the eve of Independence.[28] In short, Santha Rama Rau's privileged childhood predisposed her to appreciate the connections between cosmopolitanism travel and politics—and especially between Indian nationalism and transnational mobility.

Santha Rama Rau's first book, *Home to India,* not only announced her arrival on the literary scene: it established her credentials as a cosmopolitan traveler on the very threshold of a postcolonial India. As she framed it at the start of the narrative, such cosmopolitanism depended on an identification with and allegiance to Britain and things British for its vision and its cachet—articulated here through the idiom of orientalism. Set in 1939, the book chronicles Rama Rau's return to her grandmother's house in Bombay, and to India more generally, for the first time in nearly a decade. Though born in India, Santha Rama Rau sees herself as a foreigner in her own land—someone who is "homesick for London" and recognizes India in a vague sort of way from "Hollywood's Orients."[29] Drawing on a twentieth-century practice among elite Indian women writers of conjuring domestic space as the nation, Rama Rau stages her grandmother's home as all of India. Thus the Colaba house emerges from the very first pages of the book as a space whose interiors represent local tradition, even as they open onto the entire subcontinent—all of which Rama Rau can experience simply by walking "across the deep veranda in to the cool twilight of the house."[30] The embeddedness of this narrative practice in colonialist assumptions is difficult to ignore in *Home to India,* where a creeping orientalism undergirds Rama Rau's performance of Indian-but-not-quite identity. In the first instance, Rama Rau insists on calling herself a "tourist" in her grandmother's home. As such she is appalled by pigeons in the bedroom, surprised by the presence of a radio in the drawing room, and bemused by her grandmother's determination to reconcile her to her destiny as a proper, high-caste Indian woman. Both Santha and Premila see themselves as explorers, at least of a certain privileged landscape:

yacht clubs and the Taj Mahal Hotel figure prominently, though they do also take the train to Delhi to experience the winter "social season."[31] Their promontory perspective on "home" and "India" produces both as tourists sights: "out of the way places" which require them to "rough it" and above all to be schooled in their own "national" identity—as chapter two, "On Learning to be an Indian," suggests.[32] There is a touch of self-mockery in this, of course, and some stylistically naive melodrama as well ("already Europe and the war seemed like a half-remembered movie").[33] Nor are we in a position to doubt Rama Rau's true affection for her grandmother. But the fundamental "strangeness" of her grandmother's world is constitutive of how Rama Rau sees India—all the more so as her grandmother speaks Hindi but not English, while Rama Rau speaks English but not Hindi. Their relationship is the primary tourist scene of the book, one in which the grandmother serves as the authentic, hopelessly regressive female figure whose quaint views and household routines are the occasion for wide-eyed ethnography of the imperially-minded nostalgic kind.

This is not to say that *Home to India* presents a static view of India, or even of Rama Rau's own take on it. She was clearly unsettled by what she saw and equally determined to represent the shift in her initial reactions to conditions in India, both economic and social. If the return to "home," and specifically to her grandmother's house, produced an identity crisis in the young Santha (who was 16 when she came back to India, and 19 when writing about it),[34] *Home to India* can be read as an exercise in crisis management: an attempt to create and maintain a secular identity that is not at odds with orientalist (British) and nationalist (Indian) visions, but strives to reconcile them by taking local conditions into account without renouncing the geopolitical perspective of the traditionally "cosmopolitan" traveler. Again, I use "secular" here to mean both non-religious and worldly in the traditional cosmopolitan sense: a double meaning which is crucial for understanding how—through what kinds of narrative strategies—Rama Rau reworked the script offered her by the Colaba house and its inhabitants. If her grandmother stands in for a certain strand of Brahminical traditionalism, Rama Rau's mother acts as the translator of "Indian" ways for her culturally estranged daughter, as the following exchange illustrates:

I wanted explanations for . . . problems and conflicts which, I was now beginning to think, had been played up to me as a foreigner while I was abroad. What about caste? My grandmother made a great point of our being Brahmins, and while I secretly enjoyed a slightly superior feeling, I told myself sternly that the principle was vicious. Once I put the question to Mother, who explained that the barriers of caste, which had had a purpose and a meaning in one period of India's development, were now obsolete and were disintegrating rapidly, no matter what my grandmother liked to believe.

"As industrialism here gets underway," Mother said, "more and more Indians will move to cities. And in apartment houses and restaurants you can't be choosy about who lives next to you or with whom you eat; *if*," she added, "we are allowed to get our industries underway."

"What about the untouchables?" I wanted to know.

"That was originally a barrier against disease. The poorer classes of Indian society thousands of years ago were, as they are today, more susceptible to disease than those in the higher economic brackets; so the villagers took the only steps they knew how to protect themselves. These people were made to use different wells from the rest of the peasants. Today we are working very hard to change all that, both to check disease and to remove the social prejudice. You should know that Gandhiji"—the ending signifies affectionate respect—"has taken up their cause and has renamed them 'Harijans,' or the 'Chosen of God.' "

I felt that I had to scrap all my preconceived ideas and start collecting a new set. "I always thought of India as full of so many religions and races and languages that there was bound to be tension." Mother replied, "People's religion is their own business, and I think they would, given a chance, have only a friendly interest in other creeds. Nobody can be *converted* to Hinduism. You are either born a Hindu or you're not, and that's all there is to it, so there is no reason in the world why we should fight religious battles; we have nothing to gain by it. As for languages, I have found that one can travel over most of India speaking Hindustani and be understood. It is true that in the far south they talk Tamil. But there are countries in Europe much smaller than India whose populations are forced to be bi-lingual and even tri-lingual, and no one feels their unity is seriously jeopardized."[35]

Here Rama Rau's mother stakes an ideological position which is simultaneously—if complexly—orientalist, nationalist, *and* cosmopolitan. She has the same promontory view of "these people" as many colonial officials, ethnographers, and tourists of India during two centuries of the British rule, with the same humanitarian sympathy that could go along with such a perspective. She is pro-Gandhi specifically at the site of caste, at a time when by no means all nationalists supported his harijan campaign or saw it as constitutive of Indian nationalism per se. And, as a critic of narrow European definitions of linguistic pluralism (and, by extension, of Eurocentric versions of cosmopolitanism), she advocates a historically specific cosmopolitan vision: one rooted in convictions about India's capacity to participate in "universal" projects like industrialism and, of course, nationbuilding.

In many respects, Dhanvanthi Rau articulated what Kwame Anthony Appiah calls "rooted cosmopolitanism"—a politics which argues "not just . . . that everybody matters" but which "celebrates the fact that there are different local human ways of being, while humanism is consistent with the desire for global homogeneity."[36] Dhanvanthi's was, of course, also a profoundly Nehruvian vision: Nehru's convictions about India's connections with, and lessons for, the larger world were well known by the late 1930s, and even make their way into Rama Rau's text in episodic form.[37] Although she had grown up inside this vision, especially in the transnational context of "Round Table" London, encountering it in India inaugurated what Santha Rama Rau referred to as "my political education."[38]

The rest of *Home to India* tracks Rama Rau's educational development, mapping it onto a travelogue of India which moves gradually outward from the house at Colaba to New Delhi society and eventually into the heart of nationalist political circles (chapter 18, "Parlour and Nationalist Politics"). What follows retains the character of an orientalist ethnography, and more than simply residually. Santha and Premila venture into the bazaar, for example, to see how much a *pice* will purchase: "it seemed to us incredible that one could buy anything at all for half a penny, but apparently millions of people were doing it."[39] Their trips to Kashmir and Tibet have the same kind of "slumming it" cast to them, all the more so because Rama Rau continues to frame her account in the language of curiosity, tourism, and discovery and to differentiate herself and her sister from "real Indians." The fact that the Kashmir trip brings them into contact with photographers from *Life* magazine reinforces the touristic quality of the narrative. When a group of Tibetans rejects the peaches the photographer offered them but keep the tin they came in, Rama Rau remarks, "The people we met along the way were a constant source of diversion."[40]

Such comments are quite typical of how Rama Rau dramatizes her return from exile and her attempts to negotiate the relationship between her elite status and a certain kind of cosmopolitan / nationalist politics *in situ*. At the same time, as *Home to India* progresses, she represents herself as increasingly invested in *critiquing* Western visitors and registering her dissatisfaction with British imperial views about India. Although this critique produces a more knowledgeable and sympathetic view of Indian nationalism, the long-term effect of Rama Rau's political education is not an embrace of India but a geographical reorientation of a different order. As *Home to India* draws to a close, Britain is eclipsed as the source of culture, knowledge, and possibility, to be replaced by America—which, as Santha recalls, "seemed to all of us a remote and wonderful land: freedom, education, democracy for everyone."[41] The causes of this reorientation are incidental but cumulative: she meets Kamala, the daughter of an American woman and an Indian man whose commitment to civic reform impresses her; she talks with Sarojini Naidu, former Indian National Congress (INC) president, who lectures her about the machinery of democracy as the basis for a future self-governing India; and she is introduced to Americans in Bombay through her mother's organizational connections. Although the reasons for her decision to go to college in the United States (she opts for Wellesley from among the Seven Sisters schools) are never fully addressed in the text, the choice is nonetheless significant.[42] It signals a break not just with Raj traditions but with certain elite Indian nationalist ones as well: rather than being "England-returned," Rama Rau will be "America-returned" instead. Choosing the United States over Britain as the site of her education, political and otherwise, is also a dramatic break with the Anglo-Indian world of her parents, revealing the bildungsroman (the novel of development) at the heart of *Home to India* in the process.[43]

Home to India launched Santha Rama Rau's career as a minor literary celebrity. It was critically acclaimed in the *New York Times* and she was heralded as the embodiment of "East meets West."[44] "It was a strange time for me," she wrote, recalling her college years, "half in love with America, with its driving energy, its earnestness, its kindness, and its extraordinary beauty, half deploring its ignorance of conditions in the rest of the world, its smug self-righteousness, and its assumption of privilege."[45] As tempting as it is to credit her experience of living in America with this frustration and disillusionment, I want to argue that it was her experience of traveling throughout the postwar world in the 1950s with a view toward translating that world to American audiences that is primarily if not uniquely responsible for the ongoing crisis of cosmopolitan identity that characterizes her work. America—and Americans—cast a shadow over her entire corpus, troubling not just her aspiration to be a citizen of the world but her convictions about what it meant to be Indian as well. If some of her critical success was derived from the self-consciously staged orientalist tack she took for narrating her discovery of India, her next book adopted an even more didactic approach to the question of a cosmopolitan identity in a postcolonial world. *East of Home* (1950) finds her in full professional travel-writer mode as she journeys from Japan to China through Southeast Asia during tumultuous political times. Rama Rau's travel narrative is shaped inexorably by the fact that she begins her tour in the midst of Occupied Japan. To those Indians like the Rama Raus who had been Gandhians in the pre-1947 era and wished to see the fulfillment of Gandhian nationalist ideals in the immediate aftermath of both war and independence, Japan was a reminder of the complexities of "Asian" identity as well as a challenge to the national aspirations of a newly independent India. After the fall of Singapore in 1942, the Japanese were in a strategic position to make good on their claim to be "liberators of the Asiatic peoples." What's more, Subhas Chandra Bose's Free India Provisional Government (1943) urged the total mobilization of Indians in Southeast Asia behind the Indian National Army as part of a military offensive in northeast India—in consultation and cooperation with the uppermost levels of the Tokyo high command.[46] The defeat of combined Indian and Japanese troops in 1944 and the death of Bose in an airplane crash shortly thereafter effectively put an end to this particular incarnation of the pan-Asian movement, though this did not prevent India from seeking diplomatic ties with Japan after the war.[47] Rama Rau found herself at the center of this new geopolitical situation: her father was appointed the first Indian ambassador to Japan and, because her mother rejected the job, she was designated his official hostess.[48] In contrast to *Home to India, East of Home* features Rama Rau's father as the authority on worldly affairs and the interpreter of postwar politics rather than her mother, who in fact makes hardly any appearance in her writing in the 1950s.

A career diplomat, Rau senior took rather a dim view of his young daughter's naiveté, and especially of her "shock" at seeing war-torn Tokyo for the first time. The extent to which Santha Rama Rau's apprehensions of "the East" are set up, if not determined, by his diplomatic perspective may be gleaned from this anecdote, which opens the book:

> My father, who feels less need to talk than anyone I know, made one of his rare comments. "Americans," he said, "get homesick so easily."
>
> "And I suppose we don't?" I said. "East is east, and . . ."
>
> "It's all very well," he told me, "to be flippant about it, but you have only traveled in the West, and you know nothing about your own continent. Here you now feel a foreigner to the Japanese; soon you will feel increasingly foreign to the Americans and Europeans. After all," he said unemphatically, "you belong to Asia, you know, not just India."
>
> "Yes," I said, not believing him.[49]

East of Home is, in many ways, the fulfillment of this prophecy. At every turn in Japan and indeed throughout her "Asian" travels, Rama Rau is confronted by a critique of American power and a call to identify with "Asia" or the Orient as a transnational phenomenon.

Given the neocolonial status of the American conquering force in Japan in 1947 and after, this can hardly be surprising. That Santha Rama Rau identified with, and actively defended, the Occupation forces is somewhat more provocative. At one level, such an identification was perhaps inevitable, given her family's nationalist connections and her father's diplomatic status; this is especially so as the diplomatic corps in India was officially designated as "Occupation personnel" in Tokyo in 1947, with all the privileges, both official and unofficial, that that entailed.[50] Occupation personnel ate food flown in from the United States, for instance; they rode on the trains and had access to cars while the mobility of the Japanese was severely curtailed by the expense of petrol and the general breakdown of the urban infrastructure. In her capacity as hostess for her father, Rama Rau socialized with General MacArthur and his wife when they were in Tokyo. Structurally at least, this gave Rama Rau a kind of colonial perspective on the Japanese; the "Japan" which emerges in her account is thus a defeated imperial power but also an emerging colonial one by virtue of the American occupation. Rama Rau clearly understood this, though her critique was not of the American military presence but rather of her father who, she claimed, "seemed relatively unimpressed by the curious Occupation dream world in which we saw the Japanese on the streets, requisitioned their houses, used their movies and clubs, but never met them."[51]

Elsewhere, Rama Rau's narrative suggests her own take on the complex relationship of imperialism, colonialism, and the new world order as she encounters remnants of what is left of "high" Japanese culture in the immediate aftermath of war, defeat, and occupation. In the excerpt below, Rama Rau recounts a meeting with the mother of a member of the Japanese reconstruction government, Mrs. Matsudaira:

The ground floor had one long room with a veranda opening onto the garden all along one side. Beyond that there was only a kitchen. The main room was divided into two with the usual light wooden Japanese partitions. It had tatami matting on the floor and parchment window panes. The old lady began the conversation on a light diplomatic level, chatting in good, careful English about Europe and people. Her husband, as ambassador for the old government of Japan, and she had traveled over most of Europe and America, stationed first in London, later in Paris and still later in Washington. Her daughters went to school in Cheltenham and were presented at Court, of which she made rather an amusing story about the difficulty of keeping ostrich feathers in the straight, heavy, Japanese hair. I gathered that she and her family had been among the most powerful in prewar days, with several town and country houses and all the attendant luxury, but she made no reference to her change of circumstances. The whole conversation had a most unreal quality like a scene from one's childhood.[52]

This lost cosmopolitan world is especially poignant for Rama Rau because of its resonances with her own family history, wrapped up as it was in world travel cut short by the war, though in very different circumstances. At the same time, it allows her to construct Japan as the past: not primitive in any kind of organic way but thrust into the past because it has been overtaken, both literally and figuratively, by a new world order, albeit one of an uncertain future. Her response is wonderment, even pity; in what was perhaps an unconscious imitation of the classic American soldier's gesture, after she leaves the Matsudairas, she sends her monthly ration of chocolate to the children.[53]

Rama Rau's encounter with Japan and, more specifically, her exposure to pan-Asian attitudes and aspirations were structured in large part by her access to the world of powerful men her father's position gained her. She was also influenced by her husband-to-be, Faubion Bowers, a major in the U.S. armed forces, an employee of Occupation administration, and a connoisseur of (and later, academic expert on) Japanese arts, especially kabuki.[54] When he takes her to her first kabuki performance, they go backstage afterward to meet the famous kabuki actor Kichiemon. As she relates the experience: "I did not know how to bow, or how low to bow, so I gave him the Indian greeting of folded hands. He stared at me and his first words were to ask me to drape my sari over my head. Then he said, 'Now I see that India is really the mother of Asia.'"[55] What she may not have known at the time was that Bowers used the kabuki scene (and his power as an aide to MacArthur) as a cruising ground—something she would discover as their marriage unraveled, at least in part over Bowers's sexuality.[56] If knowledge about sexuality is implicit in all claims to cosmopolitanism, Rama Rau's experiences "east of home" make that point vividly clear, even as they reveal the differentially gendered character of such claims.

Despite the fact that the Japan which her father's and future husband's connections brings to her sightline is what shapes her initial encounter with "the East," as in *Home to India*, Rama Rau represents her developing political education as an effect of encounters with powerful women figures who compel her, with their "insider" knowledge and frank political commitments, to admit her own ignorance and confront the complexity of perspectives that postcolonial geopolitics brings into view. The first is a

Miss Hani, an instructor at the Jiyu Gakuyen (Freedom School—where Rama Rau also does some teaching) and a proponent of progressive, mixed (boys and girls) education. Hani's mother laments how hard the project of coeducation is in a traditional culture and bemoans what little help they have in running the school because there are no servants available. "You are an Asian," she tells Rama Rau, "so you will understand how strange that seems here."[57] Rama Rau's time in Japan is punctuated by recurrent references to her "shared" Asian identity. When she tells Hani she too aspires to be a teacher, Hani replies that "to an American I would speak about salary, but . . . we understand each other, and I would not insult you with such a discussion."[58] And when Hani asks her to tell her about the West and Rama Rau says she doesn't really know anything, "Miss Hani smiled as though she had expected just such Oriental humility from me."[59] Any number of these experiences accumulates, leading Rama Rau to reflect that "there is a curious solidarity between Asians of which I had never been conscious until I went to Japan, and here I began to notice it in my own attitude too."[60]

Significantly, Rama Rau's own attitudes do not take shape without conflict, both direct and indirect. Her father needles her about her Western presumptions and prejudices, and at least one student at the Jiyu Gakuyen challenges Rama Rau's critique of Japanese imperialism, especially because of its "atrocities." Those come in any war, the young female student responds:

> "Well, the Allies did not go around beheading captured airmen," I said on surer ground.
> "Yes, those should be punished. But is it worse to behead a man than to shoot him or hang him or kill him with an atom bomb?"
> "It seems barbaric to the West or rather," I said, thinking of the far worse atrocities that the West has been guilty of, their concentration camps, and torture chambers, "to the democracies." Then I amended that to "to Americans," because of the atrocities of democratic countries in their Asian colonies.[61]

Here as elsewhere in *East of Home,* Rama Rau exceptionalizes the United States and sidesteps the relationship between the American Occupation and imperialism *tout court*. She also displays the extent to which her claims to expertise are forged through encounters with Asian women who help her, by challenging her, to arrive at the kinds of postcolonial knowledge that was not generally available to American audiences. This is evident in the replay of her conversation with a Japanese woman journalist, Kumiko Nomura, who declares (upon hearing of Gandhi's death in 1948) that she loved the Mahatma because he was for "freedom for Asia . . . that was what brought him close to our [Japanese] hearts."[62] Their exchange as Rama Rau recorded it is worth reviewing in full:

"Oh heavens!" I said, in final exasperation. "Wars and murder, conquests and concentration camps, people dead, and people wounded, and everybody poorer and the world unable to right itself for ages afterward —why do we all have to pretend that . . . it was for freedom or some such thing? Why can't you, Kumiko, be honest and say it was for economic gain, or you had to, or from fear—"

"Almost all one's actions are from fear, I think [Kumiko replied]. We were afraid of fighting, but other fears, stronger fears, made us fight. But you," she said calmly and furiously, "an Indian, you should understand what we did. You, at last, have your freedom in your country, and you are the first nation in Asia to do that. But the rest of us? Are we not in chains? The Dutch, the French, the British rule Asia. In China, Americans try to build up their idea of a 'good government' with bullions and dollars. Siam is so small, and every Western nation has a share in her government. And now we, the last to be subjugated, are a conquered nation too. Oh," she said painfully and in despair, as though it was an old sore, "if only you had helped us . . ."

"You should be thankful," I said, sounding like a governess, "that you are occupied by the Americans. They are doing more to get your country on its feet than you could ever have done."

"But," she said, surprised into pleasantness, "that's not what I was talking about. . . . I was talking about Asia and its freedoms. Look at the movements that have started now, since the war, in Indo-China, Indonesia, in Malaya and Burma, didn't we organize them, arm them, lead them to 'democracy'"? She put the word in verbal quote marks. "It was only possible for them—weak countries—to fight their conquerors after they had seen the white men beaten. Beaten by Asians, working for Asians—that was when their prestige vanished and the subject peoples had morale enough to revolt. That is why you should have helped us. After the war," she finished quietly, " 'the democracies' returned those nations to their foreign rulers. Like all wars, it ends in mysteries . . ."

She picked up her teacup. "Come, let us drink to Asia's freedom. It is what Mahatma Gandhi would have wanted, I am sure."[63]

Given the ways in which middlebrow America apprehended Japanese women at the very moment—that is, as passive subjects and, in the title phrase of a 1944 *Saturday Evening Post* article, "The Unhappiest Women in the World"—this stark and ultimately humbling exchange may have had as powerful an impact on *Home to India*'s readers as their encounter with the would-be cosmopolitan Rama Rau herself.[64] Kumiko's passionate discussion of "Asian freedoms" offers Rama Rau a history lesson—thus contributing to her ongoing political education and, not incidentally, shoring up her own position as a cosmopolitan expert on the postcolonial scene by allowing her visibly to draw on the authentic voices and experiences of "natives."

Beyond recounting the sheer drama of this geopolitical debate, Rama Rau stages a crucial moment in her postcolonial education here, one in which she comes face to face with her own prejudices, not least of which is her patronizing attitude toward Kumiko (" 'You should be thankful,' I said, sounding like a governess"). But rather than accepting the Japanese woman's authority, Rama Rau responds to her provocations by organizing a pan-Asian trip, proposing to Bowers and some of her friends that they "tour" Indo-China, Thailand, Malaya, and Indonesia as well as China. Her account of this trip forms the bulk of *East of Home*, in which she effectively tries to work out "the problem" of "the East" for herself and for her readership—which is (as the Harper Brothers imprint indicates) largely an American one. Her literary mechanism for doing so is instructive: for after this heated discussion with Kumiko, Rama Rau herself rarely takes up for the United States as she has done in the exchange above. Instead, she allows America to be represented in the figure of her friend Clare Harris, a female equivalent of the "ugly American" who appears in *East of Home* almost a decade before the emergence of that term in William J. Lederer's and Eugene Burdick's book of the same title.[65]

Though Rama Rau tells us that Clare Harris is an American who works for the Public Relations Office in Occupied Japan and that she has been dispatched to research the "new Japanese woman," we know little else about her personal details—except that she epitomizes, and unabashedly, Klein's idea of Cold War orientalism.[66] In fact, as Rama Rau told me when I asked her in 2004, Harris was an amalgam of many Americans she met— tourists, journalists, and others—during her tour of Asia. Rama Rau tries taking Clare to kabuki plays but Clare isn't interested, dismissing them as "feudalism" and "perverted." In China, Clare is shocked and disgusted by the "scenes of confusion and uninhibited atmosphere" of the city streets, where mock fights and obstreperous market bargaining are every- where to be seen—not to mention dead bodies unattended to. " 'How appalling,' Clare would say, or, 'How callous—they just walk by.' "[67] And their discussions with a Miss Wang over the lack of a Western-style women's movement make Clare indignant. When told that "the Chinese woman occupies a position of great serenity and dignity in her family," Clare sits straight up and replies: "Do you mean that a Chinese woman looks forward to being no more than a wife and mother[?]" Such scenes recur throughout their trip and give the narrative a dramatic edge it would not otherwise have had. The trope of the "ugly American" is thus not just a straw figure but is crucial to the pedagogical aims of the book as a whole. Clare's sins are many, and they are highly gendered as well. Not only does she "shop European" everywhere she goes but she provokes politically charged discussions with "natives" and her friends alike—a tendency which Rama Rau stops short of calling unbecoming, though her unease at Clare's audacity is nonetheless clear. In Siam, Clare wants to know why the government collaborated with the Japanese. In Bali she demands to have Eastern marriage practices explained to her satisfaction and asks other more politically dangerous questions which her Balinese interlocutors try politely to parry. And at Angkor she insists on a con- versation with Bowers motivated by her frustration that people they meet seem to think that America is always to blame. "It was the same in

China, and now here," she complains. "We're wrong if we do send arms and wrong if we don't. Why does everyone expect handouts from America?"[68]

Rama Rau occasionally intervenes in these discussions, as when she defends the dramatic violence of kabuki as customary rather than simply backward-looking, commenting that she was "rather surprised to find myself arguing as an 'Asian' to a 'Westerner.' "[69] But for the most part Rama Rau absents herself, representing the conversations in a realistic, "as they happened" mode—one in which she emerges as an observer, a student even, of the political lessons on offer. Most often Clare is sparring with men in these exchanges, whether it is a local dignitary or Faubion Bowers—who often gets the last word. In response to Clare's perceptions that America could do no right, Bowers replies (in what Rama Rau calls "a puzzled voice"): "Isn't that strange, I was just thinking that we were the ones who expect handouts. We want Asia on our side and expect it to conform to our way of thinking."[70] If Clare had a retort, Rama Rau does not record it, leaving the impression in this instance as she does across the whole of *East of Home* that Clare is repeatedly silenced by both political and philosophical wisdom so persuasive that there is no possible response—at least not one that Clare has the capacity to imagine. Rama Rau thus implies that in the face of rational argumentation offered by either "authentic" natives or a "professional" expert such as Bowers, Americans like Clare are quite literally dumbstruck. Clare is a caricature, and a narratively effective one at that. She also functions as Rama Rau's ventriloquist. She asks the kinds of questions which Rama Rau, given her investment in displaying the tension between her attraction to the cause of Asia and her sympathy for (even identification with) American power, was interested in raising for her American readers in order to underscore the dilemmas and the unique contributions of the Cold War cosmopolitan. In the meantime, Clare also comes to represent the very kind of expertise to which Rama Rau offers herself as a counterpoint. While she may be sympathetic to American power, unlike Harris she is not its representative in Asia but rather an ex-centrically mobile cosmopolitan who has acquired expertise not simply by being Indian but by studying Asia as an Indian from other Asians. And she offers this cosmopolitan expertise apparently unthreateningly, in the guise of travel writing pitched at American consumers just as Asia was emerging as one of the major global flashpoints of the 1950s and 1960s.[71]

All of which leads us to ask, what exactly is on display in *East of Home*, to what political purposes and with what ideological effects? "The East" itself as a series of tourist sites *and* as a pan-Asian "whole" is clearly one of the spectacles that the book produces—evidenced as much by the way the chapters carve out the local ("China," "Indo-China," "Siam," "Indonesia") as by the map at the front ("The route of Santha Rama Rau"), which literally centers Asia for the reader. On display too of course is India's place in the postwar order. It is of Asia but ahead of it; it is superior to Asia, not simply because of its "success" at independence but because of the capacity of people like Rama Rau (and at a higher geopolitical level, Nehru) to act as translators of the world beyond the West and to navigate the new world order with old world civility.[72] In addition to Rama Rau's class position, her Brahminical Indian background gave her a privileged status over the fallen British, the unsophisticated Americans, and the multitude of East Asians who peopled the postwar stage. Equally powerful is the gender politics that the figure of Clare—and by implication, Rama Rau herself—enacts for readers. Although she is a person of privilege, traveling on her father's money, Rama Rau is nonetheless the quintessential "modern" woman, circulating all over the globe as an independent single female and giving new meaning to "the East as a career." But in contrast to Clare—or at least, when Clare is present—she often does not speak, let alone speak her mind, allowing Clare to draw the fire and Bowers to pronounce the definitive political statements. Moving "east of home" renders Rama Rau less certain of herself than when she went home to India. And, I would argue, although she is no less disposed toward a certain species of orientalism than in her first book, the promontory perspective which characterized that story is now attributed to Clare while Rama Rau, equally aloof but less unselfconscious about it, ends up in a position of ambivalence. Rama Rau is still a self-avowed cosmopolitan, and an expert one at that, but she is also one whose *inherited* confidence in the possibility of its disinterestedness is more precarious than when she began. This unstable position, with its embrace of the pedagogical power of cosmopolitanism and its residual dis-ease with the status of expert, was perhaps one of the only ones available to a diasporic Indian woman in America, a woman who was subject to an orientalizing gaze herself simply by virtue of being an Indian woman in public. Her ambivalence about the possibilities of a triumphalist, heroic model of cosmopolitanism operates, significantly, as an interesting contrast to what was on display at Bandung itself, where Nehru and Chou En-Lai especially performed decidedly masculinist models of postcolonial cosmopolitanism in the context of fading British imperial power and the realities of the new American / Soviet superpower system.[73]

As *East of Home* moves to its conclusion, Rama Rau becomes more critical of "the West" but less inclined to include the United States in that designation; she is simultaneously less identified with India and more comfortable with her newfound Asian identity. In many respects she anticipates de Mel's "lateral cosmopolitanism," with "lateral" signifying a gaze that moves horizontally across Asia rather than vertically with respect to the West.[74] To be sure, there are moments when Rama Rau is actively critical of the United States in Japan, especially with respect to the war trials, which she deemed "one of the most expensive and futile projects the Occupation had embarked on."[75] And she is chastened by both Clare's brazen Americanness and the challenges to American neo-imperialism which women like Hani and Kumiko pose to her. The book ends with her recording Bowers's rant: Americans are so ignorant of Asia, they know no Oriental languages—a fatal attitude, in his view, while "the world . . . is growing bigger every day."[76] And yet the implication is that such knowledges—of Eastern languages, arts, politics, people—are necessary for, and instrumental to, the success of the United States' new role in the decolonized and decolonizing world. Bowers may not have been an apologist for the regime, but as an employee of the Occupation and the personal aide to no one less than General MacArthur himself, he was not a critic either. A linguistic expert of the kind that would end up imagining, creating, and defending the project of area studies in U.S. universities in the late 1940s and after, he was "perilously close to those sensitive American specialists unleashed to 'uplift' the post-war world."[77]

The same may be said of Santha Rama Rau, for whom Bowers's earnest, benevolent, and utterly un-self-critical embrace of things "Eastern" stands as the model political position at the end of the book: one that she implicitly valorizes and even mimics. In this sense, the political education she stages in *East of Home* is a reorientation on several levels: from India to Asia via America, from tourist to emergent expert via Harris and Bowers—two very different models of expertise she implicitly rejects in order to fashion her own. On their last stop in Jakarta, while taking photographs of the ruination left in the wake of the Dutch colonial regime, her group is hailed by a soldier. "Are you for the Republic?" he calls out. " 'Oh yes,' we shouted back decidedly" is the reply. This would-be populism is tempered by the advantages her elite status affords her—"Before we left . . . we had dinner with President Sukarno and his wife. It was like being at home again"—but the message is clear: Rama Rau has embraced the spirit of pan-Asian solidarity as her parents did that of Indian nationalism as against the old order, European colonialism.[78] We might reasonably conclude that what Rama Rau does by the end of *East of Home* is to domesticate the unbridled and uncritical cosmopolitanism of *Home to India,* so that travel east of home produces a political reorientation from one colonial power (the post-imperial British) to another (the neo-imperial United States) and a new register for domesticity (feeling "at home" with the new Asian nationalisms) as well. Rama Rau does so by accommodating pan-Asian sympathies without countenancing the full, and one must say radical, implications of such an ideology for the new world order. In this sense, and importantly, hers is not the same kind of pan-Asianism articulated by Kumiko; that incarnation is unavailable to her as an extranational figure, someone in sympathy with the postwar American global project.[79] In this respect she echoes not only Bowers but aspects of American foreign policy more generally in the years leading up to and following Bandung.

In the end, Rama Rau's domestication project is more than figurative: Clare pairs off with one of their traveling companions and by 1951, a year after the publication of *East of Home,* Rama Rau marries Faubion Bowers. Their "companionate cosmopolitanism" was relatively short-lived, as they were divorced by the late 1960s, but it shaped Rama Rau's life as well as her apprehensions of Asia and "the East" in ways she recognized even half a century later.[80] In the interim, *Home to India* and *East of Home* inaugurated a series of careers which Rama Rau's ambivalent cosmopolitanism afforded her over the course of her long life as a diasporic figure in America. Prime among these was as a writer for *Holiday* magazine, where her participation in the series "The New World of Asia" that ran in the 1950s offered a wider audience of American readers models for a particularly gendered variety of Cold War cosmopolitanism that Rama Rau had begun to articulate in her first two books. Santha Rama Rau's contributions to the series did much the same thing for the Asian destinations she covered as her work in *East of Home* had done. Whether it was the Philippines, Cambodia, Burma, Ceylon, Indonesia, or India itself, Rama Rau was at pains in her *Holiday* articles to emphasize the multicultural character of all these places—and, I would add, the ways in which the history of migration, contact, and commercial connection inside "Asia" proper had left its imprint on what contemporary travelers encountered. In this way she attributed to Asia not just a cosmopolitan sensibility but a cosmopolitan genealogy that predated that of the West. She too contrasted the sites she covered with well-known destinations both in Europe and in Asia itself (comparing Jaipur, for example, to "Kyoto and Peking, or even Paris").[81] Or "Borobudur, a Buddhist stupa, carries in Asia as much religious authority as, say, Chartres does in Europe."[82] In so doing she effectively equalized "the East" and the West, marking out intra-Asia comparisons and further decentering Europe as the originary locale of tourism or commercial travel value. These maneuvers, in turn, made legible new cartographies of and for cosmopolitanism that had not been previously visible, at least not to Americans on a mass-consumption scale. They not only complicated assumptions about Asia's inertia and cultural uniformity; they stood in stark contrast to the orientalist representations that writers like James Michener contributed to the magazine, representations in which places like Japan stood still rather than moved with and even ahead of the times.[83] What's more, with her presumptively "native" access—access which the editors at *Holiday* underscored—Santha Rama Rau suggested that the new maps these glossies drew had long been part of local knowledge, thus underscoring the provincialism of the would-be American tourist even as they opened up new cosmopolitan vistas to a middle-class public drawn to Asia by virtue of American foreign policy maneuvers but with little or no knowledge of its histories or its regional specificities. In this sense, Rama Rau particularized "Asia" beyond an orientalizing whole as much by her status as an insider as by her travel writing per se.

Given her earlier work and her postwar American sympathies, it is not perhaps surprising that an older strain of orientalism made its way into Rama Rau's cosmopolitan visions in *Holiday* magazine. One example of this was the focus on "native" women in the venues she visited, complete with images of them that sometimes depicted waist-up, frontal nudity (as in the case of Bali) to grace the articles in the "New World of Asia" series.[84] Another is the tendency to single out India as a leader in Asia—to view India as "prima inter pares," if you will. Rama Rau's insistence on the influence of Indian culture throughout Southeast Asia is a thinly veiled chauvinism—a chauvinism admittedly offset by her genuine admiration for other Asian civilizations, which she stops just short of seeing as derivative of Indian influences both here and more generally in her corpus of writings.[85] The essay by Han Suyin (a Eurasian medical doctor and the author of *Love Is a Many Splendoured Thing*) on Singapore offers an excellent example of this India fetish as well. Its powerful image of a street scene with two Indian women and a Chinese "coolie" is designed to illustrate the juxtaposition of cultures as well as the contrast between tradition and modernity. The caption reads: "a coolie shuffling past the erect, chic young modern-thinking Indians." It is a phrase evocative of the tensions in this period between India and China in a postwar, post-colonial world—as evidenced most famously in the vexed pas de deux between Nehru and Chou En-Lai at Bandung, but equally in the American anxieties with India's flirtation with Chinese-style communism.[86] The fact that these celebrated Asian women could and did participate in the reification of Asia as an epistemological object of American consumer modernity can only be surprising if we imagine that there is any place outside the regimes of proliferation and containment which orientalism set in motion—or if we believe that cosmopolitanism could so easily shake its orientalist past, even and especially in the context of the new world of Asia.[87]

To some degree, the semi-imperial role accorded to India (vis-à-vis Japan and, with it, "East Asia" more generally) in Santha Rama Rau's writing in the decade before Bandung is derivative of the Nehruvian vision of Indian nationalism to which her parents' generation subscribed. The pan-Asian dimension of that vision stemmed at least from the 1920s, when C. R. Das had suggested the formation of an "Asiatic Federation" and Nehru himself had encountered Chinese delegates at the 1927 Brussels Congress sponsored by the League Against Imperialism.[88] Influenced by such events, Nehru had emphasized India's centrality in Asia at least beginning with the publication of his *Glimpses of World History* in 1942. Here he mapped the subcontinent's geographical location as a rationale for India's indispensability to the much-anticipated post-imperial world order and, after 1947, he used that same rationale for constructing the very bases of non-alignment. "Whichever problem in Asia you take up, somehow or other India comes into the picture," he wrote in a speech to the Indian Council of World Affairs in 1949. "Whether you think in terms of China, or the Middle East or South East Asia, India immediately comes into the picture."[89] If the boundaries of "Asia" were quite capacious, India's role was no less critical. For while Nehru decried the possibility that India should or would become the leader of Asia, he nonetheless insisted that India had a responsibility for "taking the initiative sometimes and helping others cooperate."[90] This attitude was enshrined in the planning for and the execution of the first (and last) Asian Relations Conference in Delhi in 1947—where Nehru's emphatic claim that he (and India with him) was not seeking the leadership of Asia was met with some skepticism.[91] As T. A. Keenleyside has argued, what Indian intellectuals and leaders (from Tagore to Gandhi to Nehru) wanted and what Congress was prepared to enact with respect to a postcolonial pan-Asian agenda were two very different things.[92]

At the moment, we await a comprehensive cultural reading of Nehru's pan-Asianism and its meanings for postcolonial India more generally; we also lack as full an understanding as we need of the range of postcolonial Indian nationalists' responses to the challenges posed by participation in a newly global yet highly regionalized new postwar order. In the meantime, Rama Rau's travelogue offers us an elaborate example of the cultural politics of pan-Asianism during this post-imperial, neo-imperial moment, even as it registers both the gendered subtexts and the contradictions of Cold War cosmopolitanism for a non-Western elite in the generation during and after Nehru. Given the ways in which that elite helped to shape both Indian foreign policy from Delhi and the image of India abroad from New York (especially through V. K. Menon and Nehru's sister, Vijaylakshmi Pandit, both representatives for India at the

United Nations in this period), their cosmopolitan presumptions—and the semi-imperial ideologies and practices they in turn generated—cannot easily be dismissed if we are to historicize the ideological work of geopolitical culture in the age of Bandung.

Nor was Asia the only object of an emergent semi-imperial gaze as it operated in Santha Rama Rau's writing in the years leading up to Bandung. She wrote two pieces on Kenya, one for the *New York Times* (1953) and one for the *Reporter* (1954), a now-defunct New York City magazine, which brought African nationalism into view as an example of contemporary challenges to colonial rule *and* as a cautionary tale for American readers with respect to the "problem" of race. As she had in *East of Home*, Rama Rau cast herself as a sympathetic observer in Kenya, parsing the triangulated landscape of race relations in Nairobi (white, black, brown) and, arguably, offering a more multifaceted view of African nationalism (as embodied both by Mau Mau and Jomo Kenyatta) than American readers were likely to get from either British or American correspondents.[93] Rama Rau spoke with candor about the racism of white settler colonialism in East Africa and the limits, practical and political, of a "terrorist" movement like Mau Mau. So, for example, her *New York Times* piece emphasized the insularity and presumptive racism of "the pink gin set" in Nairobi, underscoring whites' contempt for Africans and the cultural bankruptcy of white settler racism. She painted a vivid, detailed, and (as she had with Clare Harris in China) a deliberately caricatured picture of a white supremacist state that was militarized not only officially but privately as well, with European dinner parties routinely ending with a revolver rollcall—"you're armed, of course?"—before the guests headed home for the evening.[94] While she recognized that white racism and the "social insults" it daily entailed must be "deeply wounding to the Africans," however, Rama Rau's sympathies were not with the insurgents. Her *Reporter* piece, which was occasioned by her trip to Africa during Kenyatta's trial, produced an ethnography of Mau Mau that focused on the "terrifying" and often coerced oath-taking rituals by which Kikuyus were initiated into the organization, and it reflected an unflattering, partial picture of African nationalism to an American readership increasingly (if belatedly) alive to the growing "race relations" problem in its own midst.[95]

ferent Africa"—one of "big communal dances" and general "gaiety."[104]
Thinking no doubt about her audience, Rama Rau talked about identify-
ing with the Danish author Karen Blixen's experience of Africa. And
while there was more travelogue narrative in this piece than in the two
more "serious" ones discussed above, including that lively engagement
with streams of local history and transnational culture which had by now
become Rama Rau's signature, her emphasis was on the "magic" of
Africa. There were no individual Africans named save a pair of "Watussi
girls," and Kenya's political crises and racial struggles were all but completely occluded in this representation.[105] Three newspaper articles on
Africa are, to be fair, not exactly comparable with two full-length books
on Asia. And yet no account of Santha Rama Rau's career as a Cold War
cosmopolitan—of her career as postcolonial expert—would be complete
without attention to them, not least because her unmarked position as an
expatriate Indian national structures the kinds of Cold War cosmopolitanism and postcolonial expertise she sought to project in this context. Although she never references them expressly, I want to suggest that Nehru
and the Indian National Congress are a shadow presence, hovering over
both of Rama Rau's essays on Mau Mau and evocative of the ways that
Brent Edwards has suggested W. E. B. Du Bois functions as "the shadow
of shadows" in the career of Ho Chi Minh.[106] Kenyatta's career in Britain,
and especially his circulation through metropolitan spaces in Europe and
in Moscow, make him, potentially at least, a candidate for the cosmopolitan nationalism of which both Nehru and to a lesser degree Rama Rau
herself had become the embodiment by the 1950s. Rather than serving as
the explanatory framework for his later political convictions, Kenyatta's
career path was "baffling" to Rama Rau, beginning with the fact that
he "doesn't, for example, know when he was born" and continuing with
his unconventional and largely self-made education (farm labor, meter
reader, Harold Laski student).

Years later when I asked her about Kenyatta she called him a "very
charismatic character" and "a cross between a Hampstead intellectual and
a mountebank"—a phrase she had used in the *Reporter* piece as well.[107] "I
think there was a lot of showmanship in him. But he had traveled, and had
seen the whole communist setup in Russia. He saw it as a place where
everyone had equal opportunities and there was no color bar—sort of the

opposite of Kenya."[108] Though she backed away from this interpretation in 2005, in the context of Mau Mau, Rama Rau cast doubt on the efficacy of East African nationalism in part because of the unorthodox cosmopolitanism of its leader. Surely this is about differences of class, and about the ways in which discourses and material structures of "racial difference" are coded and circulate through colonial, and here a partially postcolonial, history. But it is equally, and interdependently, about hierarchies of racial and cultural difference *within and among* colonial possessions of the British empire past and present in 1953-54—hierarchies of black and brown with long histories in imperial discourse, despite what practices of coexistence, cooperation, and collaboration may have also occurred on the ground.[109] These hierarchies are very much on view in Rama Rau's *New York Times* story, which features the following observation:

> Outside the hotel, standing in the brilliant crystal sunlight of Kenya, on one of the city's busiest streetcorners, there may be a group of Masai tribesmen barefoot, carrying their spears, dressed only in a dusty blanket slung over one shoulder and with their bodies and hair rubbed with red ochre. Possibly they may be in town to shop or perhaps to sightsee. A group of Indian school children wheel by on bicycles on their way home for lunch. Veiled Muslim women of Arab descent may be peering at the things displayed in shop windows—cloth from India, canned goods from England, dresses from South Africa.
>
> These three main population groups—the Europeans, the Asian and the African—live in the same city with a high degree of mutual exclusiveness or, as a friend described it, as a racial pousse café, each element necessary to the whole, each retaining its separate identity and, in the opinion at least of most Europeans and some Indians, a disastrous and unpalatable failure when the various elements mix.[110]

If only in terms of the way her gaze moves—and in turn, directs ours—in these paragraphs, the racialized presumptions of Rama Rau's cosmopolitan vision are starkly realized. Not only are women of Arab descent absorbed into the category of "Asian"; they, along with Indian schoolchildren headed for a hot lunch at home, are ranged against barefoot Masai tribesmen who loiter, perhaps with a purpose, perhaps not. And the

Indians and Europeans agree not just on the failure of racial mixture but on its unpalatability as well.[111]

We can't say with certainty whether Rama Rau shared Kenyan Indians' views on "racial mixture," especially given the fact by the time she wrote on Mau Mau she herself had married Faubion Bowers. And again, it needs to be said that Rama Rau was not completely without appreciation for the plight of Africans or for Kenyatta himself, whose role in the Kenya African Union she at least recognized. And yet although she never names Nehru as a countermodel, she represents Kenyatta as such a desultory figure that the contrast with Nehru—someone whom Americans were coming to understand, if not exactly to like, as cultured, intellectual, and recognizably British, despite his own anti-British career—is hard not to read off Rama Rau's representations. At the very least, her curt description of Kenyatta as "a stocky man with an ugly, powerful face" invites comparison with the way Nehru was treated in the American press: the combination of his non-alignment and his intellectualism made him a highly effeminized figure in print culture and State Department correspondence alike.[112] It also stands in stark contrast to Rama Rau's characterization of Nehru's "swift, incisive, impatient intellect" elsewhere in her writings.[113] In my 2005 interview with her, when I asked her to compare them, she began by commenting on their shared socialist commitments and ended up saying that Nehru was "absolutely, transparently honest and Kenyatta did have a side of him that was untrustworthy."[114] If not exactly dishonest, Rama Rau's 1954 Kenyatta is unattractive and certainly not intellectual, and the contrast with Nehru points to a competitive politics of colonial and postcolonial masculinity that was threaded through hierarchies of race and class even as it helped to produce, by fixing, those categories themselves.[115]

Both Rama Rau's *New York Times* essay and her article for the *Reporter* were, moreover, almost completely devoid of women, in stark contrast to her Asian travelogues. The *New York Times* piece featured a series of photographs of white settler men in defiant poses; where African men appear they are either dimly recognizable as "native backdrop" or literally as ancillary, as in the photo of several from the African auxiliary patrol.[116] The one exception to this is Rama Rau's reference to the white mother who can't leave her daughter alone in the garden for fear of her being snatched by Mau Mau agents.[117] In the narratology of empire, both mother and daughter are classic white female victims, and there are no African Kumikos to challenge this representation or to offer Rama Rau insider knowledge; indeed, there are no African women at all. As significantly, the hero of the *Reporter* piece is not Kenyatta but his English lawyer D. N. Pritt, whose cynical, opportunistic, and above all legalistic line about the trial—"it is more important to fight this case than to win it"—she uses as a dramatic endpoint to her narrative.[118]

Rama Rau recognized that Kenyatta's trial did not mean the end of Mau Mau but rather the beginning of "one of the most inflammatory chapters in history—the political and emotional self-assertion of the Africans in the eastern, central and southern countries of their immense continent."[119] If we ignored the word "inflammatory," it might be possible to read this as an anodyne statement, even an agnostic one, with respect to the "problem" of African nationalism. But given the tensions over racial hierarchies in Africa and the circumstances through which the postcolonial Indian state came to a public embrace of the project of African nationalism in both parliamentary debate and on the world stage, we do so at our peril. In the years between Independence and Bandung, the Indian government's interest in Africa was focused on, if not strictly limited to, the problem of Indian settlers in South Africa and East Africa.[120] And although "Asia and Africa" were paired in Nehru's rhetoric as part of his vision for the postwar world, it was always in that order; and it was clear pretty consistently from 1947 onward that it was Asia that was to take "responsibility" for spreading "freedom . . . out over the whole human race."[121] What's more, Nehru's speech at the Asian Relations Conference in Delhi in 1947 articulated a patron-client relationship in which Africa was specifically imagined as the object of such Asian responsibility.[122] Bandung indubitably ratcheted up the stakes, both symbolic and real, of Afro-Asian unity in the face of Western anxieties about the insurgent nationalisms of the Third World, though it did not necessarily interrupt the logic of clientism through which India saw Africa, at least until events in Algeria in 1956 and the Congo in 1960 (where, incidentally, India made an army brigade available to the United Nations in 1961) compelled a more explicit commitment to Afro-Asian brotherhood.[123] The nature of this clientism (which was one structural manifestation of the phenomenon of "semi-imperialism" that

I have been using to describe Rama Rau's discursive maneuvers) is perforce complex. Nehru himself articulated a developmentalist logic of African nationalism through what he called (echoing Nkrumah) in 1958 the growth of "the African personality"—a logic that was accompanied by all good wishes and exhortations to Indians to find solidarity with the new postcolonial regime in Ghana, for example.[124] The conference of African students that Nehru had opened in Delhi in 1956 was a more concrete expression of that commitment, even as it located the anti-colonial training ground squarely in India. Nor should African agency be discounted here. As the testimonies of some delegates from Zambia under Kenneth Kaunda suggest, there were some Africans who appreciated Nehru's insistence on the link between Asian and African struggles, calling him "Nehruji" and recognizing in him the architect of "Afro-Asianism."[125]

As James Ferguson reminds us, such articulations of African modernity were as vital and necessary as nationalism itself, even if they were expressed in part as clientism in a developmentalist register. At the same time, and as Nehru understood, postwar modernity meant "global status . . . [i.e.,] the condition of being first"—and of course, of being able to recognize and make globally visible, those "others" who came behind.[126] Given the geopolitical realities that were developing in the 1950s, then, Santha Rama Rau's Kenyan pieces offer not just a pre-history to the solidarities set in motion by Bandung; they mark out many of the lines of tension as well—some imprinted with older British imperial legacies, others more freshly minted in light of new postcolonial realities, America's postwar global aspirations among them. For one of Rama Rau's accomplishments in her *Reporter* essay was to translate Mau Mau into terms that Americans could appreciate. Near the start of her article on Kenyatta's trial, she noted that the Europeans in the colony called Mau Mau " 'the African Stern Gang' or sometimes a 'Ku Klux Klan in reverse.' "[127] The Stern Gang (technically, Lehi: a Hebrew acronym for *Lohamei Herut Israel*, "Fighters for the Freedom of Israel") was a Jewish paramilitary group at work prior to the founding of the State of Israel; the Klan, for its part, was garnering increased publicity in the postwar period as it saw opportunities to both fuel and capitalize on anti-black violence in the South.[128] The juxtaposition of these two terms, and the comparisons they evoke, speaks directly to the ambivalence Rama Rau registered about what she saw in Africa in the early 1950s, and to the position she was cultivating as a postcolonial expert for an American audience. On the one hand, the Stern Gang was an anti-colonial organization which attacked mainly British targets; on the other hand, there was nothing redemptive about the Klan; and at the end of the day, both of these analogies were drawn directly from white settler usage in ways that, whether by design or effect, offered American readers an imperial vantage point refracted through two "inflammatory" sites in contemporary U.S. policy and culture. As in *East of Home*, Rama Rau delivered an "Indian" postcolonial perspective that underscored her own cosmopolitan identity (world traveler, world commentator) but did so via an appreciation for American neo-imperial sensibilities. In the case of Mau Mau and the Klan metaphor, she broached at least the possibility that America's race relations might be viewed as a problem of domestic colonial management and containment. Given that *New York Times* coverage used the word "Negro" to describe Africans in the context of Mau Mau, that leap of interpretation would not have been so very great for readers.[129]

Such an interpretive possibility has, moreover, important resonances with recent work on the links between Cold War ideologies and civil rights activity,[130] not least because it adds a layer of transnational complexity often alluded to in those new histories but rarely fully explored: that is, it foregrounds the role of India and Indians in shaping the cultural and ideological terms through which the United States struggled to become, and to imagine itself as, the post-British imperial world power after 1945. Frenise Logan's work on racism and Indian-U.S. relations is now more than twenty years old, but it deserves revisiting for the arguments she makes about how and why Indians in India articulated their views about American racial policy toward "negros" in the almost ten years leading up to Bandung. What she tracks is a resistance in the Indian press to American claims to fitness for world leadership given the persistence of Jim Crow in the U.S. South.[131] Such sentiment is the very kind that made the State Department anxious about non-alignment in general and Bandung in particular. It is also quite a different angle of vision from Santha Rama Rau's. Work like Logan's can and should be used as the basis for new histories about how and under what conditions Indians of all classes, castes, and political / geographical locations have embedded histories of

British colonialism in and articulated global power through reference to contemporary U.S. politics—and how and under what conditions they did not, since of course South Asian history need not and should not be completely absorbed into either American imperial history or, for that matter, into a paradigmatically "Bandung-and-after" history either. In the end, Santha Rama Rau may not be representative of "Indian" voices in India, in America, or in the spaces in between—though if we concede that, we must, I think, admit that representativeness as a standard for measuring worthiness for historical consideration is one enduring historical legacy of colonial ideologies and practices themselves.[132] In any case, her career does offer us a concrete example of how India and Indians have facilitated American identification with and disavowal of British imperial hegemony, as well as how flexible cosmopolitanism and its agents have been in their encounters with modernity, postcolonialism, and history.

Rama Rau herself is a particularly vivid example of how "discrepant subjects of globalization" can and often do function as cosmopolitan ones—particularly, as Caren Kaplan has observed, when they are women emerging in post- and neocolonial moments.[133] Given the extent to which "practices of othering internal to the East" are a commonplace of state imaginings and national image-management in the modern world outside the West, the orientalisms and the racialisms at the heart of Rau's cosmopolitan self-fashioning may not be as remarkable as we might expect.[134] If Rama Rau contributed in a minor way to the remapping of Asia and, to a much lesser degree, Africa in the American mind in the 1950s and 1960s, the effects of such work were not limited to her "Third World" travel writing. Rama Rau published *My Russian Journey* in 1959 —after allowing it to be excerpted in part in the pages of *Holiday*—to great acclaim.[135] As she told me in one of my interviews with her in 2004, she went along with Bowers who was then working on a project about the Russian composer Vladimir Scriabin. And she emphasized more than once that she did not perceive *My Russian Journey* as a travel book but rather as a more intimate glimpse into Russian life.[136] It is a bit of a challenge to sustain this interpretation of the text, which, while it has its moments of close reading and cultural analyses, moves from city to city and site to site in ways reminiscent of *East of Home* especially. For our purposes, what is significant is the attention Rama Rau focuses on both

Uzbekistan and Tashkent—places that she suggested belonged "as much to the poor continent of Asia as to the Soviet Union."[137] As elsewhere in her work, the realities of the Cold War superpower system left their mark on her apprehensions of Russia: Bowers and she are especially interested in seeing the old town of Tashkent as a way of understanding "what it was all like before 'Soviet development.' "[138] Her description of Tashkent operates from the presumption that it was like any other market town in Asia because, she observes, "the smells and noise were instantly familiar to me from India."[139] The Asian character of Tashkent is confirmed for her at every turn, as when they witness classes of children at Tashkent school studying Hindi and especially as they toured Samarkand—much to the distress of their Intourist guide, who tried unsuccessfully to hurry them back to Tashkent.[140]

Although Santha Rama Rau does not reference it, Indians had of course had a longstanding interest in Russia, with Rabindranath Tagore's visit there in 1930 among the most well known connections between Indian intellectuals and "the Russian people."[141] The Soviet Union too was a site of keen interest for Indian foreign policy makers, both despite and because of India's non-alignment position during this period. In the contexts of Indian writing on Russia, Rama Rau's allusions to its Asian connections were not unusual; but in the universe of popular coverage of things Russian in the United States, the move was a bit more provocative, if not exactly controversial. Rama Rau does not exhibit the same kind of Indian-chauvinist or orientalist view on Tashkent or even Samarkand as she did in *East of Home*, in part because *My Russian Journey* marks her out as a savvier traveler, less concerned with representing her own political education (she was thirty-six in 1959) than with producing an ethnographic view of Russian life.[142] And yet highlighting her own—and her family's—cosmopolitanism remains a preoccupation of the narrative, exemplified most pointedly by the fact that she and Bowers traveled through Russia with their son Jai and his African American "nurse," Ruth Camm, to whom the book is dedicated. Rama Rau was apparently unaware that what Kate Baldwin calls "encounters between black and red" (that is, between Russians and African Americans) had been going on at least from the 1920s—encounters which left their imprint in many spaces of Soviet life and, of course, also circulated back into American culture, both black and white, at home.[143] The spectacle that their "family" group apparently produced on the streets of Russia dominated the introductory pages of *My Russian Journey:* "one child of four dressed in a cowboy hat, one very beautiful Negro girl, one Indian, one American. Of all of us, the only one who might have passed as a Russian was the American."[144] This is all that Rama Rau makes of it in the narrative, yet the implication is clear: for all the Asianness of the Russian landscape, she herself is not in danger of passing, at least in part because she had Ruth Camm in train. That ads for the book produced by Harper and Brothers capitalized on the spectacle suggests that the "contrast" between black and brown was perceived as useful for selling Santha Rama Rau.[145] It is surely a testimony to the politics of what scholars have come to call Cold War/civil rights culture that in Russia it was an African American "domestic" who threw the Indianness of an Indian woman into bold relief—not just for Russians or even Rama Rau herself, but for her American readers as well. That Rama Rau's own cosmopolitan credentials were equally secured by such a putative cognitive dissonance is also powerful evidence of the ways in which race and gender together worked to shape the cultural politics of translation that she undertook in her travel writing writ large. In contrast to her sense of affinity with fellow Asians, Rama Rau here performs an identification with as well as a disavowal of Ruth Camm, the sine qua non of her mobility, *and* the companionate cosmopolitanism that is on display by the end of the 1950s in ways that it was not at the start of her writing career. As the following chapter will illustrate, and as Santha Rama Rau's accelerating public career enables us to appreciate, translating India and Indianness as carriers of a certain species of Cold War cosmopolitanism could not but be articulated through discourses of race and gender, with colors from black through brown through white operating as implicit standards of both American imperial "progress" and Indian self-realization in a postcolonial world.

2

Interpreting British India in Anglo-America

The Cultural Politics of Santha Rama Rau's

A Passage to India, 1960–2005

I believe in aristocracy . . . if that is the right word, and if a democrat may use it. Not an aristocracy of power, based on rank and influence, but an aristocrat of the sensitive, the considerate and the plucky. Its members are to be found in all nations and classes, and all through the ages, and there is a secret understanding between them when they meet. They represent the true human tradition, the one permanent victory of our queer race over cruelty and chaos. Thousands of them perish in obscurity, a few are great names. They are sensitive for others as well as for themselves, they are considerate without being fussy; their pluck is not swankiness but the power to endure, and they can take a joke.
—E. M. Forster, *Two Cheers for Democracy*

When David Lean's film version of E. M. Forster's 1924 novel *A Passage to India* opened in the United States in the late fall of 1984, Vincent Canby of the *New York Times* called it a "wonderfully provocative tale, full of vivid characters, all played to near perfection."[1] The film went on to receive eleven Oscar nominations and several major awards, including Best Actress (Peggy Ashcroft for Mrs. Moore) and Best Film from the New York Film Critics' Circle. Reviews in Britain were less favorable, focusing not only on Lean's interpretation of the widely read if controversial novel but also on some of the misadventures which had befallen Lean and his crew while filming in India.[2] And even some American critics—Canby included—damned with feigned praise by suggesting that *A Passage* was a miraculous comeback for the seventy-six-year-old director in the wake of the commercially and critically uninspiring *Ryan's Daughter* fourteen years earlier. In spite of all this, the movie was a headliner during what is arguably the most important moment in the annual American cinema cycle, Christmas and New Year's: not only did it receive a glowing two-page review in the December issue of *Time* but it was also the final cover story of the magazine for 1984.[3]

Historians and film critics continue to debate the place of *A Passage to India* in Lean's oeuvre. Regardless of its aesthetic limitations or its actual success, it is clear that the movie (together with Richard Attenborough's 1982 *Gandhi*) helped to galvanize a long narrative arc of Raj nostalgia in the United States—or, more accurately, it contributed to the convergence of commercial and cultural nostalgias for the British empire in India which began in the mid-1980s and lived on until images from the 1990 Gulf War, 9/11, and the war against Iraq gave rise to a traffic between Britain and the United States of new, more aggressive, and more expressly anti-Arab forms of orientalism. Lest anyone doubt the deluge of Raj memorabilia that such nostalgia generated in this very compressed time frame, the release of Lean's 1984 film coincided almost exactly with the airing of Paul Scott's *The Jewel in the Crown* on PBS's *Masterpiece Theater* (December 15, 1984). Nor were these the two only Raj extravaganzas to capture the American middle-class imagination at this particular moment. Steven Rea, writing for the *Chicago Tribune* in the winter of 1985, commented that as the new year unfolded the United States was about to be overtaken by images of India, chiefly as a consequence of the 1985–86 Festival of India which, in cooperation with major American universities, art museums, and cultural organizations, sponsored a variety of exhibitions from Los Angeles to Chicago to Washington, D.C., about the culture, history, and art of India.[4] Even the much-celebrated fiftieth anniversary of Indian independence in 1997 did not produce the same level of spectacular attention to India as the mid-1980s witnessed.

To be sure, other, edgier productions complicated the American landscape of sentimentalized imperial consumption during this, the height of the Thatcher years. *My Beautiful Laundrette* (1985) and *Sammy and Rosie Get Laid* (1987), for example, offered very different translations of "British India" in the context of economically depressed and strife-torn London. But while these did play in U.S. theaters and acquired something of a cult following, they did not participate in contemporary imperialist nostalgia—in part because Stephen Frears and Hanif Kureishi (the directing and screenwriting team for both films) were expressly critical of the dominant racial and sexual politics that were and are among the legacies of the Raj. Significantly, although *My Beautiful Laundrette* premiered in 1985, neither of Frears's films performed the same kind of ideological work as Lean's film, playing in stereo, as it were, with a whole range of cultural commodities which advertised a long-lost, once-great empire to an elite American public captivated more generally by admiration for and fascination with Victoriana-for-export. *A Passage to India* was, in short, trumpeted as David Lean's latest epic at a historical moment when there was a peculiar cultural density of things Indian on offer to certain strata of the American consuming public. It was an extended moment when "India" was being actively staged by a variety of interests, commercial and political—not as a sovereign nation but primarily, and repeatedly, as the site of a former world imperial power. Indeed, even when India-for-export items emanated from postcolonial India rather than from post-imperial film studios in Britain "proper," they succeeded in echoing the Raj in uncanny ways. The National Council of Science Museums in India presented a "festival of science" exhibition in conjunction with the Art Institute and the Museum of Science in Chicago that was to include "eight Indian craftsmen who will demonstrate native techniques of woodcarving, silver filigree, bronze casting, marble inlay, silk and cotton embroidery, brocade weaving, calligraphy and gemstone cutting."[5] This was a late-twentieth-century replication of a late-nineteenth-century metropolitan imperial spectacle, that of the "native" craftsmen featured at the 1886 Indian and Colonial Exhibition in London—a species of exhibitionary orientalism that has been scrupulously historicized by Saloni Mathur.[6]

Much has been written about the kinds of 1980s imperialist nostalgia which Lean's *A Passage to India* both appealed to and helped sustain.[7] Less effort has been made to understand the back story of that phenomenon, or to appreciate the ways in which Raj preoccupations of the fin de siècle were rooted in both the exigencies of the post-Bandung world order *and* the culture of Camelot that arose in the context of John Fitzgerald Kennedy's aborted presidential term, 1960–63. Traces of this pre-history can be found in coverage of Lean's 1984 film, which referenced Santha Rama Rau's dramatization of Forster's novel, first in Oxford, then in London, then on the Broadway stage between 1960 and 1962. In fact, Canby's 1984 review of the cinematic version of *A Passage to India* opened with a story that had circulated widely twenty years earlier when Rama Rau's play debuted—that of Forster's very public and uncharacteristically effusive reaction to the Oxford production:

> "How good the actors were," said Forster. "And how pleased I am that there were so many of them. I am so used to seeing the sort of play which deals with one man and two women. They do not leave me with the feeling that I have made a full theatrical meal . . . they do not give me the experience of the multiplicity of life."

Canby went on:

> Later, as P. N. Furbank reports in his fine biography, "E.M. Forster: A Life," Forster called absurd the play's review in the *Times* of London that described it as being about "the incompatibility of East and West." According to Forster, he was really concerned with "the difficulty of living in the universe."[8]

Canby's review praised the film as a "respectful, handsome" interpretation of the novel that would have pleased Forster. His observations also invoked several decades of literary criticism about the 1924 novel, which had raised hackles for both its attempt to bridge differences between East and West and its failure to engage empire at anything more than a personal level.[9] In his review of Lean's film, Canby replayed these themes, pitting a confident high cultural, proto-imperial analysis (echoing Kipling's "East is East" phrase) against the more universalist, ostensibly less imperialist interpretation of Forster himself (which posited a kind of existential angst not specific to the violences of imperial rule). Canby's invocation of the longer history of *A Passage to India* for an Anglo-

American readership is remarkable above all for the rehabilitation of Forster it entailed. In Canby's view, the film did what the novel had not—that is, it made a persuasive case for the transcendent liberalism of Forster's vision of India. This is all the more provocative given the fact that Forster himself had resolutely rejected all attempts to make films from his novels during his lifetime.[10] Canby's comments were but the opening salvo in what was to become an unusually rancorous public debate about the merits of the film as well as its authenticity vis-à-vis Indian culture.[11]

If Canby's review rehearsed a longstanding literary debate for an American middle-class audience curious about reproductions of the Raj, it also depended on a little-known history of that debate which centered on Rama Rau's stage play of two decades earlier.[12] As Canby revealed, long before David Lean packaged the Raj for Anglo-American consumption, Santha Rama Rau had used Forster's novel to interpret British imperialism, India, and Indians to a transatlantic theatergoing public—a role she continued to play in the mid-1980s and beyond as she saw her vision of *A Passage to India*, of Forster, and of India itself sabotaged by Lean's film and the publicity it received. This chapter offers a genealogy of *A Passage to India*'s circulation as an emblem not just of the Raj but of India and of America's relationship to it in the second half of the twentieth century, in part by historicizing Rama Rau's role in shaping the terms upon which Forster's novel was understood and appreciated. It also tracks the ways in which the drama of interracial sexual desire and ambiguity resonated with contemporary concerns about domestic American race questions and the problems associated with decolonization and the emergence of a highly racialized Third World. At what was perhaps the peak of her writing career, Rama Rau identified herself with Forster's peculiar anti-imperial vision and, in the process, became a very public spokeswoman for his particular interpretation of India and Indians at a moment of diplomatic spectacle and tension between the postcolonial Indian state and the American superpower.

When you do a Google search for Santha Rama Rau, it generates hundreds of websites, the majority of them linked in some way to her role in shaping the screenplay for David Lean's *A Passage to India*. Some attribute the screenplay to her, others to David Lean; at least one, a link to a 2001 article from the Sunday *Tribune* (India) entitled "Stories that Make Authors Rich," captures the history of her fractured relationship to the film by reporting that Rama Rau "figure[s] in the list of credits as having done the screenplay."[13] The author, Manohar Malgonkar, goes on to recount that he asked Rama Rau "how someone like her, a friend of Forster's who had interpreted the book so well in the stage version, had taken such liberties with the screen version. It turned out that she, too, was just as dissatisfied with the film version [as I was], and had actually walked off the set, as it were, when they were filming it. The inclusion of her name in the list of credits must, she believed, have been a term of the contract."[14]

Rama Rau's feelings about the film version of Forster's novel are a matter of public record, and I will discuss her self-representations about the nature of Lean's script below. Meanwhile, her role in making that film possible was crucial, and it began with a casual dinner conversation with Cheryl Crawford in New York City sometime in the late 1950s.[15] When I interviewed Rama Rau in New York City in March 2004, her narrative of the genesis of her script was vivid and detailed, offering a glimpse into her access to the glitterati of the period as well as a portrait of herself as a kind of accidental dramaturge. Crawford, one of the members of the Theater Guild and a Broadway producer (she, Elia Kazan, and Lee Strasburg had been involved with Tennessee Williams's plays *Camino Real* and *The Rose Tattoo*), remarked that it was strange that there had never been a play on Broadway about India or by an Indian. Rama Rau replied that this was not for want of good material. According to her account, it was she who suggested that a dramatization of *A Passage to India* was called for "because there are enough English roles in that . . . so . . . you don't have a cast of entirely unknown Indians."[16] Crawford threw down the gauntlet and "that summer I must have had a lot of time on my hands," Rama Rau recalled, "and I wrote it." Crawford was both startled and dismayed. " 'You must be joking,' " Rama Rau recalled her saying when Crawford first saw the script. " 'You have three changes of sets and thirty-six actors and no roles for a star. It's financially impossible.' "[17]

The agency representing Rama Rau, William Morris, kept plugging, and the script was sent to producers on both sides of the Atlantic. Rama

Rau remembered being nervous because she knew even then that Forster was adamant about not wanting any of his novels dramatized. This had even been the case when Satyajit Ray had approached him, she recalled, and Ray was someone Forster genuinely admired. Rama Rau wrote Forster directly—"out of the blue and very tentatively"—telling him how the idea of writing a play version of *A Passage to India* had come to her and asking him if he'd be interested in reading it. "I absolutely sent it to him on spec," she recalled.[18] "He was very prompt in answering his mail, particularly if it was an Indian writing," Rama Rau recalled. "I heard back in a week." Eventually they met in Cambridge, where she went to his rooms in King's College. "My hands were shaking, I was terrified of the great man." But ultimately she remembered him as "a rather modest, stooped gentleman who was just as ill at ease with me as I was with him." In our conversation Rama Rau expressed surprise that Forster had not been more critical of her script. She recalled that his comments were mainly on the stage directions: "Mrs. Moore wouldn't nod, she would bow" and the like. He gave her the impression that he had no ideas about changing it or making it more "accessible" (her word) to the audience. She took all this as acquiescence to the idea of a stage production, which Forster later confirmed via letter to both Rama Rau and Cheryl Crawford.[19] When Frank Hauser, a British director, offered her £200 for her script she accepted. Its first venue was a semiprofessional one, the Oxford Playhouse, where it opened on January 20, 1960.[20]

At this juncture we can see with particular vividness the extent to which Rama Rau not only helped to make *A Passage to India* a vehicle for interpreting India to the West but was also instrumental in setting the Raj nostalgia machine in motion in Britain and America, at least in its visual and cinematic incarnation. In his capacity as producer of her rendition of *A Passage* in Oxford, Hauser found (in Rama Rau's words) "a simply marvelous Pakistani actor to play Aziz"[21]—Zia Mohyeddin—who went on to appear in Lean's 1962 *Lawrence of Arabia*, in James Ivory's 1970 *Bombay Talkie*, and, following a stint in Pakistan and a return to Britain as a critic of the Bhutto regime, in the BBC / PBS miniseries *The Jewel in the Crown*. Rama Rau's *Passage* was the occasion for more than one star turn. When the play came to New York in January 1962, Mohyeddin came with it, and Sayeed Jaffrey was also a member of the Broadway cast. Both he and Mohyeddin appeared in the 1965 BBC television production of the play and Jaffrey ended up in Lean's movie version as Hamidullah.[22] That same year he was in the adaptation of M. M. Kaye's *The Far Pavilions* (in the movie version of which Amy Irving later appeared in blackface as Anjuli, a young Indian widow) and several Indian films as well. Interestingly, Jaffrey also appeared in *My Beautiful Laundrette*—the only actor to "cross over" from Raj nostalgia to cultural productions that were critical of the Raj in the mid-1980s.

In Rama Rau's memory, "all the London critics went tooling up to Oxford and gave the show rave reviews."[23] *Time* magazine had encouraged this interpretation, reporting at the time that the play brought "full organ tones from the London critics," in part because Rama Rau's transformation of the novel into a play was the equivalent of "rewrit[ing] the Bhagavad-Gita as a sonnet."[24] In fact, the *Times* of London, while conceding that she had adhered faithfully to Forster's original (including by preserving much of the original dialogue), called it "by no means a novelist's play"—and the review as a whole took a somewhat ambivalent position on the relative merits of that achievement.[25] Rama Rau also recalled Forster's speech at the time, in which he praised not only the play but Rama Rau's willingness to take time away from her own writing to rework his novel.[26] That speech was given play in the United States as well, where the London opening was noticed in several venues. *A Passage to India* made its way to London's West End and eventually to New York via Lawrence Langner, then president of the Theater Guild.[27] Over forty years later, Santha Rama Rau recalled with equal parts delight and wonder that the marquee had proclaimed " 'A Passage to India' " by Santha Rama Rau"—with the tag-line "Based on the Novel by E. M. Forster" in much smaller letters.[28]

The New York stage version had "certain changes" that, from the vantage point of 2004, Rama Rau remembered as "unfortunate."[29] In fact, the play underwent a number of revisions both in Oxford and in the wake of its transatlantic crossing, some of which are evident in the draft script held in the Harvard Theater Collection. Most of these represent cuts in or simplifications of dialogue, though the three original acts were also rearranged, compressed, and subdivided.[30] Significant changes had already been made to the Anglo-Indian club scene while the play ran in Britain, mostly at Frank Hauser's suggestion. This was apparently in response to critics: as he wrote to Rama Rau, "many people felt and still feel that the English were 'caricatured.'"[31] Hauser acknowledged that Forster had written that scene in the novel "with a sting" because he had wanted to dramatize the arrogance of "Empire-builders" who "could, and did, behave like spoiled children." And in fact this was a scene that had come under fire from literary critics over the years for its almost clownish representations of Anglo-Indians. Hauser, for his part, objected to the fact that the scene pitted "nice Englishman against nasty Englishman," and he suggested that Rama Rau make changes,

[which] might remove the implication that we are trying to make fun of the Club members. Goodness knows you've toned down from the novel, just as Forster had from real life; but because of the extraordinary historical change that has come about since the book was written, what must originally have been the most startling section has now become the most conventional. It's quite wrong to approach a section in a play by trying to mute it into acceptability . . . but in performance a roundness is missing from it which is wonderfully there elsewhere, and if it is to have the same import the cast should be able to approach it entirely convinced that their characters are speaking absolute common sense—and persuade the audience of the same thing . . . the poor things [the Anglo-Indians] get such a beating by the end that there's no fear of disturbing the balance of sympathies![32]

Here both Hauser and Rama Rau collaborated in reshaping what Revathi Krishnaswamy calls "the paternalism of the Turtons and the Burtons" in the novel: Santha Rama Rau responded within the week by sending Hauser revisions that cut some parts, amended others (she tried to make one of the Anglo-Indian ladies, Mrs. Turton, "bossy but commonsensical," for example), and added a passage to Mr. Turton's speech in the club scene that critiqued Fielding's "liberal" ideas about better relations between Indians and Britons and effectively questioned the wisdom of "equal terms" between the races.[33]

There is evidence in the Harvard Theater Collection to suggest that there was criticism of even that rewritten club scene when the play was proposed for Broadway. An unsigned document dated January 22, 1962, entitled "Comments Re: Suggested Changes in A Passage to India" and presumably written by someone in America, complained that "the whole first part of the scene is dependent on those biddies and the head of the colony whom we have never seen before." In my 2005 interview with her, Santha Rama Rau speculated that it might have been written by Lawrence Langner but she couldn't be sure.[34] Of concern to this critic was the character of Adela, whom s/he wanted to make more "hysterical." S/he wanted a confrontation between Quested and Aziz, not Fielding, in which it would be clear that "it is terrifying to him, and should be to the world at large, that an accidental, momentary aberration of Miss Quested, or indeed anyone, can so easily not only ruin a 'little person' but indeed be devastatingly damaging to a whole 'little people' and in so doing the play really not only indicates but pinpoints a humane and political respon-sibility."[35] The bitterness of these comments, directed at the Quested character, is matched only by their allusive reference to the story at the heart of the play: that of a possible sexual encounter between a white woman and a brown man. Though entirely unspoken, the specter of the Jim Crow South, and of lynching for African American men even sus-pected of approaching white women, is difficult not to read off a text like this written in the early 1960s, especially given the last lines about "hu-mane and political responsibility."

Frank Hauser had in fact anticipated attempts to "Americanize" the play. As early as April 1960, when A Passage to India was in London, he wrote to Rama Rau: "You will be glad to hear that 2 Broadway types who attended with Sam Wanamaker said in the first interval that the play was slow in coming to its point. As one of them put it, 'We all know that the Indian guy is going to fall in love with the girl, so why don't they get down to it?' As a friend of mine remarked, they had come to see 'Up in Quested's Room.' Thought that would please you."[36] It is impossible to know with certainty what changes were actually performed (as opposed to the ones Rama Rau suggested in the script housed at Harvard).[37] At least one American critic—John McCarter of The New Yorker—found Adela Quested's "hysterical declaration that Dr. Aziz had tried to take liberties" with her in the cave "unsettling," which might be an indication that this part of the script had been tinkered with along the lines suggested above.[38] Forster wrote to Rama Rau expressing concern that "the longer the play runs, the more it is being altered to meet the supposed wishes of its American public . . . have you observed deterioration?"[39] She replied ruefully that "yes, the play had to be changed. In some cases for the better, in my opinion, in some cases for the worse." She informed him that due to American "union regulations" the script had to be cut by twenty minutes, but she did not indicate where. "Inevitably," she told him, "the cuts changed the shape of the play to some degree, but worst of all made it necessary to reduce what is already a coarse medium to an even coarser and more odious level."[40] The intensity of this comment is as intriguing as its obliqueness, especially given the "muddle" in the caves that was at the heart of the sexual drama between Aziz and Adela.[41] Did Rama Rau feel that the cave scenes or the characters of Adela and Aziz had been sexed up for Broadway? Her response to this question when I asked it of her in 2005 was a resounding yes. Forty years on she was able to conjure how "miserable" she was about the Broadway production because of the all the accommodations to the American audience around the sex question. And she was still amazed by the fact that the producers thought that changes in Adela's character were the only way Americans could appreciate the play—that is, the producers believed Adela had to be "made a hysteric, [someone] who was overpowered by, and falling in love with, Aziz. This had to be the reason for her breakdown."[42]

Reviews of the New York production were generally enthusiastic.[43] Newsweek admired Rama Rau's "subtle, perceptive" if only "fitfully dramatic" rendition, while The New Yorker praised Rama Rau's adaptation for "skillfully convey[ing] the tone, style, wit and wisdom of the original work—an achievement that merits our devout admiration."[44] The New York Times declared it "a clever dramatization" and "a fine, moving evening in the theatre."[45] Several of these reviews were cited in the Illustrated Weekly of India, which also published full-page photos of the actors and Santha Rama Rau and Faubion Bowers.[46] American reviews dwelt hardly at all on the story of sexual encounter that shaped the play as it had the novel. Most focused on the infamous club scene as much if not more so than on the cave, with Time entitling its review "Bridge Party" to the ironic double entendre of a social gathering that was far from a bridge between the races.[47] Equally significant for our purposes is the cultural politics of the *Times* reviews, which worked hard both to situate *A Passage to India* on the contemporary global scene *and* to use it as evidence of how nationalisms of all kinds could be transcended in a new America-centered postcolonial world. The attention given to Zia Mohyeddin in the press coverage is especially instructive in this regard. *Newsweek* appreciated Mohyeddin's "naïve and puppy-lovable" rendition of Aziz, "who bubbles over with the desire to make at least one Englishman his intimate friend."[48] Howard Taubman's opening night review for the *New York Times* also emphasized the director's good fortune in having "the gifted Pakistani actor" to play Aziz.[49] His follow-up piece a week or so later waxed equally rapturous: "Here is Dr. Aziz, the play's focal character. Mercurial, proud, touchy, talkative, gallant, this young Moslem physician is an amusing and appealing human being. In his eagerness to be ingratiating, his fear of offending and his almost morbid suspicion of rejection, he personifies an Indian of goodwill in the Twenties. How brilliantly Zia Mohyeddin, the Pakistani actor, conveys his amiability and the quicksilver of his moods!"[50] This yearning for a pre-1947 Muslim man, cast as "Indian" in a way that neatly erases the role of the British colonial state in fostering communal difference (not to mention the violence of Partition itself), is a salutary reminder of the many and sedimented layers of imperialist nostalgia which emerged in the twentieth-century American public sphere well before the canonical 1980s.

In the wake of Edward Said's *Orientalism* and Mrinalini Sinha's trenchant work on the "effete" Bengali male versus the "manly" Englishman, it is easy (and frankly, tempting) to remark upon how crudely orientalist these characterizations are.[51] But if there is a historically intelligible lack of self-consciousness about reproducing such baldly ethnocentric and gendered stereotypes, it was not due to a correlative lack of political awareness. *Newsweek*'s review began by remarking on the context of the 1920s, when "the subcontinent was in a ferment and British colonists were self-righteously keeping an inferior race on the other side of the color line." It finished by observing that the estrangement between races was "a sad ending to an old story, and the suggestion in Miss Rau's version . . . is that it is an ending to be expected in stories still being written."[52] Taubman of the *Times* drew attention from the very start of his first review to what he called the "timeliness" of the play's story lines, even as he credited India with having "settled" the problem of colonial independence:

> The pertinence of "A Passage to India" is on two levels. There is the obvious immediacy of the collision between Western colonialists and the dark-skinned peoples seeking to rule themselves. If this problem has been settled in India and in other lands, it rages with undiminished force in parts of Africa. There is the timeliness in the deeper and subtler conflict that divides even people of good will. Have the bitterness, misunderstanding and ferocious pride of other years been tempered by the new day of freedom? Or is the work of healing wounded minds and hearts still to be done? When one recalls the edginess that rises recurrently between Americans and Indians, one knows that the delicate problems between peoples are as urgent in the Sixties as in the Twenties.[53]

In the latter part of this passage, Taubman was undoubtedly referring to the tensions at the foreign policy level between India and the United States over India's non-alignment policies, tensions that had recently been made manifest by Nehru's visit to the United States in the fall of 1961, just a few months before Rama Rau's adaptation of *A Passage to India* opened on Broadway. Although Nehru had been greeted warmly by John Fitzgerald Kennedy upon his arrival at Andrews Air Force Base, there was mutual suspicion on both policy grounds and, as Andrew J. Rotter has written, with regard to their respective gender performances as well. Not just Kennedy but Eisenhower and Truman before him viewed Nehru's neutral stance between the two superpowers as evidence of his effeminacy, a category they and their contemporaries evinced with descriptors like "delicate," "graceful," "fluffheaded," and, of course, "intellectual."[54] Rotter argues that in contrast, and partly as a result, American officials preferred to deal with Pakistani leaders in the period 1947–65. Prime Minister Liquiat Ali Khan was, to quote one assistant secretary of state, "a man you could do business with."[55] State Department officials under Eisenhower were delighted to discover that some Pakistani generals could even play golf—they were men who, in other words, had the additional advantage of being predisposed, by training and background, to embrace militarism and its ancillary recreational cultures as the basis of a successful postwar/postcolonial political regime.[56] Nehru, for his part, viewed Kennedy as a leader without spine, vigor, or conviction.[57] In the run-up to the Cuban Missile Crisis (October 1962) and the context of the general Cold War enmity between the United States and the USSR more generally, Nehru's unwillingness to stand with American foreign policy made these gendered performances a high stakes game. They are, I want to suggest, one important context in which reviews of *A Passage to India*—with their frank, self-indulgent relief at Mohyeddin's "amiability"—can be framed.[58]

While Taubman had only alluded obliquely to them, John Keating, another contributor to the *Times*, channeled these diplomatic tensions more elaborately into his discussion of the play and its cast. Keating's March 1962 article, "Meet Mohyeddin," focused on the actor, emphasizing the difference between the character he played on stage ("an impulsive, wildly kinetic, ripely sentimental, puppy-eager adolescent of a man, compulsively talkative and always in motion, even while sitting down") and Mohyeddin himself. Aziz was, of course, a Muslim character, but we find attributed to him all the hallmark characteristics of the effeminate Bengali Hindu. If Aziz was in danger of being read as or through Nehru, Keating established Mohyeddin as a decidedly "Pakistani" figure. Robust and multidimensional, Mohyeddin emerges as someone who, despite his transnational biography (son of a university professor, he had been to school in Lahore and Australia, received training at the Royal Academy of Dramatic Arts in London and returned to Pakistan in the mid 1950s to found the Karachi Arts Theater where, among other things, he had helped to stage a production of O'Neill's *Long Day's Journey into Night* and an Urdu adaptation of *Julius Caesar*) and his apparent seduction by America ("since his arrival in New York he has been beguiled by our taxi drivers . . . [and] dazzled by the beauty of the city at night"), professed his desire to return to Pakistan, which he saw as his ultimate personal if not professional destination.[59] In this sense, in Keating's piece, Mohyeddin redeems Aziz and ultimately India as a place where postcolonial questions of all kinds have been "settled," not least through the Partition of the subcontinent into separate and apparently compelling homelands for temporary, cosmopolitan exiles.

And yet the cultural politics of staging *A Passage to India* on Broadway was not just refracted through an India-America relationship; the specter of Britain as a former colonial power and as the site of a shared linguistic and cultural history was still very much a part of the equation. The figure of Mohyeddin himself made that triangulation indubitably clear. For one thing, his acting success in Britain—where, as a result of his work in *A Passage to India* in the West End he was nominated as the season's outstanding new actor—helped to distance him from the comparatively provincial Aziz (as did the fact that Mohyeddin enthusiastically ordered and drank a martini at lunch). But Keating also suggested that Mohyeddin was a cannier reader of global power politics than Aziz, and that he (Mohyeddin) knew it: "Where a 1962 version of Aziz might be expected to be almost unbearably patriotic, Mr. Mohyeddin seems to have gone beyond nationalism to a conception of himself as a citizen of the world. An expatriate for most of the last twelve years, he considers London his home and is, in fact, a British citizen."[60]

Mohyeddin's capacity to value his Pakistani identity while appreciating the benefits of mobility in an Anglo-American world arguably made him a likeable and above all a familiar figure to a *New York Times* audience—in contrast to the bumbling, ingratiating "adolescent of a man," Dr. Aziz. Nor was this merely a matter of Keating's interpretation. On several occasions during the interview, Mohyeddin himself offered indubitable evidence of the differences between himself and Aziz—and, in the process, laid claim to intimate knowledge of the linguistic and psychological workings of British cultural power:

"One of my favorite lines in the play," he remarked at lunch the other day, "because it tells so much about the type of pre-Independence Muslim that Dr. Aziz is, is his anxious response to Fielding's irritated exclamation at dropping a collar button. Aziz is in the next room and he calls out, 'Anything is wrong?' Not 'Is anything wrong?' or 'Anything wrong?' In that one short sentence, you know that he has, of course, never been to England, never 'lived' in English, so to speak, and that even his intercourse with the English on a personal, informal, social level has been limited."[61]

This astonishing anecdote accomplishes a number of things. It reassures readers that Mohyeddin is not Aziz precisely because he has mastered the intricacies of the English language and can evaluate what the details of its usage signify. It underscores the Pakistani-yet-cosmopolitan identity that is to be prized over the amiable but naïve, risible, and eminently dismissable Aziz. Above all, it alerts elite American, theatergoing Forster aficionados—and, of course, would-be ones as well—to the fact that because they are in a position to appreciate what the exchange between Aziz and Fielding means about the difference between East and West (and, by extension, about the realities of a decidedly masculinist Anglophone colonial world order), they too have a cultural claim, at the very least, on the postcolonial legacies of the British empire.

Whether Mohyeddin knew of the parallels between Aziz and Forster's love interest, Syed Masood, on whom the character is said to have been based, is not clear. In any event his attempt to distance himself from the character he played, especially in this highly charged scene of dress and undress, suggests dimensions of the "imperial erotic" at the heart of *A Passage to India* that the American press did not, and perhaps could not, directly countenance.[62] This, despite the fact that *Time* reported on that very scene as follows: "before the ladies come, Fielding cannot find his back collar stud, and the puppyish Aziz plucks out his own and forces the principal to take it." According to the reviewer, this situation "dryly summed up" "his position, India's and Britain's."[63] If interpretations of Mohyeddin the man tried to suggest his performative independence from Forster's script for Aziz, critical evaluations of Santha Rama Rau in the wake of the Broadway production positioned her in a more contingent fashion, emphasizing not her distinctiveness from Forster but rather her fidelity to his vision and hence her achievement as the authentic translator of his 1920s view of the Raj and of India to the stage. This is not to say that there was no negative press about the play. Taubman, for example, did not approve of either the "villainy" or the priggishness of the Anglo-Indians in the story. At the same time, he did not distinguish Rama Rau's version from Forster's in this instance—and, as the rich body of secondary literature on *A Passage to India* attests, this had been a very audible criticism of the novel from its first appearance in the mid 1920s.[64] Taubman found parts of the play a "patchwork," but overall he felt that "in view of the novel's complexity of texture and subtlety of sensibility, it is astonishing how much of its atmosphere, emotion and thought have carried over to the stage."[65] Embedded in the *Times* reviews was a series of pedagogical interventions, mostly implicit but instructive nonetheless. Although, as noted above, he objected to the characterizations of Anglo-Indians, Taubman conceded that they echoed much of the "foolish, ignorant proponents of white supremacy . . . at large today"—a more explicit, but still comparatively oblique, reference to civil rights movements then gaining steam and, increasingly, headlines, in the early 1960s. Dilating on the limits and possibilities of adaptation in his second review, he went on to declare that "even when it inhabits a less [than] exalted level, adaptation has its uses. It can bring into the theatre characters whose freshness is enchanting and whose humanity is touching. It can dramatize ideas that quicken our minds and enlarge our sympathies."[66] Toward the end of the review, he put an even finer point on it: "The play ends shortly after the trial [of Aziz], but finds occasion to emphasize, in moving dramatic terms, the great divide of injustice, humiliation and misunderstanding that keeps apart even men of goodwill. Although 'A Passage to India' never sermonizes, it is pertinent in a world that cries out for the bridging of ancient chasms."[67]

Though his referents are never specified, it requires no great interpretive leap to imagine that Taubman (no less than his readers) may have had in mind the struggle for racial equality "at home" or—in the wake of what he called "the specter of British domination" which exerted a "brooding" mood over scenes in the play—the ongoing challenges of racial relations in a postimperial world. What Taubman just hinted at, others more directly addressed.[68] As Poppy Cannon Whittier observed of the tension between Aziz and Adela in her review for the *Amsterdam News*, "and so starts a chain of reactions all too familiar in stories of our own South."[69] In this sense, critical reception of *A Passage to India* ratifies what much of the new scholarship on the cultural politics of the Cold War in America has been suggesting in the last decade: namely, that discussions of "domestic" racial issues were often, if not always, entailed by a consciousness of the pressure of racial difference which decolonization had brought to bear on communities and states across the globe.[70]

A critic like Taubman who worked to create distance between Aziz and

Mohyeddin strove, in other words, to collapse Rama Rau and Forster, in part to deliver, or perhaps more accurately, to interpret, the message of *A Passage for India* to an audience increasingly exposed to, and appetitive for, the kind of Cold War cosmopolitanism Rama Rau herself embodied. Equally striking is the extent to which such maneuvers tend to occlude Rama Rau's agency in the process of making *A Passage to India* available to New York, if not American, audiences. This impression of Rama Rau as merely a ventriloquist for Forster, as well as for his views on empire and India, is especially remarkable because by the time the play debuted on Broadway, she had established herself as an author in her own right and as an intellectual presence to be reckoned with on the East Coast cultural scene. Not only were all her books prominently advertised and reviewed in the *Times* and elsewhere; she was a regular contributor to *Holiday* magazine, *The New Yorker*, and the *Times* itself, mainly as a book reviewer but also as an occasional feature writer.[71] During the 1950s and early 1960s she consistently reviewed books for the *Times* about India and by Indians; in the two years before the opening of *A Passage to India*, she wrote a number of prominent reviews for the *Times*, including a major piece on the misrepresentation of India in Western fiction.[72] Rama Rau was also a fixture on the social scene. Whether as a result of winning literary prizes or of attending Asia Society events or of appearing in the gossip columns (as she did when the *Times* learned of Langner's intention to bring the play from Britain to the United States),[73] Rama Rau had become a minor celebrity in the local but influential circles of metropolitan New York by the time her dramatization of Forster's novel opened.

Here it is worth remarking on the kind of treatment Rama Rau had received among the "smart set" since the debut of her first novel, *Home to India*, in 1945.[74] Orville Prescott reviewed *Home to India* for the *Times*, calling it "slight, unpretentious and . . . charming," a "personal, informal, chatty book."[75] Adorned with an image of a partially head-scarfed Rama Rau, the review emphasized her "aristocratic" Brahminical origins and the privileged view this gave her as a tourist of and in India. In Prescott's view this did not disqualify her, but he was clearly discomfited by her connections to the Nehru family and her "complete allegiance" to the Congress Party. Nonetheless, thenceforth Rama Rau received notice in the *Times* with uncommon frequency, in part no doubt because of her father's position as Indian ambassador. *Home to India*—and later *East of Home*, as well as her other books—was prominently advertised. The ads sometimes featured Rama Rau looking forthrightly at the camera, arms crossed: not defiantly exactly, but with an air of prepossession that is both jaunty and serious, combining a fashion pose with a look of the Wellesley "new woman" frankness. When she got the contract to write *East of Home* it was itemized in the *Times*, as was her arrival back in New York in 1948 with her mother and her sister's children, accompanied by a photograph on page 5. She was also cited when she attended charity balls, fashion shows, and the like throughout the 1950s.[76] All this was a measure, no doubt, of her status as the daughter of a high-ranking Indian diplomat, but it also testifies to her growing stature as a writer and as an honest, if not an unbiased, authority on India in America.

Nor was coverage of her work limited to the *Times* or *The New Yorker*. From the appearance of *Home to India* onward, Rama Rau was reviewed in local and regional newspapers like the *Kansas City Star*, the *Christian Science Monitor*, and the *Hartford Courant*, where her subsequent books received regular and generally positive coverage for their informality, "direct approach," and lack of dogmatism.[77] Many if not most reviews, regardless of what part of the country they came from, emphasized her ability to bridge East and West. As the *New York Herald Tribune* put it in a review of her first novel, *Remember the House*, "Santha Rama Rau seems to write from a Western mind and from an Indian heart."[78] Or, as another review of the novel suggested, "Miss Rau does much to make the myriad faces of India plainer to the Western eye."[79] The *Cincinnati Inquirer* went so far as to suggest that *Remember the House* deserved "to be placed on the shelf next to E. M. Forster's *A Passage to India*."[80] Rama Rau's popularity notwithstanding, her authority as a political presence in the New York public sphere was increasingly derived from her role as regular reviewer of books on India for the *Times* in the 1950s and 1960s. The first of these reviews was of Andrew Mellor's *India since Partition* in 1951. Mellor was an English journalist who worked for the London *Daily Herald*. Thus Rama Rau's first piece for the *Times* was an endorsement of his "factual approach" to a subject riven by what Rama Rau called "violent partisanship."[81] To be sure, Rama Rau also reviewed novels, like Ruth Prawer Jhabvala's *Amrita* and Khushwant Singh's *Mano Majra*, both in 1956.[82]

But each of these contained political interpretations of the Raj and its aftermath, whether focused directly on Partition or not—interpretations Rama Rau was not shy about commenting on.[83] In fact, the question of politics dominated profiles of her and her work from the start, anticipating the ways in which reviews of her *Passage to India* script would, as we have seen, refract the diplomatic tensions between the United States and India during the Cold War.

Even those who attempted to trivialize her work inevitably came to grips with her loyalty if not to Nehru per se, then to larger post-independence Congress Party commitments. In his review of *East of Home* in 1950, for example, Orville Prescott again categorized Rama Rau's work as the "informal, pleasantly engaging" sort, labeling the second book "mostly a gay, feminine, chatty book, more concerned with dancing than politics."[84] Yet as with *Home to India,* Prescott revealed his discomfort with the political positions Rama Rau articulated in an ostensibly lighthearted travelogue. He bridled in particular at her sympathy for the Japanese, "forced," as he put it, "to live beneath the rule of the triumphant Americans." He went on:

> Probably Miss Rau takes a deliberate humorous pleasure in needling her prospective American readers. Certainly one can only applaud her originality when she remarks that she lunched with General Douglas MacArthur and then never refers to him or the luncheon again. What American could have resisted the temptation to expound his views of McArthur's views? But when Miss Rau refers to the Vietminh movement in Indo-china as the "Resistance" she obviously is not being humorous. To her sympathetic eyes the Vietminh is a nationalistic war for freedom. She is certain that French rule in Indo-china is inexcusable, and that Communist control of the Vietminh is exaggerated or unimportant.[85]

Prescott pulls back from this highly politicized engagement with a book that is, in his view, essentially "chatty" and "feminine" by concluding that "such political jottings are of minor importance in *East of Home.*" Moreover, he ends the review by commenting that the most "remarkable" thing Rama Rau learned on her travels is that "Balinese women take thirty-five less days than other women to have a baby!"—thereby effectively cordoning *East of Home* off in the domestic rather than diplomatic realm.[86] Prescott's unease speaks directly to the ambivalent figure Rama Rau had become in the Cold War American public sphere: a "society" woman with political opinions and a growing reputation as a reliable authority not just on India but on the larger world stage in the era of Bandung as well.

The fact that Rama Rau was a woman clearly played a role in this unease, for the majority of those who moved between high society and the world of politics both before and during Camelot were high-profile men who did so without jeopardizing their credentials as either "genuine" intellectuals or effective opinion makers. As George H. Douglas has documented, the elites who had dominated the "smart set" in American culture since the turn of the century relied on the very confluence of cultural and political capital that Rama Rau enacted in both her own books and in her work for the *Times* and *The New Yorker*.[87] It is also true that by the late 1950s such venues were beginning to come under scrutiny as excessively feminine and therefore not considered sufficiently "serious." Taking direct aim at what he perceived as the feminization of the "smart set," Tom Wolfe famously derided *The New Yorker* as "the most successful suburban women's magazine in the country" and "a national shopping news."[88] Though neither Douglas nor Wolfe comments on it, the "smart set" was almost exclusively white, though, arguably, the further to the left of the political spectrum one got, the more integrated it became. Critical discourse aimed at disqualifying Rama Rau relied more on gender than on race for its rhetorical power. For someone like Prescott, the fact that she was Indian was reflected in her politics, but it was not mobilized to suggest she should not or did not have legitimate political views; to the contrary, it accorded her a legitimacy, albeit a startling and unsettling one.

This "smart set" milieu was one important context in which Rama Rau worked to create a role for herself as an Indian woman knowledgeable about India in ways that an admittedly elite American audience should credit, but it was not the only one in the years leading up to and surrounding the attention that her dramatization of *A Passage to India* received. All manner of American public figures were visiting and writing about India between 1950 and 1965, many with a new-found realization of the global stakes of those representations given the standoff between Nehru and a succession of American presidents, and many with a sense of the translatability of India's exoticism from the political to the cultural realm (and back again). To give just two pertinent examples, both Chester Bowles, the American ambassador to India and Nepal (1951–53), and his daughter Cynthia wrote memoirs in this period that used India as a backdrop. Cynthia's book was called *At Home in India* (so evocative of Rama Rau's earlier title) and was in the very same vein as Rama Rau's first book, narrating as it did Cynthia's experiences as the daughter of famous diplomatic parents. Rama Rau reviewed the book for the *Times*. It was an elegant and favorable review, though Rau did comment somewhat mischievously that Indians had learned "so much about Americans" from the Bowleses, and she ended her review somewhat proprietarily by saying that "as far as Indians are concerned, it will be a pleasure to welcome Miss Bowles home."[89]

I would not like to suggest that Rama Rau was anything but sincere in her embrace of Cynthia Bowles's book. But by the late 1950s the metropolitan public sphere was becoming increasingly crowded with India-wallahs and India images produced at the intersection of diplomacy and celebrity, and never more so than in the year right before *A Passage to India* opened on Broadway in 1962.[90] In January and February 1961, Queen Elizabeth II traveled to India, the first British monarch to do so since her grandfather, King George V, visited there in 1911. With Prince Philip, she attended state functions, gave speeches, went tiger-shooting, flew over Mount Everest, and was greeted by a succession of "wild" crowds. The *New York Times* coverage was lavish, featuring dozens of articles and sumptuous photographs under headlines like "India Hails the Queen" over the course of the five-week tour. The *Times* reported that several socialist protesters were arrested when they tried to march on the Governor's House in Bombay where the queen was staying, but this was the only sour note reported.[91] While the queen was indubitably a figurehead in this period, she was an important postimperial symbol as well. Before she left India she gave a radio broadcast in which she expressed confidence that the visit had "set the seal of a new relationship between India and Britain" and that "the new Commonwealth which came into being in 1947 was firmly based in the hearts and minds of the people."[92]

By November 1961 the *New York Times* was reporting that Jacqueline Kennedy was also planning a "personal and private" trip to India and Pakistan. According to the *Times,* the idea for the trip originated with Field Marshall (later President) Ayub Khan and the invitation was brokered by John Kenneth Galbraith (then the U.S. ambassador to India).[93] The *Times* noted that "since India and Pakistan are in dispute over several matters, it probably would not have been politically possible for Mrs. Kennedy to visit one . . . without also going to the other"—even on a "personal and private basis." The article says nothing directly about the fact that her visit to both also prompted disagreements between the United States and India, though the rest of the piece is devoted to anticipating the discussion of differences, especially on the question of nuclear arms, which President Kennedy and Nehru would be discussing during the latter's upcoming visit to Washington.

Jacqueline Kennedy's trip was in fact rescheduled a number of times, first at Nehru's suggestion and then in response to India's forcible seizure of Goa in late 1961, an action of which the Kennedy administration heartily disapproved. The delay meant that the nature of the trip that eventuated in March 1962 had changed from personal and private to "semi-official"—making it, as the *Times* put it, "one of the most formal informal visits" ever made to India.[94] Mrs. Kennedy's trip was more anticipated and more scrupulously covered than Queen Elizabeth's had been: her arrival in Delhi was front-page news, with photographs, and full-page stories continued throughout the twenty-day tour of India and Pakistan. She was pictured in hospitals handing out lollipops to children, at the Taj Mahal, at state occasions in Benares, atop an elephant in Jaipur. She was seen most often on the arm or in the company of Galbraith, though the *Times* did feature her with Nehru as he "dabbed red powder" on her forehead "in a traditional celebration marking the Hindu festival of Holi."[95] The trip to Pakistan was equally faithfully covered, though the photographs were fewer and focused on the horse given to her by President Ayub Khan (they also rode a camel in Karachi).[96]

Galbraith leaves the impression in his 1969 memoir, *Ambassador's Report,* that the greatest challenge of the visit was in managing Jackie's unwieldy and unprofessionally organized entourage.[97] The *Times* coverage, in contrast, makes evident the political stakes, at home and abroad, of the tour, which occurred against the backdrop of discussions in public and in private not just about nuclear questions but also about India's attitude to the China border question. But again, the United States' relationship with Britain on the world stage remains, if not central, then at the very least part of the larger frame in which India and South Asia more generally were cast at the start of the 1960s. For Jackie Kennedy's return to the States was circuited through the UK, where she lunched with Queen Elizabeth II at Buckingham Palace. "I had a wonderful English lunch," Mrs. Kennedy was reported as saying; and she and the queen talked "mostly about India."[98] Lee Radziwill, Jackie's sister, had traveled with the entourage throughout India, and she lived in London, so it was logical enough that their tour should end there. Yet, of course, even an "unofficial" visit like this one was a highly staged affair, designed no doubt to juxtapose the American First Lady with "real" royalty and hence to underscore the power of the Kennedys' emergent celebrity to emulate royalty as well. It is crucial here to see the culture of celebrity as embedded in the political and especially the diplomatic world of the Cold War, as the ubiquitous presence of Galbraith before, during, and after Jackie's "Indian tour" illustrates. If Santha Rama Rau played a comparatively small role in this drama, we can nonetheless see how even her minor celebrity—through the intertwined political cultural discourses surrounding *A Passage to India*—was being harnessed in the public sphere as evidence of the ongoing purchase of Anglo-Indian and Anglo-American connections.

Plans for Jackie Kennedy's trip to India and Pakistan unfolded in the pages of the *New York Times* at the exact moment that *A Passage to India* opened on Broadway. The play thus propelled Santha Rama Rau into the spotlight at a time when India was being represented as a pawn in a geopolitical game with several axes, the Anglo-American one prime among them. How did Rama Rau's response to the play's success participate in this cultural politics, if at all? In contrast to the London *Times*, which featured an article on her with a photo when *A Passage to India* was just opening in London, the *New York Times* carried no interviews with Rama Rau about the play.[99] Rama Rau did, however, write a number of pieces for various venues to coincide with the Broadway production. One of these was an introduction to notes from Forster's diary of his first trip to

India in *Harper's Magazine* in February 1962.[100] Here she praised Forster as "the most renowned contemporary English novelist" and celebrated his capacity to see India from a perspective that "an Indian national can never have."[101] Her *Theater Arts* piece of February 1962 was called "A Passage to Broadway" and more directly underscored her role as cultural translator of "the most famous work of Britain's Grand Old Novelist" from "Cambridge via Bengal" to New York.[102] In it she recounted her initial dinner table conversation with Crawford, the meeting with Forster (in this version she was "giddy with joy" that he was willing to allow the stage play), the circumstances of the Oxford production, and the travails of getting actors, sets, and Equity details in order. Rama Rau made no reference to the changes in the play that the Broadway production necessitated; nor did she talk about her disappointment with the "coarseness" to which the New York production had been reduced. Instead, she emphasized her excitement and terror at this newfound celebrity, comparing her relationship to playwriting with drug addiction ("How do you persuade yourself to leave the stuff alone?"). She also cast herself as the carrier of a certain message about colonialism, a particularly Forsterian message, from the page to the stage:

> [*A Passage to India*] represented the first time that an Englishman — incidentally the most celebrated novelist of his generation — had found the courage to look at the colonial British from the outside, in the harsh understanding light of truth. This would have been enough of an occasion to give his book praise, even though it shocked and offended the die-hard colonialists of Britain at the time. But then add to the fact that in *A Passage to India* Mr. Forster had the courage to do something that none of his colleagues were able or willing to attempt. He gave us real Indian characters, acting in genuine Indian ways, thinking as Indians in their own society and philosophy, and *all in the same novel!*[103]

Rama Rau made it clear that her reasons for choosing Forster's novel were highly personal ("it was part of my childhood, my education, my view of both India and England") but were also politically specific to the 1950s and 1960s:

By the time that I decided to make a play out of it, India was a free nation, running its own government, and after years of struggle it was possible to be friends—really friends on a equal basis—with the British. At the same time, the colonial situation, or variations on it, continued in many other parts of the world, even in countries that count themselves democracies and feel that because rights under laws are guaranteed to colored races the social and emotional problems can be ignored. Anyone who has read about the happenings in the Congo, or anyone concerned with the fate of the Freedom Riders in the South, knows that this is a far more intricate situation than is comfortable for a person of good-will or a persona of international thoughtfulness. Indeed, how can you be friends with a "lesser" race until the real questions raised by the situation are completely understood? This is what Mr. Forster was trying to say in his novel. This is (however ineptly) what I have tried to express in my play.[104]

Rama Rau's invocation of contemporary decolonizing struggles and the U.S. civil rights movement not only echoes Taubman's *New York Times* review of *A Passage to India*; it once again speaks to the ways in which Cold War contemporaries understood that the historical legacies of British colonialism had implications for American domestic racial conflict. Here we find Rama Rau explicitly using Forster and his novel as a peda-gogical tool—indeed, as a model for how imperial mentalities might be represented, critiqued, and ultimately challenged for Cold War audiences in the United States.

In putting *A Passage to India* to work politically, Rama Rau was by no means unique, of course: the political messages of the novel had been debated since its publication. As recently as 1954, just a year or two before Rama Rau began to draft her play, Nirad C. Chaudhuri observed in the pages of *Encounter* that *A Passage to India* was nothing less than a "verdict on British rule in India." Although in the end he dismissed the novel for its determination to understand power as an individual rather than as a structural affair, Chaudhuri suggested that it had done more for British imperial politics than it had for English literature.[105] Meanwhile, Rama Rau's *Theatre Arts* essay was one of several public accounts about *A Passage to India* in which she trumpeted Forster's novel as an object lesson for contemporary geopolitical problems in the wake of colonialism—

accounts that interpreted Forster himself as an exemplar of principled anti-colonialism and the embodiment of classic English gentlemanliness. Indeed, Rama Rau's genealogies of *A Passage to India* were also routinely praise songs for Forster himself. In her 1962 essay Rama Rau emphasized his moral probity: in the face of queries about selling the rights to his novel for a film version, Rama Rau recounted that Forster had been resolutely opposed. This was not for want of trying to persuade him on Santha Rama Rau's part; she and Natwar Singh tried to convince him at one stage that an Indian production would be the most faithful to his novel—as opposed to (in her words) "some ignorant 'we-got-to-get-some-bare-breasted-girls-into-that-shot' type from Hollywood."[106] "It is wonderful to know someone who can't be bought," she commented. "It is wonderful to know a novelist who is, as critics like to say, 'a classic in his own time' "—especially when, as she remarked, there was a quarter of a million dollars on the table.[107]

In actuality, Forster was not disinterested in the business side of his writing, and he was happy to see the New York play close when he realized the extent of the cuts in royalties that he and Rama Rau would have to take to keep it open.[108] His response to the constant queries about movie rights is best summarized by his comment to Rama Rau in 1960: "Miss Strauss [Rama Rau's agent] has already reopened the question of picture rights. 'No go,' I am afraid. You must all wish me out of the way!"[109] Because Forster had no agent—he didn't even have a telephone—Rama Rau found herself fielding questions about the movie rights for *A Passage to India* almost from the start of their acquaintance. In this context at least, she was not above having a little fun with Forster's image. In an interview in her Manhattan apartment with *Show* in February 1962, she "gave an imitation of the 83 year old novelist's response" to film requests: "She lowered her voice and spoke slowly in a clipped British accent: 'If I had wanted to write a play, I would have written a play. I have written a novel!' "[110] *Show* dubbed Rama Rau "the lively impersonator," and the anecdote suggests that for all her principled defense of Forster she had the ability to take a joke that the great man professed to admire (*pace* the quote from *Two Cheers for Democracy,* above).[111] As significantly for the kinds of cultural politics that the play set in motion, Rama Rau became his agent in both a symbolic and a very real sense—with material consequences for the eventual production of the 1984 David Lean film. In 1964, Rama Rau contributed an essay to a collection called *E. M. Forster: A Tribute*, edited by K. Natwar Singh on the occasion of Forster's eighty-fifth birthday. Singh was a member of the Indian delegation to the United Nations and a long-time Forster admirer.[112] The volume featured an impressive lineup of Indian personalities (including Mulk Raj Anand and Raja Rao). The fact that Santha Rama Rau was included among them testifies to the fame her writing and her involvement with *A Passage to India* had gained for her in the almost two decades since the publication of *Home to India*. In fact, it was Rama Rau who first approached Forster about the volume on behalf of Singh, and it was she who tried, unsuccessfully at first, to shop the book around to various publishers in the United States with whom she had connections.[113]

Rama Rau's essay in the Singh volume rehearsed the backstory of the New York stage play in slightly more detail than in the *Theatre Arts* piece, but as befitted a collection in honor of Forster, its effect was to underscore his role as a novelist of "the human predicament." Here she praised *A Passage to India* (the novel) again for its development of Indian characters who were not just "Gunga Din," suggesting that it stood in stark contrast to what she dubbed the "Lean Bronzed Horseman School" of literature on India which in her view contained no politics, no humor, no social up-heavals.[114] Rama Rau's admiration for Forster remained rooted in its authenticity vis-à-vis India:

> the most astonishing aspect of the book for many Indians was that it had the courage to talk and think from the inside of the Indian mind in all its many divergencies, and still convince *Indians* that it was telling the truth . . . he persuades you, by characterization and without a word of exposition, that his Indians are speaking to each other in their own language, and yet catches the special lilt and idioms of Indian-English when they are talking to the colonial British.[115]

Here, Rama Rau used the dramatization of the novel as an occasion for observing its, and Forster's, timelessness rather than its specificity. It was a novel that, in her view, did not "date," for its political sentiments rose above its history. According to Rama Rau, "there were two facts that even the less than academic audiences of London could not ignore: first, Mr. Forster had truthfully explored a moment in history; and second, similar moments are being lived by human beings almost anywhere in the world."[116]

Rama Rau's emphasis on the humanitarianism of Forster's vision—his emphasis on friendship and his signature theme, "Only connect"—might be read as a depoliticizing move. In fact, as I suggested in the introduction to this book, she was echoing the connections reviewers of her own work had made between his writing and hers—which, for at least one critic, "faithfully endorses Forster's strong plea for simple human contact."[117] Rama Rau shared Forster's utopian liberalism, his conviction (articulated again in the epigraph to this chapter) that it was personal relationships between like-minded cosmopolitans (such as himself and Rama Rau) that had the power to transcend the vagaries of colonialism.[118] This was Forster's political vision, and it was—or came to be—Rama Rau's as well. In the Singh collection, Rama Rau observed that the novel and the play with it dealt with issues contemporary to the 1960s, and she ended her paean with a series of questions that began with a focus on India and ended by opening up more generally onto the postwar postcolonial world:

> Can we, after blaming the British for their lacks, arrive ourselves at the hope of both governing and "connecting" with the mass of underprivileged Indians, the millions who are still in a position we used to share? The thoughtful British must have faced many of the same paradoxes. To get back to Mr. Forster's basic questions in *A Passage to India*, are friendship, cooperation, life, love, the brotherhood of man impossible until the first steps to political freedom are achieved? Are good intentions enough? And most important, can the subjects who become the rulers keep from perpetuating both a human and a political dominance?[119]

In contrast to her work in *Home to India* and *East of Home*, Rama Rau appears here to be turning her critical gaze away from former and current imperial powers (Britain and the United States) and toward the postcolonial Indian state and its rulers themselves—using Forster expressly as her agent for interrogating their nationalist and even their democratic aspirations.

If Forster—that exemplar of high English modernism—seems like an unlikely stick with which to beat the Nehruvian regime, in fact there is a certain postcolonial logic here. For one thing, Rama Rau was an admirer of Britain and England within it. As she commented in a review of Nirad C. Chaudhuri's *A Passage to England* in 1960,

> It is one of the odd ironies of history that years of domination should have prepared us, at last, for deep understanding and affection. Of course, we were lucky to have England. The English tradition is a great one, English literature *is* probably the most splendid in the world, the countryside is beautiful, the people (in their own country) civilized, and English institutions have left their imprint on a far greater area than their colonies encompassed. One thinks with commiseration of the Indonesians who were educated in Dutch.[120]

In this context, not only did Forster's rehabilitation as the embodiment of universalism rescue British imperialism from its unsavory past and thereby offer Americans an ennobling philosophy about (if not a model of) imperial power; it also spoke to a postimperial Indian elite steeped in an appreciation for things English. (Harrow- and Cambridge-educated, Nehru famously dubbed himself "the last Englishman to rule India" and was renowned for his Anglophilia.)[121] Like Rama Rau's essay on Forster in the Singh volume, her rehabilitation of him in the 1960s was undoubtedly aimed at an American audience, and it offered some lessons for a would-be imperial power—especially one that, despite its sense of affinity for things English, was skeptical at best about how the British had dealt with empire in its last stages.[122] As a reviewer for *Time* of her first novel, *Remember the House*, remarked, her Forsterian vision "puts in a novelist's terms an Indian psychological dilemma, which in the terms and the person of Nehru irritates the West: just as the British were disliked more for their law and the incorruptibility of their law-givers rather than for their conquest, so Americans seem to be disliked and resented for their quixotic goodwill rather than their 'dollar imperialism.' In the presence of envy, gratitude is impossible."[123] Rama Rau, for her part, felt that it was in India that "the Forster gospel reached its full expression."[124] In this sense, Rama Rau's cosmopolitanism is once again not a view from "nowhere." In style and in substance it falls short of what Rebecca Walkowitz has called "critical cosmopolitanism," even as it underscores the possibilities and the limits that the pressure of postcoloniality could place on the career of that phenomenon.[125]

If her identification with Forster, both self-generated and critically ascribed, permitted Americans to appreciate the similarities and differences between British imperialism and its U.S. successor, it also arguably addressed Indians involved in the creation of a new role for India on the world stage and drew them into discussions about the nature of national and global power in the context of the Cold War. Given her own family and social connections with the ambassadorial world, the United Nations, and the Nehrus themselves, in other words, Rama Rau was undoubtedly directing her comments at a diasporic as well as a transnational Indian elite. The Indian journalist Kusum Nair called this the Indian "cocktail circuit," and it included the likes of Natwar Singh and Madame Vijay-lakshmi Pandit (Nehru's sister)—Indians who read the *New York Times*, were affiliated with the UN, attended Broadway plays, and helped to shape American foreign policy toward India in New York and Washington, by both official and unofficial means.[126] By the time David Lean's film hit movie theaters twenty years later, however, Rama Rau was more concerned with shaping public perception of Forster and her relationship with him over the stage play and the screenplay than she was with geopolitical concerns. This was the case in part because after the 1970s Rama Rau ceased to have the same cultural influence she had had enjoyed in the quarter of a century before (see chapter 3), and in part because the fortunes of India vis-à-vis American foreign policy had shifted measurably since the death of Nehru in 1964. And yet, if Rama Rau was less connected to the political world than she had been, she was no less determined to secure Forster's image in the face of the version of *A Passage to India* that Lean ended up staging in the film.

After Forster died in 1970, his share of the movie rights reverted to King's College, Cambridge, where his literary executors persuaded Rama Rau to sell it because the college needed the money.[127] Although Lean had approached Rama Rau for a film version of the script and she had drafted one for him, he did not rely heavily, if at all, on it for the movie that eventuated. From the start Rama Rau's disagreements with him were about the structure of the story. Whereas Lean wanted to dramatize the novel in its entirety, she had ended her play with the trial because she felt that "you couldn't put the whole last section of the book on stage . . . a lot of the argument that comes up in the last section I tried to 'cram' into the court scene."[128] Of the section where Aziz wanted to show Fielding the monsoon, she said, "Well, rain to an Englishman is not particularly interesting on stage."[129] Lean found all that too "drab" and opted to set that bit in Kashmir. When I interviewed her in 2004 she told me that when Lean had Aziz living on a houseboat she protested, as she did when he set Holi and Dewali both in spring ("which," she said, "would never happen. It was not only inaccurate but especially so in Kashmir, where they don't celebrate Hindu holidays anyway."). It was these inauthenticities that Rama Rau dwelt on twenty years later, lamenting that the movie was "so full of really crass misunderstandings, like the feet dangled [together] in the water—Muslim [Aziz], Brahmin [Godbole], and Miss Quested— sharing water between these totally diverse people in the same tank. . . . Of course Alec Guinness as Godbole was an absolute scandal—he was making fun of the part, hamming it up and making it into a joke. I wrote an eleven-page single-spaced letter to Goodwin and Braybourn [the producers] pointing out all of the things that were totally impossible in India . . . [and] of course the whole last section was totally absurd."[130] Guinness, for his part, remembered his role "as a comic-cuts character without the necessary oriental mystery."[131] When I offered the opinion that the movie was surely something of a success, Rama Rau replied, "I would say not a financial success but a cultural success," and she attributed that to the fact that critics in the United States had not read the novel. Critics in India who had done so gave it totally different kinds of reviews, she claimed, and the movie opened and closed in Delhi within a week.[132]

One of Lean's biographers, Kevin Brownlow, interviewed Rama Rau for his 1996 book and she told much the same story there. Perhaps not surprisingly, Lean's interpretation (as reproduced by Brownlow) characterized the struggle between Rama Rau and himself as one between a writer and a movie director. But Lean also represented the disagreements he had with Rama Rau as a function of her determination to be the custodian of Forster's memory. Lean had seen the play in London in 1960 at the Comedy Theater and told her, "I nearly sat down to write you a letter saying 'Please tell me the story of our film on a half a sheet of paper.'"[133] They corresponded for some time about how to structure the play, how to represent what went on in the caves, and about each character and its development. But when he saw her script he felt it was unworkable for the screen, and according to Brownlow he wrote the final version in very short order in a hotel room in Delhi. Rama Rau was distressed by this turn of events, objecting to new scenes and especially to Lean's vulgar approach to "Forster's oblique, equivocal approach to Adela's sexual malaise."[134] Rama Rau, for her part, told Brownlow that "David used to call me 'the Keeper of the Flame' (not as a compliment) because . . . I kept referring him back to Forster's very dramatic, visually arresting novel."[135] "Keeper of the Flame" was a phrase she also referred to when I interviewed her almost ten years later.[136]

To be sure, Rama Rau took issue with a number of Lean's artistic choices; as suggested above she abhorred his encouragement of Guinness's mockery of the Godbole character as well as other inaccuracies of representation. These were second only to the very well publicized arguments several of the major players in the movie had with Lean—including Peggy Ashcroft, Judy Davis, and Victor Bannerjee. Bannerjee (the movie's Aziz), for example, railed against Lean's insistence that he do a "chi-chi" accent, remarking that "playing one Englishman's idea of another Englishman's idea of an Indian isn't my scene."[137] Rama Rau and Lean also disagreed over how to render Adela's character. Brownlow records that Rama Rau not only objected to Lean's "vulgar" approach to Adela but also to Lean's insistence that Aziz was a stand-in for Masood, the Indian with whom Forster had had a romantic relationship and to whom the novel had been dedicated. In her 1952 introduction to Forster's Indian diary in *Harper's Magazine*, Rama Rau had suggested that it was actually Saeed, "Mr. Forster's host during his visit to Hyderabad, a young Moslem working in a provincial part of India," who had served as the model: "the reader can see the outlines of a sketch for the character of Aziz in the novel."[138] Rama Rau did not mention this in our initial conversation, and her correspondence with Forster at the time that *A Passage to India* was first staged in the 1960s suggests that (with the exception of his delight at the news that Aziz would be played by Mohyeddin),[139] he was more concerned about the positioning of the half-clad punkah wallah on stage than he was about the details of Adela and Aziz and the caves.[140] I don't want to suggest that this omission on Rama Rau's part grew out of any sense of prudishness. Indeed, when I asked her about it in a later interview she was quite candid about her belief that Forster didn't have a sexual relationship with Masood; and though she didn't recall having written about the Saeed possibility in the *Harper's* piece, she volunteered that she had gotten that information from a friend of Saeed's family in Hyderabad named Akbar Hydari.[141] In an earlier interview she was equally forthright about the fact that her first marriage, to Faubion Bowers, had broken up in the context of his self-avowed homosexual practices.[142] This is a dimension of her life story it is not possible to have a full apprehension of, and its impact on her championing of Forster is also a matter of speculation. At the very least, it adds a postcolonial dimension to Joseph Boone's argument about the homoerotics of orientalism by highlighting the complex circuitries through which such erotics may be translated in and through mass-market culture—including through the agency of an Indian woman.[143] In the end, Rama Rau remembered Forster's preoccupation with the punkah wallah—the "most overt and full-blown embodiment of homoerotic desire" in the novel, as Krishnaswamy has called him—in great detail, speculating that "I think he [Forster] saw him [the punkah wallah] as a sort of symbol of India that sees things come and go—it's sort of a god-like attitude, but I think that's how Forster saw India. He saw the British as a sort of passing phase in the history of the place."[144] Down to this last comment in 2005, Rama Rau was invested in interpreting Forster, and in protecting him and his posthumous image from, for want of a better word, Americanization by the Lean movie, its subsequent publicity, and its long life in the American imagination (including my own).

This association between Americanization and sexualization had been operative in the London production, as we have seen through Frank Hauser's correspondence from 1960. According to Brownlow, Lean was cognizant of American sensibilities about sex and was keen to render the caves narrative in accordance with those attitudes.[145] Rama Rau's own take on Americanization in the 1980s had perhaps less to do with sexuality than with the material corruptions of the move business, as is evidenced in her 1986 article for *Grand Street* (a now-defunct New York City magazine), which contains the longest, most elaborate public account of the making of the stage play rendered by her—and refers, tellingly, to the Lean film not at all. In this essay, entitled "Remembering E. M. Forster," Rama Rau focuses on the 1960s story of her play, privileging the novelist's anti-materialist strain, opposing it to "the reality of Broadway economics," quoting extensively from his letters to her, and rehearsing his by now well-known rejection of the possibility of making film rights available to anyone. In light of Rama Rau's strong disapproval, horror even, at the way the film turned out, the *Grand Street* essay can be read as an attempt to cast Forster as everything that Lean is not: impervious to Hollywood's call, deeply invested in Indians' appreciation for the novel, and despondent over the changes in the play made to appeal to Broadway.

Perhaps most significantly, Rama Rau identifies completely with Forster in this narrative, recalling, "I thought the cuts had coarsened and weakened the play. The snatches of dialogue intended to make it more 'relevant' to an American audience and inserted, at the producers' insistence, during the frantic nights of rewriting in Boston [in its pre-Broadway run], seemed hopelessly out of tune with Forster's work."[146] Without alluding at all to Lean's movie, Rama Rau makes clear her ongoing role in preserving and promoting the "real Forster," who emerges, not incidentally, as a lively character in the 1960s drama of *A Passage to India* that Rama Rau managed to produce in several American print culture venues. The essay ends with her recalling that when the producers announced that Forster and Rama Rau would have cuts in their royalties, Forster said, effectively, fine: what I wanted to happen, happened: your version of the play opened on Broadway and Zia got the audience he deserves.[147] In the context of the publicity storm around Lean's film's debut, Rama Rau's message is clear: the play was closer to Forster than Lean could ever be, as is evidenced by Forster's endorsement. She is not, however, content to leave it at that. She ends the essay by recounting how Helen Willard of the Harvard Theater Collection wanted to archive the correspondence between Rama Rau and Forster. According to her, although Forster promised the documents, he couldn't find them, offering that he tended to "destroy matter which does not seem to me of primary importance"—thus pitting his almost otherworldly modesty against Lean's well-known braggadacio.[148]

In the end, then, the real pairing here is not Forster and Lean but Rama Rau and Forster. Her championing of him and his vision in *A Passage to India*—both in her play and in her public recuperation of him from both Hollywood and the more general American scene—should be understood as an attempt to underscore a version of the Raj in which an English-modernist universal brotherhood triumphed over a Kiplingesque East-will-be-East pessimism. Indeed, the ex-centric and eccentric effects of his sexuality—which enabled or required Forster to question the paradigm of social reproduction at the heart of British imperialism—were arguably matched by Santha Rama Rau's differently dissonant position as an extra-national Indian subject in Cold War America—which in turn predisposed her to embrace his "Only connect" philosophy not just with respect to the British empire but with regard to the new American one as well.[149] That they both articulated these perspectives from an elite vantage point speaks to the limits that class exerts on gendered apprehensions of empire; it speaks, in other words, to the structural contingency of all kinds of queer critique. In light of Krishnaswamy's claim that the novel itself was predicated on a desire not just to route homoerotic desire through homosocial friendship but to "eliminate the woman as the middle term in interracial relations," Rama Rau's very public claims on Forster also represent an attempt to restage the work of the female postcolonial critic—to insert an Indian woman's agency, as I suggested above, in the story.[150] This is all the more apposite when we appreciate the ways in which Rama Rau's own work up until the 1960s was read in the American public sphere: that is, as a storied version of "East-West" conflict—a representation of her work she did not share, not least because her view of the postcolonial world was hardly so dichotomous or, by extension, so politically naïve. In attempting to redeem Forster's vision, Rama Rau, whose own career before and after *A Passage to India* was arguably dwarfed by her dramatization of Forster's novel, strove to align herself with him: to represent to American audiences the authentic Forster and his "authentic" India as she hoped to have done herself.[151] Her identification with him both underscores her minority and gives its gendered career a nuanced meaning particular to liminal historical space "between" Anglophone empires that the postcolonial Cold War in America makes visible.

Another possible postcolonial reading of this story is to highlight the ways in which Rama Rau functioned not just as an interpreter of British India in America but also as a carrier of elite Anglo-Indian values to a Cold War United States intelligentsia that was beginning to appreciate in cultural terms—largely through the aristocratic, Brahminical figure of John Fitzgerald Kennedy himself—the extent to which, despite its critique of British imperialist policies and attitudes, it had inherited the British imperial mantle in the new world order.[152] Forster and his vision of the Raj was a crucial aspect of what Robert Dean has called this postwar "imperial brotherhood"—a fraternity for which Rama Rau was a kind of unintentional cultural broker.[153] Although I did not pose it to her in exactly those terms, I did ask Santha Rama Rau in 2005 what she thought American audiences were seeing when they saw *A Passage to India* on stage in 1962. She replied:

> Up until very recently, when Americans thought of imperialism they thought of domination by the British. I would have thought they [the Broadway audience] would have seen the parallels [between British imperialism and American imperialism] immediately. Everyone else did. Did you read *East of Home?* [she asked me. Yes, I replied]. When I interviewed people in Laos and all over Southeast Asia [for that book] they couldn't believe that America was supporting French imperialism or Dutch imperialism [after the war]. They all thought of the United States as the first anti-imperialists, no taxation without representation and all that.[154]

Nor was she, as we can see, anything less than an agent, in many senses of the word, in this ongoing process of exchange and translation in and for the West (in this case for an audience of one: me)—though of course she knew I was writing a book about her. Such cultural work during the height of her career was admittedly dependent on the shifting ground of Anglophilia in the Cold War American scene—an Anglophilia exemplified subtly but powerfully in elite strata like the *New York Times* by the persistence of the English spelling of "theatre" in all newspaper copy throughout the 1960s. As I have implied, it would be rash to translate such culturally derivative mannerisms with pro-British sentiment per se; for as historians have remarked, the so-called special relationship was rooted as often in suspicion of Britain's lingering imperial motives as it was in convictions about the power of Anglo-saxon connection.[155] Rama Rau's success in plumping for Forster's vision of the Raj was, of course, also dependent on the posthumous career of Forster himself in both Britain and America. Had he not been recognized as "England's greatest living novelist,"[156] and also "the most authoritative voice of 20th century English letters,"[157] Rama Rau's acts of translation would not have gained what purchase they did—either in the 1960s as she brought *A Passage to India* to American audiences or in the 1980s as she defended Forster against Lean and the apparent depredations of the film industry.[158]

As Richard Cronin has observed, Forster's was in fact a minor literary achievement. His enduring power—what Cronin calls his "moral posture"—stemmed from his canniness about the fact that with the decline of the British empire (as early as the 1920s, when *A Passage to India* was published), "Englishness could no longer represent itself as a universal moral value." In doing so, Cronin argues, Forster "helped his countrymen to reconcile themselves to the impending loss of their empire by indicating how it was possible for prestige to outlive power . . . how the loss of power might become itself the foundation of a new kind of prestige."[159] If Cold War America was ripe for this kind of message, the message itself depended on a shared sense of cultural, political, and above all racial solidarity that Rama Rau did not threaten. Indeed, her Indianness—with its Brahminical genealogy, its Aryan roots, its aristocratic "pluckiness," and above all *her* capacity to "pass" as not-black and perhaps even not-brown (she was often mistaken for Italian, readers of the introduction to this book will recall)—allowed her to translate a cosmopolitan critique of Western civilization that could interpolate postcolonial nation states like India, neo-imperial diplomacy like that of the United States, and race relations questions endemic to the American domestic scene—all apparently embodied by (and of course safely refracted through) the minor but morally prestigious voice of E. M. Forster. That her acts of translation still have purchase for us today testifies to the ongoing power of Raj nostalgia, albeit as a popular site of postcolonial criticism.

Santha Rama Rau, 1945. Photo by Clara Sipprell. Courtesy of the Special
Collections and Research Center, Syracuse University Library.

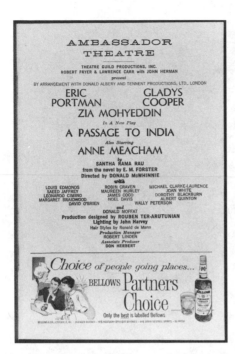

Playbill from *A Passage to India*, Ambassador Theater production, 1962. Courtesy of the Harvard Theatre Collection, Houghton Library, Harvard University, Cambridge, Massachusetts.

Al Hirschfeld drawing for *A Passage to India* on Broadway, appearing in the *New York Times*, January 28, 1962, p. 81. Courtesy of Margot Feiden Galleries, Ltd., New York.

Jackie Kennedy and her sister Lee Radziwill riding an elephant at the Amber Palace, Udaipur, Jaipur, India, March 19, 1962. John Kenneth Galbraith, United States ambassador to India, appears riding another elephant. Courtesy of the John F. Kennedy Presidential Library and Museum, Boston, Massachusetts (PC 1995).

Santha Rama Rau, 1969.
Courtesy of Getty Images.

Santha Rama Rau, New York City, 2004.
Photo by Antoinette Burton.

Home to India

Cooking with Santha Rama Rau

~~ Halfway into her introductory chapter to the Time-Life book *The Cooking of India* (1969), Santha Rama Rau lamented that "it is a point of some astonishment to me that after all these centuries of foreign contact, India and most of Southeast Asia should still be screened from the Western world by such a formidable barrier of fantasy, half-truths, misconceptions and sheer ignorance." Even the food, she remarked,

remains virtually unexplored, and a great and varied cuisine evolved from indigenous sources and outside cultures seems to have been reduced in Western minds (those that consider the matter at all) to the comprehensive and meaningless category "curry." To most of them curry is simply a floury, yellow cream sauce that can be used indiscriminately with meat or fish or chicken, and served with rice—and of course, with Major Grey's chutney. The term curry is actually an Anglicization of the word kari in Tamil (a language spoken in South India) which does, indeed, mean "sauce." Kari could, perhaps, be more accurately described as the combination of seasonings with which meat or fish or vegetables are cooked to produce a stew-like dish. No Indian cook would ever use a prepared curry powder, because each dish must have its own distinct masala. A large section of the country rarely eats rice, and as for major

Grey, he is unknown in India, though the appeal of chutney is apparently universal as a catchy verse suggests:

> Rank Injustice All things chickeny and muttn'y
> Taste better far when served with chutney
>   This is the mystery eternal:
>   Why didn't major Grey make colonel?[1]

That India remained such a puzzlement to the West, and particularly to Americans, must have been as frustrating as it was astonishing to Rama Rau, who had by the late 1960s spent the better part of her varied career as a writer trying to make India and Indians less of a mystery in and to the Anglophone world. To be sure, the equation of curry with India was a mild preoccupation of American print culture in the 1950s and 1960s, where recipes "adapted to American tastes" for it abounded.[2] That Rama Rau was reduced to explaining the real meaning and origins of curry to Anglo-American audiences after two decades of producing similar acts of translation in more "highbrow" cultural forms (travel writing, autobiography, and a famous stage play) than the cookbook is testimony both to how minor her own successes were as well as how entangled the task of mediation was in the Cold War culture of orientalism—embodied here in enduring popular Western misapprehensions about that apparently quintessential Indian commodity. But *The Cooking of India* cannot and should not be written off as a mundane project, one of the last major productions of a minor career. As Arjun Appadurai has so perspicaciously written, cookbooks may "belong to the humble literature of complex civilizations," but they tell revealing and often unusual "cultural tales" nonetheless.[3] In the first instance, Rama Rau appropriated a genre that was (at least in the context of "Indian" cooking) still very much in its infancy and shaped it to her own pedagogical ends. As we will see, she did so by engaging in considerable negotiation and at times outright conflict with her editors at Time-Life over the form the cookbook should take as well as the political messages it could and should carry in Cold War consumer culture. The result was a piece of writing that, in addition to imagining a "national" cuisine for middle-class Western and diasporic Indian consumption, ended up being part autobiography, part travelogue, part social and cultural history, and part political platform—a platform not, in the end, completely to Santha Rama Rau's liking. In producing a text that was so generically sedimented, so deliberately self-referential, and so politically charged, Rama Rau anticipated some of the narrative strategies in the cookbook career of her countrywoman Madhur Jaffrey, whose bestsellers made her name a household word for Indian cooking in Britain and the United States from the mid-1970s onward and, as Parama Roy has argued, came to personify the intimate connection between "gustatory and national memories."[4] And yet, as with her theater script *A Passage to India*, Rama Rau did more than simply set the stage for later incarnations of Raj memorabilia or imperial nostalgia. This chapter offers an account of the historical contexts in which Rama Rau produced *The Cooking of India* in an attempt to appreciate how and why her work in this, one of the most popular of realms, must be understood as a highly contested political act—an act of cultural translation and of a certain species of cosmopolitanism during the middling decades of the Cold War.

A word on the genre of Indian cookbooks is needed here. If the commercial revolution in American cookbookery was an interwar phenomenon—beginning with Irma Rombauer's *The Joy of Cooking* in 1931—Appadurai's ethnographic work suggests that the 1960s were the inaugural moment in the textualization of "Indian" food knowledge, a phenomenon that occurred largely in response to the consumerist demands of an emergent Indian bourgeoisie.[5] Arguing that food is "a highly condensed social fact," distinctive among cultural artifacts for its "semiotic virtuosity," he outlined in 1981 some of the "gastro-poetics" of South Asian foodways, focusing specifically on "the unfolding dramas" of public meals served in the context of marriage ceremonies.[6] In his more commonly cited 1988 essay, "How to Make a National Cuisine," Appadurai extended this discussion to the rise of the Indian cookbook, which he identified as a transnational process directed at an Anglophone audience by virtue of the triangular publication histories of the first generation of collections (with markets in India, Britain, and America).[7] Appadurai made a number of other observations about the crop of 1960s–70s Indian cookbooks that are germane to the making of Rama Rau's *The*

Cooking of India. Among these are the visibility of regional cuisines in these productions; the emergence of an organizational technique previously unknown to Indian foodways, the menu; the growing tension between a species of "culinary cosmopolitanism" on the one hand and rather more carefully controlled practices of "interethnic dining" on the other; and, not least, the fact that cookbooks foregrounded food preparation in ways that oral traditions (with their emphasis on customary dietary regulation and practice) had not.[8] Appadurai relied heavily for his interpretive frameworks on the studies of ethno-sociologists like McKim Marriott and R. S. Khare, whose work on food transaction and "gastronomic ideas and experiences" was also being undertaken in the 1960s, at the same historical moment that Indian cookbooks themselves gained a berth in the global public sphere.[9]

American print culture was somewhat slow to catch up to this accelerating trend. Indian cooking was discussed sporadically in popular culture venues like *McCall's*, *Good Housekeeping*, and *Ladies' Home Journal*—all venues for which Santha Rama Rau wrote, but not typically about food.[10] The subject of Indian cooking was also taken up in *Life* magazine and *New York Times* as early as the 1950s, although (as I discuss in more detail below) this coverage was overshadowed by the headlines about Indian famine that dominated the news from the postwar period onward.[11]

Parama Roy's study of the gastro-poetics of the South Asian diaspora takes the field in another direction, emphasizing the overlap between "reading communities and culinary communities" through an analysis of the highly gendered narrative strategies of the celebrated Indian cookbook maven Madhur Jaffrey.[12] The historical contingency of this emergent genre is important to specify from the outset: cookbooks of even the early 1960s—such as Attia Hosain's and Sita Pasricha's *Cooking the Indian Way* (1962)—were short on autobiographical detail and cultural context, with their spare introductory prose and their matter-of-fact, pictureless rendition of recipes.[13] Rama Rau's *The Cooking of India* shares much with the genre of diasporic cookbook which took hold in the 1970s and generated runaway bestsellers like Jaffrey's *Invitation to Indian Cooking* (1975) and, later (and to a lesser degree), Ismail Merchant's signature cookbook series, the first of which, *Ismail Merchant's Indian Cuisine*, appeared in 1986.[14] As in Jaffrey's writing, autobiography is at the heart of Rama Rau's text, which opens with an anecdote about her grandmother, who had been the organizing subject of her 1945 book, *Home to India*. Here Rama Rau recounted how, upon her return to India from her English boarding school, her Bombay grandmother had expressed concern that because Rama Rau was so tall, she might not be able to find a suitable husband in India. "Since I was scarcely 16 at the time," she recalled, "the matter didn't seem of primary importance to me, and I made the mistake of saying so. She replied severely that she had been half my age when she married."[15] As Rama Rau related it, this became the explanation for why she felt called to the cookbook project: "The episode is still fresh in my mind, and I remember my grandmother's answer rather shook me, though I had known it for years. I kept a decorous silence during the rest of the family greetings and comments, and immediately after these formalities, we were all ushered into the dining room for an elaborate meal that included all the favorite dishes of my childhood. In a way, these minor incidents summed up the two major preoccupations of my grandmother—and millions of other Indian women of all classes. Marriage and food."[16] As she had in *Home to India* more than twenty years earlier, Rama Rau used the site of her grandmother's home to foreground her own peripatetic life and cosmopolitan existence. But in this context (that of a corporate-sponsored series on cuisines around the world) and at this rather different moment in her career (when she was at the tail end of sellability rather than at the beginning of it), she staged her mobile past against two rather more fixed coordinates—North India and South India—represented by the "mixed" marriage of her mother and father respectively. This distinction between north and south—itself the expression of a kind of Indian cosmopolitanism—became the geographical, cultural, and political point of departure for Rama Rau's culinary narrative, which takes off from the perspective of "two grandmothers and their kitchens."[17]

The ostensible provincialism of *The Cooking of India*—as conjured by the apparently extreme local character of the two family kitchens—is worth lingering on, especially as it appears to stand in marked contrast to the cosmopolitan aspirations at the heart of virtually all of Rama Rau's previous writing. At least at the start of the text, Santha Rama Rau labored to establish herself as authentically Indian, as against the powerful and persuasive images of the mobile worldly woman she had striven to cultivate as a public persona since her graduation from Wellesley in the 1940s. The first chapter of the cookbook is devoted to a cursory sketch of her life, one that acknowledges the influence of her world travels on her "real," post-formal education (and in that sense again echoes the theme of *Home to India*) but subordinates those adventures to her regular returns to India—which, she says, "will remain forever 'Home' in my mind": "wherever I happened to live or travel, I felt I had to return to India at more or less regular intervals, for a year, a few months, whatever I could. Some atavistic urge made me feel, for example, that my son had to be born in India, at my parents' house, in the accepted Indian tradition. And for the last couple of years India has remained, and I hope will continue to remain, my 'Home' in all the ways that really matter."[18]

Nowhere else in her work do we find such a conventional affirmation of home; it is quite a retreat, in other words, from the cautionary tale embedded in *Home to India* or the less sardonic but no less worldly story of Asian discovery in *East of Home*.[19] Equally telling, the preface of the cookbook is called "A Passage to Indian Cooking"—a title which reveals Rama Rau's determination to capitalize on her Broadway fame even as she used it to focus her readers' attention on India per se.

Such self-consciousness about her Indian bona fides may be understood as one effect of having been asked, after a career built on travel and a certain species of global consumption, to settle down under the rubric of "Indian" cooking. But Rama Rau takes another, even more dramatic turn at the start of *The Cooking of India*. Her overdetermined identification with India in the cookbook is matched by an equally unprecedented defensiveness about her class status and hence the nature of the "cooking of India" on display in the Time-Life book. From the beginning, Rama Rau is eager to be clear that her vantage point on Indian food is structured by her own privileged life both in India and outside it. Though admittedly not "unaware or unaffected by the way that the majority of 520 million Indians lived," Rama Rau confesses that the recipes featured in the book are derived from food she knows—"from the sort of homes I have lived in and visited . . . not the daily fare of Indian villagers, about 80% of the country's inhabitants."[20]

This kind of disclaimer is not one common to Euro-American cookbooks; M. F. K. Fisher certainly did not make it in her contribution to the same Time-Life series on French provincial cooking (published in 1968), for example.[21] Unlike Fisher, of course, Rama Rau had no reputation as a cook or culinary savant, and her celebrity as a travel writer may have given some pause about her qualifications for writing a cookbook. On the other hand, given the overlap of the domain of travel with that of dining and, by extension, cooking, the work of translation Rama Rau undertook in *The Cooking of India* was a logical enough outcome of her well-known career as a mediator between things Asian and the West. As such it hardly required an apology for the class-based perspective that had, after all, become the hallmark of her work by the late 1960s.

It seems likely that Rama Rau staked out the parameters of the "Indian cooking" to be found in her book so deliberately because she knew that the majority of Americans from the mid-1940s onward would have associated "food" and "India" not with "cuisine" and its high culture connotations but with famine, starvation, lower-caste suffering, and Asian economic failure more generally. It is no exaggeration to say that for at least two American generations following World War II, impressions of India *tout court* were dominated by headlines about food crises produced by drought—crises imperfectly managed by postcolonial leaders, barely staunched by high-profile if controversial American government intervention, and of course deeply entrenched in Cold War politics.[22] Given the fact that before Pearl Harbor the majority of Americans sampled in national polls could not even locate India (or China) on an outline map of the world, the association of India with hunger is all the more significant.[23] If the mantra of the consumerist postwar generation was "think of the starving children of India," this was no mere fantasy: images of gaunt Indians of all ages could be found on the pages of national newspapers and featured as stock characters in policy debates over what to do about Asia's ailing democracies.[24] Moreover, by the mid-1950s, among the most well-known Indian novelists in America was Kamala Markandaya, who had made her reputation with the publication of *Nectar in a Sieve*—a story about the grinding poverty and hunger (both literal and figurative) produced by India's near-famine conditions, published in the United States in 1954.[25] The novelist R. K. Narayan used headlines about India-American talks on grain as an occasion for disquisitioning on ghee and its uses, but this was a rare, even a one-off, connection.[26] *The Cooking of India* certainly did not directly engage the issues of famine and foodstuffs, but it did attempt to rewrite the association between Indian food and lack, Indian food and poverty, Indian food and global dependence on American bounty. In this sense, naming Indian cooking as "cuisine" and detailing its social, cultural, and historical meanings—especially in a vaunted venue like the Time-Life series—was possibly the most challenging act of translation Rama Rau undertook in the course of her career, countering as it did pervasive and extremely powerful images of India and "the Indian" as a drought-ridden, starving beggar.[27] As Chester Bowles, the American ambassador to India, had put it in 1964, "Is India really unable to feed herself?"[28]

It was also, arguably, the most "cosmopolitanizing" work that Rama Rau produced. Reading the locus of her grandmothers' two kitchens as inward-looking or provincial is, in short, ultimately misleading. *The Cooking of India* uses the high-caste, domestic, and potentially oriental(ist) spaces typified by her grandmothers' kitchens as occasions for dramatizing the historically rich and culturally various nature not just of Indian food but of Indian domestic preparation and consumption as well. Take, for example, her treatment of her grandmother's home in North India, which opens with a lyrical description of the early morning rhythms of the awakening household, followed by an equally detailed account of how the orthodox kitchen was created—including an elaborate rendition of how the floor was laid with cow dung, a layer that was changed daily in order to satisfy her grandmother's insistence on a "neurotically clean" space.[29] In between these two passages is a short but crucial digression about the Kashmiri origins of her grandmother's family. Here Rama Rau details how her ancestors had fled Muslim invaders three hundred years ago ("to settle, inappropriately enough, in another Muslim stronghold, Allahabad").[30] Despite being migrants—and, of course, because of it—the women of the family preserved Kashmiri customs such as brewing green tea, cooking in ghee as opposed to oil, and preferring a variety of breads to rice. Not only does Rama Rau materialize the cultural geography of Indian cooking through this story; she also outlines some of the politics of dispossession that produced "Kashmiri" food as a highly politicized as well as a culturally marked category. Nor is she shy about reminding her readers that Kashmir was still, in 1969, very much a geopolitical flashpoint.[31] But Rama Rau does not leave it at that. In addition to pointing out that the predilection for green tea was shared "with Russians on their northern frontier, across the massive stretch of the Himalayas," she is at pains to make visible the fundamentally hybrid character of even "traditional" Kashmiri cooking:

> In all of this, their fierce sense of origins, their strong feeling for the "Kashmiri Brahmin community," remained undiminished even though they were exiled in uncomprehending, if not hostile territory. So intense was this feeling that it never allowed them to realize that their food, like their manners, language, even in some cases their dress, had been strongly influenced by centuries of Muslim rule in Kashmir and later in Allahabad. Unlike most Brahmins they ate meat (though not beef); on the rare occasions when they served rice it was in the form of *pulaus* (imaginative variations of the Persian *polo*, or *pilaf*). They delighted in serving an iced sherbetlike mixture of fruit juices, a drink they had adopted from the Moghul courts of North India.[32]

Though she ends up concluding that "they were Hindus and Brahmins, and no matter how long they lived in Allahabad, they would never be anything but Kashmiri," Rama Rau represents her family as thoroughly, if unwittingly, enmeshed in an expansively regional rather than an exclusively local culinary culture, one with north Indian tentacles that crossed religious, sub-imperial, and linguistic boundaries. Even "the north" that undergirds the autobiographically inflected representations of Indian cooking that open the book is, in the end, the effect of histories of migration, displacement, cultural encounter, and gastronomic exchange. In keeping with the way she managed the combination of orientalism and cosmopolitanism that informed her early travel writing, Rama Rau retains a promontory perspective on this transregional and even transnational cuisine, to which she is indubitably and at times wryly our guide. The politics of this perspective are worth underscoring because they dramatize the stakes of her role as translator of Indian foodways to Westerners and Americans in particular: Indians are cosmopolitan, in ways they live but don't necessarily fully understand—in ways that Westerners need to appreciate through elite, indigenous observers if they are to fully countenance "the world" of food and, of course, of cultural politics more generally. Rama Rau is suggesting, in other words, that cosmopolitanism exists in India but with its own spatial references, its particular lateral visions, and its specific translocal histories.

In many respects *The Cooking of India* reads like a travelogue, in much the same mode as the travel books that helped Rama Rau make her career early on. Each chapter focuses on a different dimension of Indian food or cooking—some predictable (spices, vegetarian dishes), some designed especially to appeal to the American palate ("Barbecuing Indian Style") or the American tourist ("Glittering Festivals and Lavish Feasts"), and some quite unusual for their treatment of regional variation and intracontinental boundaries ("Venerable Specialities of the Minorities" and "Pakistan: Muslims Who Eat Meat"—to these latter I will turn in more detail, below). In all of these, Rama Rau takes the opportunity to map the complexities of cooking—from the nature of ingredients to the utensils used for preparation to the variety of settings in which food is cooked and occasions for which it is consumed, whether quotidian or ceremonial—onto a remarkably detailed cartography of "India" in all its linguistic, territorial, and political complexity. She does this by weaving stories of festivals and feasts past and present and conjuring word-pictures not just of dishes but of their constituent parts: "the calm, snowy beauty of coconut rice"; the "sweet, glassy coating" of the shakar-paras; the "rose and yellow Romani" mango.[33] More prosaically but none the less powerfully, a colorful, full-page map of the subcontinent accompanies her discussion of her North Indian grandmother's kitchen. Legible there are the major Indian states, as well as West and East Pakistan (not to mention East Bengal), as is a textual sidebar which narrates the "startling contrasts and contradictions" from north to south and east to west and, additionally, correlates differences of region to those of skin tone and food preferences.[34]

Maps were a commonplace of the Time-Life series, which by its very nature telescoped political and cultural histories into descriptions of food culture writ large. Fisher's French cookbook had one too, with an equally detailed text enumerating the cultural peculiarities of the historic provinces of France, placed practically in the same place in the text as in *The Cooking of India*.[35] There is no denying the totalizing effect that such a standardized mapping produces, even as it parses local and regional differences. Taken together, however, the images and the text in Rama Rau's cookbook work to destabilize the will to cohesion—and hence to authenticity—that the map and indeed the entire ideological project that "the cooking of India" performs. For Rama Rau insists upon the multiculturalism indigenous to India itself, using cooking and food as platforms for making an argument about the continent's storied past and the multiplicity of influences on it. As early as page 26, she actively disavows the very possibility of the "Indian" cuisine of her title:

> There is one aspect of Indian cooking that should be emphasized in advance . . . Regional and religious food habits die very hard here, and as a result there is no major body of dishes and techniques of cooking that one can combine to call a "national cuisine." In a southern city like Bombay, for example, with its huge and very mixed population, you are able to tell at once, from food eaten in a private house, what part of the country your hosts' ancestors came from, what religion they observe, and probably how extensively they have traveled and their degree of familiarity with foreign ways as well. Apart from the Maharashtrians who form the central core of the citizenry of Bombay, their state capital, there are large numbers of Gujaratis . . . There are people from Kerala and Madras, the far southwest and southeast coastal regions, North Indians from Uttar Pradesh, and Goans, many of them Christians, from the small enclave south of Bombay that was ruled for three and a half centuries by the Portuguese. There are also Pathans, from the Muslim tribes of the Northwest Himalayan frontier, and Parsis or Zoroastrians, who fled from Muslim persecution in Persia 1200 years ago to seek sanctuary in India. They settled in the Bombay area and so did Jains, Sikhs and many other smaller groups . . . In their homes you would find the distinctive food and cooking of their ancestral province and their ethnic community. Only in some "modern" Indian homes would the meal be likely to include dishes from a variety of regions.[36]

This last point is one worth underscoring, for as Appadurai's research has shown, intra-ethnic dining, whether it meant different people sitting down together or different regional specialities being served at the same meal, was still rare enough in 1960s India.[37]

By her own admission, there is more than a bit of Bombay chauvinism at work here, since Rama Rau confessed that it was there that she considered her "real home," as well as an "excellent place to begin to know India as a whole."[38] On the one hand, urban culture in Bombay was the site of well-known culinary cosmopolitanism, as Frank Conlon's work on dining out in Bombay has illustrated.[39] This was the kind of restaurant scene in particular to which Santha Rama Rau's mother referred when she spoke of mixed dining as evidence of subcontinental progress (see chapter 1). On the other hand, Bombay's claims to world-class cosmopolitanism mask a history of political culture marked by xenophobia and violence, as Thomas Hansen's work on identity in postcolonial Bombay has also shown.[40] There is, nonetheless, a deliberate and politically consequential reorientation of Western impressions of India going on in *The Cooking of India*. For although she recognized that "people will tell you that the 'real' India is in the villages," it was in her view in the cities "that you get a sense of the whole Indian experience"—an experience shaped by "history . . . foreign influences . . . religious distinctions . . . dependence on traditions, as well as the presence and lack of orthodoxy."[41] Such an attempt at decentering the village in the Western historical imagination is of course fraught, entailing as it does a developmentalist model of country-to-city-to-modernity that carries with it, in turn, its own orientalist genealogies. And yet the focus on the Indian city does serve to challenge a certain monolithic and—given the powerful imagery of a starving rural India in the American Cold War imaginary—a readily available and quite reductivist stereotype about what (and where) India was. As *The Cooking of India* repeatedly illustrates, Rama Rau was committed to materializing the multiplicity of cuisines that might be found under the umbrella of "Indian": to signal their integrity from one another as well as their relatively peaceful coexistence. In this sense she was in step more broadly with the trend to make and keep visible the regional cuisines that Appadurai noted in his study of Indian cookbooks—though Rama Rau does not, interestingly, engage in the progressive hierarchy of local-into-supranational which he also noted as a characteristic feature of the emerging genre.[42] In keeping with this is her use of the term "foreign" (as in, "their degree of familiarity with foreign ways"), which is ambiguous: it could refer to exposure to international or intra-Indian differences. In this sense, Rama Rau's cookbook narrative is designed to reveal the cosmopolitan foodways and cuisines "natural" to India qua India, rather than a cosmopolitanism with presumptively Western coordinates and vectors.

Rama Rau's grasp of history and her willingness to deploy it as evidence of the polyglot nature of "India" is the most consistent narrative technique she uses to achieve this end. Citing India's legacy of conquest "by armies, traders [and] immigrants from all over the world" and the equally diverse profusion of faiths that resulted in part from it, she emphasizes the ways in which these influences shaped everything from the spices ground by itinerant grinders to the range of her South Indian grandmother's breakfast dishes.[43] Pickles provide an occasion for talking about the active fifteenth-century trade with China; Kashmiri lamb, for reminding readers of the region's location at the intersection of Tibet and Afghanistan; and Goa curry, for a history lesson on the voyage of Vasco da Gama.[44] At least one contemporary cookbook—Hosain's and Parsicha's *Cooking the Indian Way*—emphasized the impact of cultural and racial diversity on Indian cooking, but not nearly in the depth that Rama Rau did.[45] The lavish images that grace the text of Rama Rau's *The Cooking of India* contribute to its overall cosmopolitan effect. While the photos tend to fix highly local peoples and specialties, they also illustrate the variety of a singular and well-known commodity like rice, as the photo of sellers at the market in the vegetarian chapter (and her discussion of the twenty-five different kinds of rice) demonstrates.[46] Her treatment of pepper is typical of how histories and images come together to underscore what is a notoriously distinctive "Indian" ingredient; in her view it cannot be understood without a genealogy which lays bare the traces of early modern colonial warfare, contest, and desire that propelled it to the forefront of global cooking as a quintessentially "Eastern" spice.[47]

This is, again, not to say that traces of the same residual orientalism that informed her travel writing cannot also be seen here. For what is an argument about "the inexhaustible diversity of India, the overwhelming complexity of its cultural, religious and historical heritage, its imperviousness to generalization" but a series of classic orientalist tropes of the "other"?[48] Nor is it to suggest that Rama Rau was immune to the seductions of an all-India cuisine, or that she did not account for regional and local specificity whenever and wherever it was called for (the custom of thali in Maharashtra or the "perfect" idlis of the south). The pressures of the Time-Life contract were many, and writing under the rubric of "the cooking of India" exacted its price. Moreover, as I have suggested, the overarching narrative depends on the gastronomic dichotomies Rama Rau herself sets up around the differences between her two grandmothers. And Indian readers, at the very least, would surely have recognized therein a version of the distinctively Nehruvian vision of India's glorious past, echoing in content and in form his approach in *Glimpses of World History* (1942) and "India Today and Tomorrow" (1959).[49] But the burden of *The Cooking of India* is to interrupt a coherent notion of India by translating not just a national whole made up of local variations—the very kinds of regional divisions that Appadurai and others have noted were just beginning to emerge in Indian cookbooks emanating both from India and in the West in this very period—but an appreciation for the multifaceted, even hybrid India that was and is the consequence of a particular history of incorporation through conquest: of large scale digestion, if you will. Unlike Nehru, whose vision of a global India had to do with India's impact on its neighbors both in the past and in the present, Rama Rau posited a cosmopolitanism in which India was the consequence of vectors of outside influence: cultural, historical, linguistic, and of course, culinary. And unlike Madhur Jaffrey and those Indian cookbook writers who came of age with and after her, Rama Rau used *The Cooking of India* to fashion nothing less than an account of how the nation became a site of multicultural exchange and, ultimately, cosmopolitan culture: how people "became Indian" in ways that had, in her words, "nothing to do with passports or voting rights" and everything to do with intermixture, mobility, and exposure to a variety of "foreign" influences from near and far.[50]

As such, the nature and character of India's foodways were no less political subjects than travel in Asia had been for Rama Rau—and not only because the issue of Indian hunger was a problem with genuinely global ramifications and a hot-button Cold War question. *The Cooking of India* was the result of a complex series of negotiations with a variety of print culture and corporate entities that enlisted Rama Rau in their own cultural translation projects with respect to things Indian in America and, to a large extent, tried to shape the contours of her representations of "Indian cooking." Rama Rau's first foray into writing about cooking came at the invitation of Arnold Erlich of *Venture* magazine, who commissioned a 2,000–3,500 word article from her on curry in 1967. His concern was that she make curry "understandable to the American traveler in India." He asked for "a short rundown of what curry is all about, how important in the Indian diet, and the kind of curry available that the traveler ought to investigate. The piece should tell us where regional specialities are available and what is contained in the dishes. Hopefully you will indicate in which cities and restaurants the various curries you recommend are available."[51] Rama Rau complied, opening her article with an anecdote about her mother's compromised attempts to make curry in America for Americans who had no clue about the various spices needed to carry out such a feat.[52]

Erlich's belief that restaurant culture was universal was of course mistaken. Though public eateries were just beginning to emerge on a large scale in India, in part in response to an increasingly monied and mobile Indian middle class, in fact such dining was comparatively rare, both in India and in comparison with Europe and the United States—a fact which did not prevent scholars like R. S. Khare from noting it in their ethnographic work on Indian food cycles by the mid 1970s.[53] Erlich may have been misled by the eruption of Indian restaurants in New York City in the 1960s, among them East of Suez on East 58th Street (which featured "Javanese, East Indian, Chinese and American" food), Nataraj on West 112th Street, and, by 1971, Nirvana at 30 Central Park South.[54] His misconception may be responsible for the fact that by the time she wrote *The Cooking of India*, Rama Rau felt compelled to open with a pointed statement about the absence of such public eating venues in India—a fact which helped underscore her emphasis on domestic space as the focus of her concern. The conditions under which Rama Rau came to write *The Cooking of India* were somewhat different, though they may have been prompted by the appearance of the *Venture* article, since so much of the writing she did resulted from her exposure in a wide variety of print culture outlets from the 1950s onward. Her correspondence with one of her agents at William Morris, Owen Lassiter, indicates that Time-life paid her a substantial sum in the form of a base fee for the book, in addition to a $200 signing bonus.[55] As far as I am able to tell, this was the most money she had ever received outright in a contract, which must have made the pressure to produce enormous—all the more so since the scale, if not the exact amount, of the advances for the Time-Life series was a matter of public discussion. As Craig Claiborne, the famous American chef, put it in his *New York Times* review of M. F. K. Fisher's book in the series in 1968, "the volumes are reportedly financed by one of the largest budgets in cookbook history, so much so that one wag has said, 'they're throwing money to contributors like it's so much rice.'"[56] Given the associations with rice and poverty, rice and Asia, this is an instructive idiom in which to be addressing the profits of turning Indian cooking into "international" cuisine. The money aside, there was a series of logistical and technical problems the likes of which Rama Rau had never experienced in over twenty years of writing to contract. In the first instance, her editors at Time-Life (Bill Goolrick and his boss, Dick Williams) were not happy that she was doing the bulk of the writing out of New York and in India, in part because communication was slow or delayed between them, in part because in their view she disappeared for great lengths of time just before the final manuscript was due. Their concerns on this score were a major theme of the correspondence between New York and Bombay in the year leading up to the publication of the cookbook and constituted a source of considerable anxiety for Rama Rau.[57]

In fact, the tensions between Rama Rau and the Time-Life office were more complex than mere geographical distance and missed deadlines. Material in her correspondence suggests that what Time-Life had wanted at the outset was a book called "The Cooking of India and Indonesia"—a culinary combination she did not balk at in the beginning because she had a passing familiarity with Indonesian food. As she put it, she understood that "historically and culturally, the ties between the two countries are very close"; she felt that she could "fill in the colour, the background the manner of serving meals, etc." But, she added,

> this, of course, would be only incidental to the actual food which I made no particular study of while I was there. I lived for a while in Bali, and could give a fairly accurate picture of what both the daily food and the raja's feasts are like (Bali is the only other entirely Hindu country outside

India). Oddly enough they do eat beef there and it is of a very delicate and delicious quality—the cattle themselves look quite different, more like large, docile deer. Equally, I have lived both in villages and in Jakarta in Java, have eaten food from village bazaars and at sultan's palaces. Sumatra . . . I know much less well, having only visited there for brief periods.[58]

The Time-Life editors had suggested she make use of the expertise of George E. Lang, who had been responsible for setting up the Indonesian Pavilion at the 1964–65 World's Fair in New York. They may also have known about the restaurant East of Suez on East 58th Street, which had combined Indian and Indonesian food since 1955.[59] Rama Rau suggested that Lang provide the "technical information about the food and the recipes" while she would "cope with the historical and cultural background, and could fill in what was needed in the field of present day living and the details of entertaining and the look of the country and the interiors of the homes."[60] Rama Rau's outline, dated January 22, 1968, and entitled "The Cooking of India-Indonesia," together with her annotated copy of the menu for the "Second Tasting for Indonesian Section of Foods of the World" (March 4, 1968), further suggest her willingness to comply with their desire to meld the "two" cuisines in one volume. But by October of that year Rama Rau was feeling much less happy about the inclusion of Indonesia because her space was limited and she felt she needed every word to deal with India in its own right. Writing from Bombay, she was frank with Goolrick:

What I want to suggest is that this volume should deal with India only. Bill, this is very important and I do hope that Time-Life Books can see its way to being flexible about it. I cannot emphasize too strongly that India is a continent, and writing about any aspect of it is rather like writing about all of Europe in one book. To allot nearly a quarter of the space at our disposal to Indonesia really does not do justice to either country or its food. This seems to me particularly sad since this is really a pioneering project. No book that I know has ever attempted a comparable coverage— indeed, that has been my worst headache in researching it. . . . the only alternative I can see is to cut out the background colour, customs, etc., that I have described which (judging from your reaction to the first two chapters), I think you will agree will make the book much duller really and remove whatever little fun and individuality it has. In any case for a country as little known in the West as India, a disproportionate amount of exposition, history and setting is necessary simply to make the material comprehensible to Western readers—quite apart from the important consideration of trying to interest them.[61]

Using the language of marketability with which she had become familiar as a result of years of dealing with editors and publicists, Rama Rau makes a case for India as sui generis for the purposes of a Western audience— thus throwing into bold relief both her attachment to the cultural and historical cartographies that ended up shaping the cookbook *and* revealing how and why her determination to represent a nationally specific cuisine underwrote the particular brand of cosmopolitanism that, finally, marks *The Cooking of India*.

To be sure, Rama Rau's impassioned defense of a nationally bounded cookbook was motivated in part by a series of practicalities: she did not know Indonesian foodways all that intimately; she was writing the book from India where her access to the information necessary to such an understanding was possibly limited; she was already over the word limit assigned her by Time-Life; and, not least, she was already pushing up against the deadline of November 1968 for delivering the whole manuscript when she wrote the above letter to Goolrick. As her correspondence also intimates, by the fall of 1968 she and Goolrick had had their differences over the chapters she had already delivered. He had praised her "lively" style and assured her that she was off to a "fine start" when he received the first chapter in the late spring.[62] He did, however, wonder whether "there may be a shade too much history in it for a book on food" and, later, took issue with some of her prose, deeming it too "expository" (hence her reference to exposition, above).[63] The Time-Life editors also had substantive questions. It was Williams, for example, who urged her to talk about the relationship between pulau and pilaf; and it was he who wondered, very early on, whether it wasn't "worth a paragraph or two on who in the world was Major Grey?"[64] Though Rama Rau won some of the editorial battles, she lost a significant few—the inclusion of the hackneyed, orientalist ditty about Major Grey being evidence of one of them. At the start of these long-distance discussions, the most substantive editorial comments were not always conveyed directly by Goolrick or Williams themselves; they were commonly relayed by women from the New York office, among them Irene Saint or Grace Brynolson, the picture editor. In the context of delivering the news that Williams had reservations about Rama Rau "going so far away as India" when the manuscript was so unfinished, Saint remarked, "If I had one reservation it would be that in your excellent report of the place of food in the manners and mores of your country, I miss a little bit the word and word-sensations of lip-smacking over the taste of different dishes. You tell me why certain dishes are served at certain occasions, but you don't often describe those dishes in such a way that I want to run to the store to cook them in order to taste their particular delights."[65] Later on, Goolrick especially was quite direct in his comments. By January 1969 the manuscript was overdue, and Goolrick was even more blunt than he had previously been in his comments on the draft of her latest chapter. "This chapter reflects the main problem of the book," he told her. "There are some things about it that are wonderful, and some things that are dull. Your descriptions of the festivals themselves fascinate me, but when you list foods and use the festivals as a launching pad for a lengthy discussion of sweets, you bore me . . . This is a food book, of course. But it should evoke good food—and not feel duty bound to tell the reader in so many laborious steps how he or she can prepare a particular dish. Let's leave that for the recipes, and have pure Santha Rama Rau in the text."[66] Goolrick undoubtedly knew what Santha Rama Rau perhaps did not: that the "Betty Crocker era" of cookbook popularity that had peaked in the 1950s was on the wane, and that long-time cookbook publishers like Time-Life were trying to adapt to changing market fortunes. In the United States, Peg Bracken's runaway success, the *I Hate to Cook Book*, published in 1960, not only offered relief from the stay-at-home ideology of earlier cookbook genre; it insisted that a woman had a right to expect what she called a "hands-across-the-pantry feeling" from cookbook writers.[67] Indian cooking, already perceived as challenging despite the convergence of the gourmet movement and the internationalization of cooking that the late 1950s had given rise to, needed to be streamlined, made simple for the new Bracken-savvy generation.

It should be clear by now that the emphasis Rama Rau placed on cultural and historical background in the final version of *The Cooking of India*—"pure Santha Rama Rau," as Goolrick put it—was the result of a protracted struggle with Time-Life over the very terms through which she would translate Indian food to a Western public. For while there is detail about preparation, the texture and make-up of ingredients, and, as we have seen, attention to cultural and historical context, there is very little if any "lip-smacking" description in the text. If M. F. K. Fisher's *The Cooking of Provincial France* (which appeared in 1968, a year before Rama Rau's cookbook) was Time-Life's model, it is not surprising that they were trying to push Rama Rau toward more "word-sensations." Although there is a distinct similarity between the layout and structure of the two, Fisher's book is peppered, in contrast, with phrases like "garlicky mayonnaise," "spicy vegetable soup," and "pungent bouillabaisse"—her signature style, perhaps, but not a template that Rama Rau followed.[68]

Fisher was, of course, a celebrated professional cook who had already written sensational copy for years by the time she was commissioned by Time-Life. Rama Rau had done a feature on rice and reviewed one cookbook for the *New York Times* when she took on the Time-Life volume. And she opened that review by announcing, "I have always felt that a cookbook should be kept handily in a drawer . . . along with the pamphlet that tells you what to do when the electric mixer goes wrong"—a view of the cookbook as last resort, in other words.[69] Given the specificities of Rama Rau's career—and the fact that she had largely been left alone by her editors at Harper, who offered some editorial suggestions but nothing like the radical interventions Goolrick and company so strenuously recommended—it is not entirely surprising that she had to be tutored in the pitch and detail of culinary writing, or that she resisted the Time-Life editors' attempts to shape both her prose and the final outcome of the project. On one point in particular Goolrick was confrontational in a letter to her in August 1968:

I am afraid that the text may discourage the American housewife who wants to try to cook Indian dishes. I realize from reading the text that Indian cooking is very tricky, but on p. 11 [of the draft] where you say "beyond these very general observations, as an Indian cook, you are on your own. From here only time, experience and experiment can teach you . . . " We are going to have a lot of recipes in the book, and I think we want to encourage readers to try them. The phase "you are on your own" and "experiment" bothers me. It makes it seem as though recipes are useless. Can't we say something that will make it clear that you can achieve good results if you follow the recipes we are taking so much trouble to prepare? Otherwise why have the recipes?[70]

In Goolrick's view, Rama Rau's approach was in danger of challenging the very raison d'être of a cookbook: to induce people—and the American housewife in particular—to head to the market and start cooking the dishes. This was a vastly different enterprise from, say, writing a piece on curry for *Venture* magazine, a publication that was aimed (however wrongheadedly) at the American tourist in India.

Rama Rau was clearly hampered by the fact that she was neither a cook nor a professional gastronome. But as Goolrick well knew, she was cognizant of this fact and took elaborate care to make sure that the information she was conveying—not to mention the recipes she was discussing—was accurate and, for want of a better word, authentic. For one thing, she did voluminous research on South Asia in preparation for writing. Among the books she consulted were K. M. Panikkar's *Asia and Western Dominance* (published in 1953 and destined to become a classic) and *The Wealth of India* (a dictionary of economic products in six volumes dating from the late nineteenth century).[71] For foodways and cultural context she looked at, among other things, Apte's *Social and Religious Life in the Grihya Sutras* (1954) and *Beef in Ancient India* (1967).[72] This reading was second only to the research she did on food preparation from all around India with cooks, cookery experts, and at least one professional culinary instructor. Her notes indicate interviews with Rohini Haksaa on the Hyderabad banquet and Kashmiri dishes, with Indira Talyarkham about Bengali foods and festivals, and with Dhan Nanvatty on Parsi dishes.[73] These interviews were guided (at least in anticipation, if not in practice) by lists of questions pertaining to specific subjects, such as those she posed to Thangam Philip about "spices in Indian cooking." Philip was then principal of the Institute of Catering and Technology and Applied Nutrition in Bombay, as well as the author of her own cookbook—one of the most authoritative figures, in fact, on Indian cooking in contemporary India.[74] In her case the queries—which ranged from "are there any mixtures besides garam masala that are kept for ready use in the kitchen?" to "how individual can one be about spicing?"— were typed out with Rama Rau's handwritten responses jotted down in between. Because these notes are not dated, it's impossible to know whether Rama Rau did this in response to Goolrick's concerns or in anticipation of them. I suspect the questions were drawn up and asked after his letter quoted above, which was written at the very start of the project when she was first headed to India, but she may have intended to proceed in this way from the start.

In any case, what these details tell us is how seriously Rama Rau took this particular act of translation, and how invested she was in producing a semi-scientific account of India's and Indians' relationship to food. Given how young the Indian cookbook industry was in the 1960s, Rama Rau may be said to have been present at the beginning of this generic enterprise and to have contributed to the process of converting a largely oral tradition of recipekeeping and culinary narrativizing into a literary genre and, in turn, a transnational phenomenon with a growing (and potentially profitable) diasporic audience. As has been noted, despite some highly localized and small-scale exceptions, this move to codify oral knowledge into the written word marks a significant departure in the history and culture of Indian foodways, since before the 1960s there was no sustained attention to culinary issues per se, if these are understood as having to do with preparation (as opposed to dietary practices per se).[75] And Rama Rau had to fight with Time-Life to do it, since she perceived their critiques of her thick descriptions as a call to evacuate the text of deeply personal communications she had received from local Indian experts. "Everything had to be assembled through personal contacts," she told Goolrick, "[through] finding the people who know and getting them to talk and demonstrate. I think it would be a great pity if we skimped on this virtually untouched material."[76] Once again, though she was a minor player, Santha Rama Rau participated in a major process of cultural translation that had a number of different audiences and operated in several registers—here, specifically, in the political economy of transnational consumption and the symbolic economy of an aspiring, middle-class Indian diaspora, largely though by no means exclusively located in the United States. In an important sense, she both capitalized on and helped to circulate the connections between Indian food and "dietary liberalism" that, as Keya Ganguly has shown, was to become a hallmark of diasporic Indian communities in the United States, where "the Indian meal" has become not merely cultural capital but a fetish as well.[77]

For all these reasons, the complex circuitry of knowledge out of which *The Cooking of India* emerged at this historical moment is crucial to the story of the cultural politics it has to tell. In the first instance, Rama Rau was in regular contact with Devika Teja, the wife of a UN official who was her cooking liaison with Time-Life in New York and whose photo appeared with Rama Rau's on the inside cover of the book. Initially suggested by Williams and Michael Field (a chef in his own right who was the consulting editor for both Rama Rau's and Fisher's books), Teja became a confidante and friend during the writing of the cookbook as well as the recipe tester in the Time-Life kitchens in Manhattan.[78] She was an enthusiastic supporter of Rama Rau's storied approach, praising the draft of her introduction and endorsing the use of the two grandmothers' kitchens as an organizing principle: "[it] will be of special interest to the foreigners— it fills me with nostalgia for our own home in Goa, and for our kitchen that still gets the cowdung treatment."[79] Teja and Rama Rau corresponded about what dishes to feature and what emphasis to give beef, given that it would not be served at an "all-India" dinner table.[80] Teja also recommended two popular contemporary cookbooks from India (one by "Mrs. Singh" and one by "Mrs. Oberoi")—recommendations that underscore the complex traffic in Indian cooking that was going on both in and around the publication of *The Cooking of India*.[81]

Time-Life furnished Rama Rau with a research assistant in New York, but there is no evidence that she ever put her to use.[82] If this was an all-Indian production, however, it was not necessarily self-evidently so. For at the center of *The Cooking of India* was Thangam Philip, whose *Modern Cookery* (1965) went through four editions and was sanctioned by the government of India.[83] In addition to consulting her extensively on the finer points of food preparation, Rama Rau relied on her editorial skill for parts in the book, specifically the chapter on fish and seafood. She also sent her the final manuscript before its publication. Philip wrote back that she approved heartily: "It reads like a story and can easily be titled 'Romance of Spices.'"[84] Not only was Rama Rau dependent on Philip for her expert knowledge but she used her to help navigate the demands of the Time-Life editors that she cast the book more recognizably toward the American housewife: Thangam Philip very intelligently suggested that she make two sets of recipes for the very same dishes. One the traditional, authentic, as-it's-cooked-in-India list and two, the same recipe as it could be adapted for America—substitutions, shortcuts, etc. She thought Rama Rau was in a particularly good position to be able to do this because a large part of her training was in America and she was totally at ease in both Western and Indian cooking.[85]

Here Rama Rau again displays her canniness about marketability. She also reveals the cross-currents of "professional knowledge" from India to America and back again among Indian elites, many of whom aspired to the same cultural status as those Americans designated as the audience for *The Cooking of India*. Rama Rau's relationship to Philip also tells us something about the material conditions under which the cookbook was produced. Philip was not just instrumental in the recipe department; she also proved crucial to the images of spices that appeared in chapter 7 of the book. All the photos for *The Cooking of India* were taken by Eliot Elisofon, a well-respected Time-Life photographer, under the direction of Grace Brynolson from the New York office. Brynolson was keen to have as many "recipe pictures" as possible shot in India rather than "in the studio with rigged-up backgrounds."[86] She also wanted the food in the photos "authentically" prepared, and Philip was in charge of orchestrating all of that—a role that proved to be indispensable when Elisofon got sick while on a shoot in India. Rama Rau's correspondence during this period suggests that she had to press to have Philip remunerated accordingly, and more than once. Rama Rau also billed Time-Life for the typographical and dictation services of Homai Bilpodiwala (Rs 250) and for incidentals like telegrams and stationery.[87] However minimally, Rama Rau was doing her best to keep the local economy afloat—in this case, a "local" that was constitutive of the national project of the cookbook and contingent on the transnational movements of Rama Rau and her monies, from New York to India and back again. In the end, the contributions of

Indians in India are visible only in the fine print of *The Cooking of India*.[88] Rama Rau does allude throughout the text to the fact that she had spoken with friends and family members about various issues in the text, but there is no attribution to specific individuals. The short bibliography and acknowledgment of people in India at the back of the book notwithstanding, the American-based Teja is the one whose picture is featured, while the critical role that Philip and others played in Rama Rau's construction of the cookbook would most likely not have registered at the level of the average reader's sightline. This is perhaps understandable enough. The Time-Life books were designed to be consumed as expert knowledge and as such they privileged individual authors; most if not all of them had their own resources as well as the Time-Life staff at their disposal. If nothing else, the invisibility of the Indian hands in the making of *The Cooking of India* testifies to the very real hybridities that performances of the national tend consistently to obscure, especially where commodity capitalism of the kind that Time-Life represents is concerned.

In many respects, and in spite of her overall success in creating a profoundly storied account of Indian food and its cultural meanings, Rama Rau's role in shaping what her cookbook became was actually quite limited. Nowhere is this more evident than in the battle she fought and lost with her editors over the inclusion of Pakistan in the volume. In the course of increasingly tension-filled communiqués between New York and Bombay in the fall of 1968, Bill Goolrick dropped a bombshell on Rama Rau: having cut out the Indonesia section, he now wanted to add one on Pakistan. He wrote:

> In spite of what has been said previously, we think that you have to include a Pakistan in this book at some point. You can tell us in general what Pakistani cooking is like in either of two places: where you talk about Muslim cooking in the Kashmir section or in the final section on the minority groups. We believe that for historical reasons at least, we must not leave this out. I don't think it requires a separate chapter, although we may want to do a separate picture act on it . . . I think you are quite right that Indonesia does not belong in this book, but at the same time I think we must take Pakistan into account.[89]

If this request was designed to get a rise—and to rematerialize an errant author—it did the trick: Rama Rau responded immediately. She objected to the main thrust of Goolrick's suggestion, and her reply is worth quoting in full:

> About Pakistan. In actual fact just about all the best Pakistani cooking will automatically be covered in the section on Mughlai food and *tandoori* food. I can of course mention this in the text and will in any case have to explain that all this food which is Muslim is origin was evolved throughout North-West India (of which Pakistan was, at one time, a part) during and after the Muslim invasions which reached their greatest strength in the 15th and 16th centuries. However, I am afraid that the inclusion of Pakistan in the general picture of North Indian cooking may offend modern Pakistani sensibilities. I cannot go to Pakistan myself to describe a specific dinner of the sort that you suggest because Indian nationals are not given visas to visit Pakistan unless they are Muslims and can demonstrate that they have relations there. But if [you] don't mind possible touchiness from Pakistan I certainly don't. For so many centuries Pakistan was a part of India and it has only been a separate nation for twenty years, so it really would be impossible to give an account of North Indian food without including Pakistan either specifically by name or by implication.[90]

Here we see Rama Rau, in response to Goolrick's claim that Pakistan must be included for "historical" reasons, offering Goolrick a history lesson with clear contemporary implications—implications not just for representation but potentially for marketability as well. Her reference to Pakistani "sensibilities" and "touchiness" suggests that she at least hoped that Indians, whether nationals or diasporans, would be one possible audience for *The Cooking of India*.[91] She also reveals, parenthetically but no less emphatically, that her view of "India" contained contemporary Pakistan, and at the very least that the cookbook should not necessarily be a respecter of the boundaries set up by states and passports. The politics of this position is at once resistant and conciliatory: a gambit, perhaps, aimed at representing herself as insouciant about the ramifications of Goolrick's choice even as she lays out what she sees as the potential market costs.

There is some evidence that American readers of the day were being encouraged to differentiate Indian from Pakistani food, though this is admittedly scant.[92] Perhaps Rama Rau knew that some of her competitors in the cookbook market were at pains to make clear that postcolonial national boundaries had little or no effect on culinary difference per se (at least not perceptibly by the 1960s).[93] The letter above continues with Rama Rau's recommendation that Elisofon go to Pakistan to take photos that would not overlap with the Mughlai banquet ("which is Muslim," she reminds Goolrick) or the Kashmiri wedding scenes ("also Muslim," she says, as if to make certain that Goolrick understands) already embedded in her text. These could later be incorporated, she went on, "possibly in a caption for a picture essay."[94] And she reassures Goolrick that "in fact one of the reasons I changed the Rajasthan feats to a Mughlai Banquet was to be sure that Muslim cooking, which is quite distinctive, be given its proper place and coverage."[95] In fact, Rama Rau mentions Pakistan by name throughout the book, as in the chapter on barbecuing, which opens with an anecdote about her childhood visit to her aunt in the Punjab, now "severed" from India by the 1947 partition.[96] In choosing the language that she did, she hinted at the violence surrounding the creation of the new state and signaled (however obliquely) her own political disquiet at the sundering. That disquiet is obviously more legible in her correspondence with her editors, where her reference to the legal barriers to the kinds of border crossing they wanted to instantiate at the heart of *The Cooking of India* was quite pointed. It would also have been discernible to careful readers of the cookbook—and, given the tense relationship between India and the United States over the question of Pakistan at the level of diplomacy and foreign policy well into the 1960s, not necessarily only to Indian ones.

In the end, Rama Rau mobilized a combination of compliance and tenacity in the face of Time-Life's increasingly intrusive and politically naïve demands. "In any case, I think our problem with Pakistan is not a matter of ignoring their cuisine but simply a question of fact," she told Goolrick. "A separate chapter on Pakistani cooking would really be duplicating material already in the book, yet I do see that Pakistanis might feel slighted if they are not mentioned at all. My own solution would be to give them the very full credit they deserve in the background history, evolution, and customs of North Indian cooking. It is possible, of course, that the hill tribes of Pakistan might have special dishes and might from a photographer's point of view be worth exploring."[97] This last comment is surely a bit mischievous, for Rama Rau must have imagined that Goolrick had not reckoned on tribal peoples at all in his apprehension of the subcontinent. Ever the cultural translator, Rama Rau displayed her insider knowledge to try to influence the outcome of this particular dispute in her favor. And in keeping with her view, inscribed all over *The Cooking of India*, that "India" itself was more complex and more culturally diverse than Westerners were able to grasp, she made it clear that Pakistan could not stand in for Islam or "the north" any more than India could be reduced to curry.

Ultimately, Rama Rau's intransigence won her a pyrrhic victory: she did not have to adjust her prose, but Time-Life had its Pakistan chapter anyway. They hired Mohammed Aftab—a Time-Life correspondent from Rawalpindi—to write it, accompanied by a series of dramatic photos, many of them full-page.[98] In fact Aftab's essay, the last chapter of the book, is quite short and is dominated by images rather than text. It begins with a proverb ("you cannot be a good Muslim unless you eat meat and lots of it"), dives immediately into a factual history of Pakistan's origins and statistics, continues with a condensed account of dishes and festivals, and ends rather abruptly with the recognition that Pakistan is a "fledgling nation" nonetheless unified by religion and in the process of producing "a cuisine of its own."[99] Given the quality of this piece, and given their management of the cookbook-ese of Rama Rau's writing, the editors at Time-Life must have wanted a chapter on Pakistan very badly indeed. It functions like an appendage to *The Cooking of India*, not least because, in purely stylistic terms, it is so vastly different (flatter, more matter-of-fact, and less nuanced) from Rama Rau's rich and engaging prose. For all that Goolrick and others at Time-Life critiqued what they saw as Rama Rau's excessively expository prose and pushed her to discard the naming of dish after dish in favor of more "lip-smacking" descriptions, what they got in their Pakistan chapter was very much a laundry list of kebabs, kormas, and koftas.

More significantly, Aftab's essay also turns on the very oppositions— India / Pakistan, Hindu / Muslim—that Rama Rau had worked to undermine across the whole of *The Cooking of India*. It has, moreover, an unselfconsciously developmentalist tone that stands in opposition to much of Rama Rau's approach. The following paragraph is exemplary:

> As recently as a quarter of a century ago Muslim families in Pakistan used to eat sitting cross-legged on the floor, because they believed that this created an affinity among those who were eating together. The floors usually were covered with carpets, and enormous white or flowered sheets were spread where the serving dishes were to be set. In the countryside and small towns, the custom still prevails. But nowadays a great number of Muslims have moved up to regular dining tables.[100]

Contrast this with the passage in an earlier chapter of the book, where Rama Rau discusses the "usual Indian way . . . [of eating with] our fingers":

> It may sound like a messy habit, but once you are used to it, you are apt to feel much as connoisseurs of Japanese and Chinese food feel about using chopsticks. The food, for no definable reason, just tastes better. (There is a story that the Shah of Iran, on a visit to India, was so taken by the custom that he remarked that to eat with the spoon and fork was like making love through an interpreter.)[101]

Rama Rau herself was not above invoking the "modern" Indian home, as when she observed, above, that this was the most likely place for people to see and experience regional cuisines side by side. But modernity and tradition were not the polar bases upon which her approach to "Indian" cooking was based. The invocation of the Shah as well as of a world in which readers are "connoisseurs" of various Asian cuisines reminds us of the bourgeois and bourgeois-hopeful audiences to which *The Cooking of India* was directed. It also underscores the deftness and subtlety of Rama Rau's posture with respect to this project, which offered accounts of the historical background of food and eating practices not in order to prove that Indian culture was primitive or in need of modernizing but precisely to demonstrate that it contained "modern" (which for her implied urban, non-static, multiple, and extraterritorial) streams of influence which the sovereign category of "India" could not capture.

The inclusion of the chapter on Pakistan was unquestionably awkward, especially since the organization of the cookbook was, for the most part and purposefully, as much non-national as it was non-regional. The greatest exception to this is chapter 7, "Venerable Specialities of the Minorities."[102] In the context of what Appadurai describes as the contest between national and regional cuisines in the emergent Indian cookbook industry, this chapter represents an instructive approach to the question of diversity that Rama Rau had striven to make more than simply a contrapuntal note to *The Cooking of India*. She opened with an explanatory line which, while intended to introduce the cooking and eating practices of "Jains, Sikhs, Parsis, Syrian Christians and Goans," could easily stand as a description of the cookbook as a whole: "In the extraordinary mosaic of cultures, religions and traditions that go to make up Indian life," she observed, "certain small ethnic, religious and geographic communities have evolved such distinctive manners, habits and food customs that, though indisputably Indian, they retain a definite identity of their own."[103] Guided by the combination of historical context and personal anecdote that structures the rest of the book, this chapter contains the fewest images, sketches of "two oriental" deep-fryers (one the "Indian karhai," the other the "Chinese wok") being the most remarkable. It is not self-evident from the archive whose idea this partitioning off was, and it would be easy enough to read it as parenthetical, in its specificity and self-containment, to the overall narrative of the cookbook: as tacked on, in other words, as the final chapter on Pakistan was. At the same time, it is here that Rama Rau is, perhaps, at her ethnographic best. All three of the major "minorities" (Syrian Christians, Parsis, and Goans) come in for careful and respectful treatment, with the pressure of long histories (Persian for the Parsis, Portuguese for the Goans) and the perspective of her own personal encounters everywhere in evidence. Indeed, this chapter is redolent of some of the most sensational prose in the whole volume. Describing the process of preparing a dhansak dish that she witnessed in the home of a Parsi friend in Bombay, Rama Rau waxes eloquent about what she saw, smelled, and tasted:

[When] the lentils had cooked to the required consistency, and, using a round indented wooden ladle placed in the center of the *dal* vessel, she proceeded with a rhythmic rolling of the ladle held within the palms of her hands, to break up the lentils into a sort of coarse purée. To the bland lentils she added the aromatic vegetable *masala* purée, and blended it together, tossing in the lightly fried cubes of meat, mint, chilies and coriander. When this was done, she topped it off with a cream of crisply fried brown onion. The end result was surprising indeed. Gone were the stunning hues of yellow, purple green and red. Instead we saw a light brown stew with specks of green coriander and brown onions, but the richest, most forceful and most filling meal I have ever eaten.[104]

The extent to which Rama Rau had control over how (and even whether) the so-called minority cuisines of India were placed in *The Cooking of India* is difficult to know with certainty. But the mosaic theme, the combination of the historical and the ethnographic, and above all, the resistance to any simplistic notion of "Indian" cooking arguably make this chapter the most representative of the kind of cosmopolitanism—global in its scope, deeply local without being either fixed or "traditional" in the conventional sense—Rama Rau wanted to impress on her readers as exemplary of "Indian cuisine." Given the rank orientalism to which non-Western cuisine was subject in this period—Pearl Buck's *Oriental Cookbook* is a case in point—Rama Rau's determination to make nuanced and complex observations about Indian food has to be appreciated for the culturally and politically savvy intervention that it was, whether intentional or not.[105] Rama Rau's work interrupted a steady flow of liberal American cosmopolitan appreciation for "other" foodways that anticipated later multicultural incarnations of ethnic difference. Books about "international" (by which was meant European far more often than non-Western) cooking were all the rage in the 1960s and were regularly reviewed in the *New York Times* as well as in more popular culture venues.[106] Santha Rama Rau even wrote a review of Dharam Jit Singh's *Classic Cooking from India* in 1956, praising its "pioneer attempt to persuade Americans that Indian food is not 'the gummy, pasty mess known here as curry.'"[107] However, despite the attention given to a variety of "exotic" cuisines by Jane Nickerson and June Owen, both food critics for the *Times, The Cooking of India* was never reviewed there.[108] This is in contrast to the lengthy article by Craig Claiborne on Madhur Jaffrey's love of cooking, which coincided with the debut of her 1966 film, *Shake-speare Wallah*—that is to say, almost ten years before her first cook-book ever appeared, and despite the fact American distributors for the Merchant-Ivory film (only their second) were hard to find.[109] In the end, it's possible that the fortunes of *The Cooking of India* were tied up in reviews, as the fortunes of the Time-Life series in toto had been through-out the book's production. Craig Claiborne had roundly panned Fisher's *The Cooking of Provincial France* (the first of the series to appear) on the grounds that its definition of provincial was too capacious, casting the obviously Parisian coquilles Saint Jacques as such and ignoring obvious candidates as chicken livers Bressane in the process.[110] Claiborne was unequivocal. Though he admired the prose and the authority of Fisher herself, he opined that with the "popularity of Americans in France . . . at its lowest ebb in history," Fisher's book was very likely to make things worse.[111]

If Rama Rau's foray into cooking yielded nothing like the fulsome and enthusiastic reviews of her earlier work, this need not distract us from the accomplishments of the book, nor from appreciating the ideological work it did—however "minor"—in the transnational landscape of Anglo-Indian relations in the Cold War United States. Though there were Indian cookbooks geared toward an American audience before the publication of *The Cooking of India*, none had the cachet which association with Time-Life Books (whether well reviewed or not) conferred. Rama Rau antici-pated, and helped to shape, a commercial appetite not just for Indian food but for attention to Indian foodways as an entrée into larger discussions of and discourse about the relationships between consumption, autobiogra-phy, and the postcolonial nation outside the West. She did so at exactly the same historical moment when ethnographers of the stature of Claude Lévi-Strauss were fashioning arguments about the capacity of the lan-guage of cuisine to translate culture "unconsciously" and Mary Douglas was first articulating claims about the relationship between social rela-tions, social structure, and the meal.[112] It would be more than a stretch to suggest a conscious link between these academic practitioners—who, in any event, were on the cusp of their own academic celebrity with this very late 1960s work—and the making of *The Cooking of India*. At the same time, this is clearly a historical moment when debates about the raw and the cooked were alive in discourses high and low, blurring what we know in any case to be the highly constructed boundaries between those two domains of culture. I have dwelt at more length on Rama Rau's use of historical background and context to "break up" a unified vision of India than I have on her ethnographic approach, but there is more to be said on that score. As suggested above, this is most evident in her detailed coverage of Hindu festivals and feasts—those events that Goolrick worried would be "dull" unless they were more expressly and engagingly connected to a discussion of the meals around which they were organized. Rama Rau ratifies Appadurai's sense (gleaned directly from Marriott) that foodways were changing more rapidly than the ceremonial occasions (especially marriage) in which they were so central. But despite even her careful attention to "regional observances," she is at her most unselfconsciously essentialist and nationalist when examining the "glittering festivals and lavish feasts" across the subcontinent.[113] As she puts it at the start of the chapter by the same name, "this sense of pageantry is irrepressibly Indian."[114] The photos that accompany these passages reinforce this interpretation; they are reminiscent of her *Holiday* days, though her correspondence with Time-Life suggests she had more of a hand in shaping them than she did in the "New World of Asia" series (see chapter 1).

On the other hand, Rama Rau's ethnographic approach also destabilizes "the wonder that was India" in other, subtler, ways. To give just one prominent example from the text, she offers an ongoing taxonomical discussion of the utensils and cooking devices that Indians use, refracting them sometimes through historical accounts and sometimes through daily usages. Whether via a description of the separate vessels for different kinds of milk (137) or a rehearsal of the variety of cooking pots in one grandmother's household (69, 71), Rama Rau strove to make visible the differential dimensions of Indian foodways for a Western audience, anyway, intrigued by the exoticism to say nothing of the poetics of subcontinental diets and practices.[115] Her continual return to the "local" space of the two kitchens provides a quotidian character to *The Cooking of India* that Fisher—whose text, despite the ubiquitous image of the French woman "Annie" of the photos, references French people scarcely at all—fails to achieve. Rama Rau talks through stories, and they are often other people's stories: her grandmothers', her cousin's, a Bombay friend's. To secure her own authority as the expert, the people are never named; and admittedly they all come from the same class that would be likely to read the cookbook rather than from the ranks of servants or lower-caste people. But these stories offer, I would argue, a view as differentiated as the culture of food Rama Rau succeeds in producing in *The Cooking of India*. And, ultimately, her willingness to play with her own role as ethnographer helps to achieve this end. For Rama Rau performs the innocent, if not wholly ignorant, participant-observer throughout the text. She not only asks simple but provocative questions of her interlocutors (" 'if you were hiring a cook,' I once asked an Indian friend who is a gastronome of some eminence, 'what dish would you ask him to prepare as a test of his ability?' ") but records them along with the responses for readers.[116] She also shares minimally embarrassing but instructive moments, as when she asked her cousin what kind of pepper to use in garam masala. " 'Pepper?' [my cousin] said. 'Pepper? But everybody knows you can't use pepper in *garam masala*. It catches the throat.' "[117] Rama Rau thus interrupts the most anticipated and naturalized expectation of all for consumers of *The Cooking of India:* the presumptive link between women, whether Indian or otherwise, and an inherent knowledge of cookery.

Of course, cooking only became a woman's "profession" in the modern period, both in India and elsewhere globally. In India, the ancient links between food, hierarchy, and gender were recast in the context of colonial modernity.[118] Such links had genealogies in Raj history (transmitted via Mrs. Beeton's and Flora Annie Steel's famous cookbooks) and in regional cultural practices (as in all manner of rituals organized around domesticity in Bengal, to name just one).[119] To be sure, Rama Rau's own cosmopolitan identity is rooted in her playful posture noted above. And there is no doubt Madhur Jaffrey's culinary narratives dramatized such equations with more panache and, in the long term, probably introduced Indian cooking into American popular culture with more success, both symbolic and commercial. This is not necessarily because Jaffrey was inherently more talented, but rather, I think, because her particular performance of "the Indian woman"—tied as it was to film rather than to novels and other forms of writing (like middle-brow periodicals)—was more readily harnessed to new patterns of celebrity consumption as the early Cold War period gave way to the later one, that is, just as the 1960s were coming to a close. Rama Rau's own career as a writer was, moreover, also decelerating as the 1970s began. Her second and last novel, *The Adventuress* (1970), did not enjoy the same critical reception as her work in the 1950s had.[120] At least one Indian observer of the American scene felt that by the early 1970s Americans had lost interest in India—in contrast to the decade before when "the toy was India."[121] And as her personal papers reveal, she had struggles over her writing with her editors at Dell that were similar to those at Time-Life—specifically with respect to character development, organization, and the general pitch of the story.[122] During this time as well, Rama Rau was writing less frequently for venues like the *New York Times* and *The New Yorker* and more commonly for women's magazines like *McCall's* and *Family Circle*, where she did a regular astrology feature. She did occasional pieces for the *Times* and *National Geographic* and *Reader's Digest*, and she continued to endorse books about India and the East in a variety of publications, but her heyday—especially as the go-to girl for things Indian in a certain stratum of the American cultural scene—was over just as *The Cooking of India* was being completed.[123] Seen in this light, Rama Rau's cookbook venture represents the endpoint of one arc of her postcolonial career, without being a particularly triumphal one.

And yet it remains an important example of the fate of elite postcolonial nationalism as refracted through a gendered female subject operating in and through the transnational landscapes of the Cold War. In many ways, *The Cooking of India* is more genuinely autobiographical than her self-professed autobiography, *Gifts of Passage*, which effectively strings a series of previously published journal articles together with short, interconnective narration to fashion a life-story that ends in 1961, when she was not even forty years old. Her cookbook tells a far more complex and provocative story of Rama Rau's life and career—not just as a translator of India in and to the United States but also as the embodiment of a certain generational definition of the female cosmopolitan who felt compelled to reckon with the nation in its pre-postcolonial incarnation differently and, I think, in more registers than someone like Jaffrey. Rama Rau felt responsible for, and was made (through her own active pursuit of a modicum of American fame) to be representative of, India's colonial past during the first three decades of the Cold War—an era during which all kinds of elites kept that past highly visible on diplomatic stages and in popular culture as both a screen for and a foil to American neo-imperial ambitions. In keeping with the prophetic nature of much of her Cold War work, and as the research of Ira Raja suggests, Santha Rama Rau anticipated a postcolonial hunger for food images and food metaphors among later generations of South Asian fiction writers in English.[124] If *The Cooking of India* is Santha Rama Rau's last substantive production, its making rehearses some of the challenges of navigating a postcolonial career during a new phase of Cold War cosmopolitanism, as well as the temporal and cultural limits of translating "India" in an ever-shifting, newly imperial, postcolonial age.

Cosmopolitanism by Any Other Name

Premila said, "We had our test today, and She made me and the other Indians sit at the back of the room, with a desk between each."

Mother said, "Why was that, darling?"

"She said it was because Indians cheat," Premila added. "So I don't think we should go back to that school."

Mother looked very distant, and was silent a very long time. At last she said, "Of course not, darling."

[Later] . . . I could hear Mother and Premila talking through an open door . . . Mother said, "Do you suppose she understood all that?" Premila said, "I shouldn't think so. She's a baby." Mother said, "Well, I hope it won't bother her."

Of course, they were both wrong. I understood it perfectly, and I remember it all very clearly. But I put it happily away, because it all happened to a girl named Cynthia and I never was really particularly interested in her. —Santha Rama Rau, *Gifts of Passage*

This book has emerged as part of my long-standing interest in the afterlife of British colonialism in the American public sphere. In that respect, like the phenomenon of postcolonial cosmopolitanism that it attempts to historicize, it is hardly the view from nowhere either.[1] From this vantage point (at once former, anti-, and postcolonial, as well as feminist), the story of Santha Rama Rau's postcolonial careers is a minor, but instructive, aspect of the history of British imperialism in/and the United States—a history that has yet to be fully understood, let alone fully countenanced in this age of aggressive Anglo-American imperialism. With its appreciation for things English and its semi-imperial perspective on the postwar world, Rama Rau's particular brand of Cold War cosmopolitanism not only bore traces of the imprint of the British Raj; it served as a carrier of models of postcolonial knowing that have had analogs in contemporary culture, both academic and popular, especially in recent decades. And yet, as this book has also tried to illustrate, Rama Rau was not simply an advocate of the values of what Radhika Mohanram and Gita Rajan have called "English postcoloniality."[2] She was an ardent spokeswoman for the sovereignty of a species of postcolonial Indian cosmopolitanism as well. In acting thus, she not only attempted to reterritorialize the ground of postwar postcolonialism by centering India in the American imaginary of Asia (if not the whole "Third World" as well); she unwittingly provided a critical genealogy for "new" histories of globalization, neoliberal and otherwise.[3] If the tensions between her association with the Raj and her diasporic American experience—and between a liberal pluralistic vision and a more defensive nationalist one—served as the fault lines of her career, they also meant that recognition of her *as an Indian* was refracted through a decidedly Anglo-American lens. In this respect, she once again anticipated the critical space occupied by many Indian writers in English who followed her—writers whose "Janus-faced" stance has been oriented at once toward the colonial past and the postcolonial metropolitan market.[4] Like many "disruptive acts" undertaken by women in the modern public sphere, Rama Rau's work challenged some cultural boundaries and consolidated others—in part because her careers were not only a matter of individual choice but operated within the confines of an emergent Cold War political and cultural economy. That economy, like the colonial one before it, shaped the spectacular visibility of "the Indian woman" in historically new but discursively recognizable ways, at least to those familiar with how that figure has been "sighted in circulation" in and through the West from the eighteenth century onward.[5]

As Amal Amireh, Graham Huggan, and Timothy Brennan have all argued in different contexts—and as the enduring (if also fitful) preoccupation with "the Afghan woman" and "the Iraqi woman" in the twenty-first-century West continues to testify—this kind of sighting is by no means unique to the Indian woman.[6] And while its gendered effects are differential, it remains the fate of most if not all non-Western writers in English who aspire to critical recognition in the Euro-American marketplace: a "world republic of letters" with its own imperial modalities dating from the high moment of European colonialism.[7] If the comparably minor post-1945 American fetishization of Santha Rama Rau reflects continuities, rather than stark divergences, between colonialism and postcolonialism, it also illuminates the ways in which accounts of postcoloniality that are disconnected from concrete historical contexts do not and cannot do justice to the complexity of that condition. In that spirit, this study joins recent work in the history of postwar culture such as Christian Appy's *Cold War Constructions* (2000), Christina Klein's *Cold War Orientalism* (2003), and Penny von Eschen's *Satchmo Blows Up the World* (2004)—each of which seeks to understand the links between high politics and popular culture in the postwar period but does not engage the historical fact of decolonization as an animated or thoroughgoing analytical category. Rama Rau's case adds the former British empire back into the story of American neo-imperial power during the first quarter century of the Cold War and underscores the role of India and Indians in facilitating American identification with and disavowal of the British imperial legacy through attention to travel writing, contemporary drama, and various forms of print culture. These were all popular or semi-popular media aimed at white, middle-class, upwardly mobile U.S. audiences at different moments in the post-1945 period, when Americans of all kinds were involved in imagining and creating a new imperial role for themselves in the global order—and when, as recent scholarship has shown, African Americans were increasingly seeking a world stage for the burgeoning civil rights movement, thereby making debates about race and racial difference a constitutive part of Cold War culture at home and abroad. As we have seen, Rama Rau participated in the racial economy of this culture in a variety of ways; at the very least she stands as one example of how South Asians could be mapped onto the Cold War racial landscape, especially given the association of elite Indians with the Raj. Rama Rau's eccentric / ex-centric cosmopolitanism, with all its limits and possibilities, was a function of her U.S. diasporic perspective, even as her quest to bring India to American sightlines and into emergent narratives of "world" history retained its own peculiar Nehruvian stamp. Not incidentally, the liberal pluralism of her particular postcolonial locations and identifications presages the "new liberal cosmopolitanism" recently offered as a model for the post-9/11 world as well.[8] Historicizing Santha Rama Rau allows us, in short, to appreciate her as a complexly cosmopolitan figure *and* to begin to understand the influence of India and Indians in translating British imperial and postcolonial values to a would-be cosmopolitan American public in the last half of the twentieth century.

The focus on an individual figure like Rama Rau as a pretext for tracing both the embodied histories of postcolonialism and the currents of lateral cosmopolitanism raises important and unresolved methodological questions about transnational history as a critical practice. This is especially the case since a number of scholars interested in moving beyond the boundary of colony-metropole in order to materialize and historicize lateral connections, cosmopolitanisms, and exchanges (whether in the shadow of the British or the American empire) have tended to single out individuals or pairs of people so that older traditions of political possibility might offer paradigms for contemporary anti-imperialist, anti-globalization projects.[9] Quite apart from the question of the "representativeness" of figures like Santha Rama Rau, this singularity is somewhat at odds with the imperative to historicize those social and cultural *formations* that have exceeded the centers from which they have allegedly been marginalized. In keeping with the approach of Elleke Boehmer, Bill Mullen, and Augusto Espiritu, with whose work on migrant flows and counterflows I seek company, I have endeavored to illustrate wherever possible the ways in which Santha Rama Rau's careers were not self-fashioned but were interpolated and shaped by the various economies both symbolic and real in which her work and her careers (were) circulated.[10] As I hope I have been able to demonstrate, this is less a question of Santha Rama Rau's agency per se than it is of her capacity to negotiate the machinery of critical reception in Cold War America—its historically specific forms of recognition, its particular patterns of consumption, its strategies for publicity and containment. Pursuing this line of argument requires that biography (whether as a history of lives or of careers) not be relegated to the realm of the "merely" cultural, precisely because the domain of culture intersects with and is entailed by the social, the economic, and above all the political, broadly conceived.[11] Although this echoes much recent scholarship on life histories, it runs contrary to some recent work on the genre in South Asian studies which, despite a rich and sophisticated take on the telling of lives in India and Pakistan, views the genre presumptively as a window into cultural history, despite the often overtly political nature of the material at hand.[12]

My point here is hardly to resolve the "why this writer?" question, or to offer an apologia (much less an elegy) for Santha Rama Rau herself— not least because the pitfalls of using the logic of individualism as an "interpretive grid" are many, and the payoffs comparatively few.[13] What I have done is to suggest that the various careers of a figure like Santha Rama Rau are a timely reminder that the claims to newness which a critical mass of recent "Third World" writers (perhaps especially Indians) have seen as exceptional need to be resolutely interrogated. As Salman Rushdie has famously observed, "We are Indians, but there is redefinition. India has now to admit that there are different ways of being Indian, which do not necessarily have to do with being rooted in India. This is a wonderful and exciting realisation. It is a kind of liberating realisation. This is a kind of newness."[14]

Rushdie's determination to understand his own success as phenomenal, both in historical and contemporary terms, is matched only by the investment the North American capitalist/critical establishment has in successive waves of literary novelty, especially when they appear to emanate unmediated from outside the West. Rushdie's refusal to admit to "global regimes of value" and "the alterity industry" affords the concept of cosmopolitan disinterest a whole new horizon of imaginative possibility.[15] A number of recent critics have suggested that Indian writers in English like Arundhati Roy have been more self-conscious about the metropolitan audience machine than those of earlier generations, in both their writing and their "self-promotion" processes.[16] Meanwhile, the comparison between Roy and Rama Rau with which I opened this book remains germane to my arguments about the pressures of American national-universalism on cosmopolitanism in its Cold War incarnation: for where Rama Rau aspired to a kind of Indian cosmopolitan identity, Roy more fully realizes it because she is not, as Rama Rau was, unhinged from the subcontinental locales about which she writes—and to whom she speaks—as a postcolonial critic. Nor is Roy alone, though her global celebrity far exceeds that of her contemporaries.[17] While Rama Rau may have had Indians partly in mind, she wrote from and spoke to a predominantly American audience. And with few exceptions, her reception in India (such as it was) is not preserved in her archive: just one indication of the ways in which her Americanization (however incomplete) shaped the Cold War cosmopolitan she became. In a trajectory which might begin with Pandita Ramabai in America and end with Arundhati Roy in America —and in the context of otherwise triumphalist and self-assured convictions of contemporary cosmopolitanism of the kind articulated by, say, Kwame Anthony Appiah in (of all places) the *New York Times Magazine*— Santha Rama Rau's careers offer us a much-needed genealogy of the late-twentieth-century spectacle of postcolonial cosmopolitanism and a critical, if not entirely predictive, counterhistory of its fate.[18] If they also represent a particular kind of postcolonial "upward mobility story," they suggest too how and why the socio-cultural spaces of the Cold War United States offer a challenge to the presumption that postcolonial subjects necessarily "resist a dominant bourgeois sociality characteristic of North American existence."[19]

Santha Rama Rau was a prolific author, and this book has touched on only some of her writing. Although I have done so elsewhere in brief, her career as a novelist remains to be fully examined, as does the bulk of her journalism, which I have merely sampled.[20] She also co-wrote two books in the 1970s, one of these her mother's autobiography.[21] As I noted in my introduction, of interest to me is not the totality of her professional or even her personal life but rather the consensus among critics that her destiny as a writer is one of relative obscurity because in purely literary terms (as if such terms actually existed) her careers, however various, were negligible ones. Especially if we concede that literary value is made and not born—as the Egyptian writer Nawal El Saadawi has said of her own transnational career, "it's not a matter of who's good who's bad. It's a matter of who has the power"—such a criterion seems positively beside the point.[22] This is particularly apposite in Santha Rama Rau's case, in ways that are linked to the demotic character of much of her writing. Her minority status is compounded by gender and by the "low" (and hence quite ephemeral) cultural forms her work took, especially as her writing career fizzled in the late 1960s and early 1970s. Her epigrammatic statement—"my work is not art"—testifies as much to her self-effacement in the world of belles-lettres as it does to the self-fulfilling prophecy that writers dubbed "minority" are destined to inhabit the margins of culture. In contrast to the highly portable "the East is a career" and the equally durable "Only connect," her aphorism has no legs in the literary marketplace. Indeed, by far the most reproduced quotation by Santha Rama Rau on the Internet is one with much more "high" (if also highly stylized) literary value, or at least ambitions for such:

> Really, in the end, the only thing that can make you a writer is the person that you are, the intensity of your feeling, the honesty of your vision, the unsentimental acknowledgment of the endless interest of the life around and within you. Virtually nobody can help you deliberately—many people will help you unintentionally.[23]

If the fate of the minor writer is to be reduced to a sound bite not of her choosing, the long virtual life of this quote is emblematic of what happened to Santha Rama Rau when the tastes of the Cold War public and her postcolonial careers diverged. For despite the fact that after the late 1960s she ceased to command that small corner of the marketplace she had once enjoyed, she lives on in that apparently most indefatigable of genres, the literary anthology. As early as the 1960s Rama Rau received requests to reprint her short essays, especially those that appeared in ephemeral venues like *McCall's* and *Reader's Digest*. Nor was the American publishing market the only caller: she had at least one request for permission to reprint for a pamphlet being produced by the Indian tourist industry. By far the most sought-after piece was her short story "By Any Other Name," which is about her discovery of racism while growing up in colonial India, and more specifically in an English-run Indian school which she attended with her sister Premila. Not only are the girls' names changed (to Pamela and Cynthia) by the English headmistress; Indian girls are treated like second-class citizens by being made to sit separately during testtaking, as cited in the epigraph above.

"By Any Other Name" was first published in *The New Yorker* and then in Rama Rau's 1961 "autobiography," *Gifts of Passage*.[24] In a story that reminds us once again of how Santha Rama Rau was present at the beginning of the postwar cult of literary celebrity, she told me that she did not have an agent when she sent it off to *The New Yorker* with a cover letter that began "Dear Sir." She got a reply from Harold Ross himself and sealed the deal at lunch with him at the Algonquin.[25] I would venture to say that "By Any Other Name" remains the most read work of Santha Rama Rau today. It continues to appear in a wide variety of contemporary American educational forums, from K-12 readers to college textbooks— and, if the syllabi and lesson plans available on the Web in connection with the story are anything to go by, it is still taught in grade schools and high schools around the country as an example of both the evils of colonial education and the power of a spirited child of color (in this case, Rama Rau's sister) to rebel against it.[26] In the case of at least one curriculum, the other authors on the reading list are Malcolm X and A. M. Rosenthal ("No News from Auschwitz")—and this complementary menu is far from atypical. Even where Rama Rau's short story is juxtaposed with a Robert Frost poem, it is still presented as an example of a "different" type of literature, where "difference" presumes that capacity for recognizing sameness—that is, whiteness of the American variety—that is the hallmark of liberal multiculturalism in contemporary U.S. discourse.[27]

Echoing the ways that Rama Rau has consistently anticipated critics' formulae for the domestication of Third World writers, her once-lauded postcolonial cosmopolitan past has been transformed into an emblem of multicultural idealism, in part because of its resonance with the politics of recognition that has undergirded some rationales for that project.[28] Rama Rau's association with multicultural education is a fate worse, perhaps, than obscurity, the ongoing author revenue it generates notwithstanding.[29] How and why the experience of an Indian girl under the Raj should have pedagogical value for late-twentieth, early-twenty-first-century Americans is precisely the kind of curiosity this book has sought to shed light on, without pretending to fully explain. More modestly, tracking Santha Rama Rau's variously cosmopolitan careers allows us to appreciate her as an originary postcolonial figure and to understand the role of that phenomenon called "British India" in shaping a genuinely cosmopolitan history of the imperial present as well.

Introduction

Chapter epigraphs: Nehru, "India's Foreign Policy," 1947, from his *India and After*, 231; and Spivak, *A Critique of Postcolonial Reason*, 198.

1. She also collaborated with Gayatri Devi on *A Princess Remembers: The Memories of the Maharani of Jaipur*, and with Dhanvanthi Rama Rau on *An Inheritance*.

2. Elizabeth McSherry, "East Meets West," *Hartford Courier*, June 4, 1961. Santha Rama Rau Papers, Howard Gotlieb Archival Research Center, Boston University (henceforth HGARC).

3. From the transcript of a TV show in which Santha Rama Rau appeared, *Mrs. Eleanor Roosevelt: Prospects of Mankind*. The subject of discussion was "the American image abroad," and the show was telecast in Boston, Washington, and New York on Sunday, April 17, 1960. Courtesy of the Franklin D. Roosevelt Library, Hyde Park, N.Y.

4. For Roy, see Boehmer, "East Is East and South Is South." For postwar U.S. consumer culture, see Cohen, *A Consumers' Republic*.

5. See, for example, Desai, *Santha Rama Rau* and Rustomji-Kerns, "Expatriates, Immigrants and Literature."

6. Interview with Santha Rama Rau, New York, March 2004.

7. See Santha Rama Rau, *Gifts of Passage* and Dhanvanthi Rama Rau, *An Inheritance*.

8. Gandhi's South Africa experiences are legendary. For Tagore, see Chakravarty, ed., *A Tagore Reader*; Tagore, *A Visit to Japan*, his *Diary of a Westward Voyage*, and his *Letters from Russia*. For Nehru, see his *Soviet Russia*, and Ralhan, *Jawaharlal Nehru Abroad*.

9. See, for example, von Eschen, *Satchmo Blows Up the World*.

10. See Sahgal, *Prison and Chocolate Cake*.

11. Rama Rau, *Gifts of Passage*, 93.

12. For details on Bowers, see Okamoto, *The Man who Saved Kabuki*. Santha Rama Rau was eventually divorced from Bowers and married Gurdon Wallace Wattles in 1970. "Gurdon Wallace Wattles Weds Santha Rama Rau," *New York Times*, October 9, 1970, 45.

13. *Home to India* had sold 10,000 copies by March 1945; see Elizabeth Lawrence (Rama Rau's Harper editor) to Rama Rau, March 23, 1945. By the end of 1959 *Home to India* had sold over 40,000 copies; *East of Home*, over 23,000, and *This Is India*, over 11,000. Harper and Row memo, October 1960, box 3, HGARC.

14. Rama Rau, *This Is India*, 17. For the connections between *Mother India* and Nehru's interest in America, see Clymer, "Jawaharlal Nehru and the United States," 149–50; and Sinha, *Specters of Mother India*.

15. Herbert G. Stein, "Western Authors on India Scorned: Writer Says Books are False Picture of her Nation's Culture," *Post-Gazette*, n.d., box 6, HGARC. The talk was given at the Carnegie Institute of Technology. For a catalog of some of these works see Sujit Mukherjee, "The Indias of American Fiction," in Glazer and Glazer, eds., *Conflicting Images*, 221–40. For an account of Salman Rushdie's complaint about Western takes on Indian fiction ("village life is hard," "Indian women are badly treated") several decades later, see Ghosh, *When Borne Across*, 31.

16. Gardner F. Fox, *Woman of Kali* (New York: Gold Medal Books, 1954); Edison Marshall, *Love Stories of India* (New York: Dell, 1945); Pearl S. Buck, *Come, My Beloved* (New York: Pocket Books, 1953); and John Masters, *Nightrunners of Bengal* (New York: Viking, 1950).

17. Dorothy B. Jones, *The Portrayal of China and India on the American Screen, 1896–1955*, 52–61.

18. Ibid., 62–65.

19. See, for example, Rama Rau, "Travel Bazaar: India, an Explorer's Country,"

Harper's Bazaar, September 1957, 106, 308, and her *This Is India*. This was an era when India was just being "discovered" by the postwar American tourist industry. See A. M. Rosenthal, "India Imagined, India Seen Are Often One," *New York Times*, March 3, 1957, 331; Rosenthal, "India—Fertile Land for Growing Tourism," *New York Times*, March 2, 1958, XX33; Kathleen Teltsch, "Motor Route to the Orient," *New York Times*, August 23, 1959, X17.

20. See Santha Rama Rau's cover story on India for the October 1953 *Holiday* magazine, 40, and her "Letter from Bombay," *The New Yorker*, May 3, 1952, 81.

21. This was the name of a special series in *Holiday* magazine, to which Santha Rama Rau contributed; see the issues of July 1955 (Bali); August 1955 (the Philippines); September 1955 (Indonesia); February 1956 (Cambodia); July 1956 (Laos); August 1956 (Ceylon); September 1956 (Burma); and August 1957 (Vietnam). These articles were later collected and published in her *A View to the Southeast*.

22. Klein, *Cold War Orientalism*.

23. See Bhattacharya, *Reading the Splendid Body*, 13. I am grateful to Shefali Chandra for passing this reference along to me.

24. See Leong, *The China Mystique*.

25. Quote from review of *Remember the House*, *New York Herald Tribune*, typescript collection of quotes, box 3, HGARC.

26. For *Holiday*, see chapter 1; for *Flair*, see "The Texture of India" (January 1951), 60–61. Thanks to Danielle Kinsey for this latter reference, and to George Robb for sharing in the pleasures of *Flair*.

27. See the image of her gracing Orville Prescott's review of *Home to India*, *New York Times*, May 23, 1945, 17, and the back cover photograph of her second novel, *The Adventuress*.

28. Anderson, *The Powers of Distance*, especially "Introduction: Forms of Detachment," 3–33; and Cheah and Robbins, eds., *Cosmopolitics*. As Craig Calhoun points out, there is a real contradiction between recourse to this universalist ideal and the ways in which modern cosmopolitanism has actually played out. See his "The Class Consciousness of Frequent Travellers."

29. Cheah and Robbins, eds., *Cosmopolitics*, 1. Interestingly, their definition of

the negative associations for cosmopolitanism ("Christians, aristocrats, merchants, Jews, homosexuals, and intellectuals") is taken from the Indonesian writer Pramoedya Ananta Toer; see p. 1 and footnote on p. 39. "Rootless cosmopolitanism" as applied to Jews is an epithet from the Stalinist era; see Ryan, "The Magic of 'I' "; see also "Insults for the Ideologically Informed," *http://www.cyberussr.com/rus/insults.html*. Buruma and Margalit have recently applied the term to the United States in their book *Occidentalism*, 8. I am grateful to Leora Auslander for encouraging me to consider this point.

30. See, for example, Associated Press of America clipping, June 28 [1945], box 6, HGARC.

31. For a comprehensive account of this theoretical terrain, as well as a number of trenchant critiques of it, see Vertovec and Cohen, eds., *Conceiving Cosmopolitanism*.

32. "The Twain Meet," review of *Gifts of Passage*, London *Times*, October 5, 1961 (no author).

33. A contemporary analogue of this endeavor might be Heinrich Zimmer; see his *Myths and Symbols in Indian Art and Civilization* and his *The Art of Indian Asia*, which had pictures by Eliot Elisofon, a *Life* photographer who also did the visuals for Santha Rama Rau's cookbook.

34. "New Voices of the Far East Interpreted," *Shreveport Times*, n.d., box 6, HGARC. See also Santha Rama Rau, "New Voices from Asia," *AAUW Journal*, October 1964; this was adapted from her Phi Beta Kappa address at Mount Holyoke College, April 24, 1963, box 6, HGARC.

35. *Harper's Magazine* published her very first essay, which was the seed of what became *Home to India*. See Santha Rama Rau, "Home to India at Sixteen," *Harper's Magazine*, September 1944, 360–70.

36. Santha Rama Rau to Elizabeth Lawrence, March 19, 1949; and Lawrence to Rama Rau, May 4, 1949, box 3, HGARC.

37. Berlanstein, "Historicizing and Gendering Celebrity Culture," 65.

38. Robert S. Kane, "Travel Talk," undated clipping, box 4, HGARC.

39. I have struggled with whether to name the promontory perspective of Santha Rama Rau with respect to East Asia and China semi-imperialism or sub-imperialism (the latter, à la Chiu's "Suborientalism and the Subimperialist Pre-

dicament"). In the end I have chosen "semi" both to echo the discourse of British semi-colonialism in China and to underscore the unstable character of Rama Rau's ideological maneuvers.

40. de Mel, *Women and the Nation's Narrative*.

41. Lionnet and Shih, eds., *Minor Transnationalism*, 1–21.

42. For Bandung, see Singham and Hune, *Non-Alignment in an Age of Alignments*; for pre-histories, see Edwards, "The Shadow of Shadows," and Boehmer, *Empire, the National, and the Postcolonial, 1890–1920*.

43. I am grateful to Ania Loomba for insisting on this point.

44. Among the India-based periodicals that were surveyed for this book are *Illustrated India Weekly* (which reviewed only the stage performance of *A Passage to India*); *Orient Review and Literary Digest*; *Modern Review*; *Quest* (Bombay); and *Calcutta Review*. *Thought* (Delhi) did short reviews of her early books; see Krishnanath, "Remember the House," *Thought* 9, 3 (January 1957): 13; and E. A., "The Soviet Scene," *Thought* 13, 12 (March 1961): 15–16.

45. See Robin Mayhead, "A New Indian Novelist," *JANA: The News Magazine of Resurgent Asia and Africa* 3, 11 (March 1957): 29–32. Mayhead was a lecturer in English at the University of Ceylon. I am grateful to Deborah Hughes for tracking down this journal for me.

46. Santha Rama Rau told a Buffalo newspaper that "India is offering the world a third force between America and Russia, and if we can make it work in India it probably will work for . . . most of Asia." "Experiment by India Topic for Miss Rau," n.d., box 6, HGARC. For one analysis of the "third force," see Wainwright, *Inheritance of Empire*.

47. See Bowers, *The Dance in India* and *Theatre in the East*.

48. Hal Boyle, review of *Home to India*, *Wichita Beacon*, n.d., box 6, HGARC.

49. See Orville Prescott, "Books of the Times," *New York Times*, May 23, 1945, 17.

50. Mehta recounts taking the Indian novelist R. K. Narayan to dinner at Rama Rau's in New York, where Narayan proceeded to tell her about an Indian donkey he had seen in Central Park Zoo. "Narayan went on to tell us that the animal was just an ordinary dhobi's donkey, who, with his brethren, roamed in the Indian streets by the million. But in America, apparently, he was a great success; nobody

who saw him could doubt that the zookeepers fed his vanity—an attribute never associated with donkeys in India. . . . 'I think I'll write a little fable about him for *Harper's*,' Narayan said smiling. 'Do you think they will take it?'" See his "Profiles: The Train Had Just Arrived at Malgudi Station," *The New Yorker*, September 15, 1962, 85.

51. I am grateful to both Minnie Sinha and Durba Ghosh for insisting on this point.

52. For statistics on Indian immigration to the United States, 1871–1965, see Fisher, *The Immigrants of New York City*, 11–12. For more recent work, see Rangaswamy, *Namasté America*; and Shukla, *Indians Abroad*.

53. See Khandelwal, *Becoming American, Being Indian*, 1–15. There is also a long history of Indian political activity, nationalist and otherwise, in the United States. See, for example, Das, "The Struggle of Indians to Attain Equal Rights in the United States of America"; Bose, "Indian Nationalist Agitations in the U.S.A. and Canada"; and Raucher, "American Anti-Imperialists and the Pro-Indians Movement, 1900–1932."

54. See Shukla, *Indians Abroad*, especially 133–60; Jensen, *Passage from India*; Kosambi, ed., *Pandita Ramabai Through Her Own Words*; and Chang et al., eds., *Caste and Outcaste*.

55. Isaacs, *Scratches on Our Minds*, 37–38.

56. See Isaacs, *Scratches on our Minds*, and Klein, *Cold War Orientalism*.

57. Boyle, *Wichita Beacon*. For her contempt for "Mr. Luce's" love for China over India (and its subsequent impact on *Time* magazine), see Rama Rau to Eliot Elisofon, March 23, 1955, Harry Ransom Collection, University of Texas, Austin. Buck did eventually write a novel on India, *Mandala*. Thanks to George Robb for this reference.

58. Kaufman, *The Rise and Fall of Anglo-America*.

59. Ernestine Evans, "An Indian Comedy of Manners," *New York Herald Tribune*, May 27, 1945, box 1, HGARC.

60. "Coming of Age," review of her first novel *Remember the House*, *Time*, April 16, 1956, 116.

61. Brands, *India and the United States*, 27.

62. Saadia Toor, "Indo-Chic: The Cultural Politics of Consumption in Post-

Liberalization India," *http://www.spas.ac.uk/soaslit/issue2/contents.html* (accessed fall 2003). I am grateful to Shefali Chandra for this reference.

63. *A Passage to India: A Play by Santha Rama Rau from the Novel by E. M. Forster.* See also Lago, "*A Passage to India* On Stage."

64. Lionel Trilling's analysis of the novel remains among the most insightful. See his *E. M. Forster*, 136–61. I am grateful to Jed Esty for this reference.

65. Santha Rama Rau, "Life Goes On under Mau Mau's Shadow," *New York Times*, July 19, 1953, Sunday Magazine, 10; and "The Trial of Jomo Kenyatta," *The Reporter*, March 16, 1954, 12–23.

66. I am extremely grateful to Rebecca Walkowitz for enabling me to appreciate this point.

67. Rama Rau, "The Trial of Jomo Kenyatta," 12–13.

68. Interview with Santha Rama Rau, March 2004. As the *Time* review of her first novel noted, Rama Rau played on this question of suntan and color in her first novel, *Remember the House*. See "Coming of Age," 116.

69. Rama Rau, *Gifts of Passage*, 25–26.

70. See, for example, Padma's comment on the fairness of Kashmiri girls ("like mountain snow") in Salman Rushdie, *Midnight's Children* (New York: Knopf, 1980), 57. I am grateful to Barbara Ramusack for this reference.

71. Lipsitz, *The Possessive Investment in Whiteness.*

72. See Salman Rushdie, "Outside the Whale," in *Imaginary Homelands*; Greet et al., eds., *Raj Nostalgia*; and, more recently, Shauna Singh Baldwin, "With Contempt or Love?" (text of speech given at the Centre for Canadian Architecture, May 24, 2003, Montreal), *http://www.sawnet.org/books/writing/SSB_CCA .html.*

73. Santha Rama Rau, *My Russian Journey*, and her "Pacific Adventures," *Vogue*, October 15, 1963, 106, 108, 111, 139, 140, 141.

74. Basham, *The Wonder That Was India.*

75. See, for example, "Passage to Malabar," *New York Times*, March 13, 1983, ST40; "Images of Delhi, Old and New," *New York Times*, November, 20, 1982, 1; and "Growing Up with the Arts of India," *New York Times*, September 1, 1985, A1.

76. I am extraordinarily grateful to Minnie Sinha for enabling me to grasp this point.

77. R. Radhakrishnan, "Toward an Eccentric Cosmopolitanism."

78. See Nussbaum, *Sex and Social Justice*; Nussbaum, *Women and Human Development*, and her essay "Patriotism and Cosmopolitanism," in Nussbaum et al., *For Love of Country*, 4. For SEWA, see Jhabvala and Bali, eds., *My Life, My Work*; and Rose, *Where Women Are Leaders*.

79. See Burton, *Burdens of History*.

80. Brennan, *At Home in the World*, 317.

81. Russell Jacoby, *The Last Intellectuals: American Culture in the Age of Academe* (New York: Basic Books, 1982), 7ff. Thanks to Kathy Oberdeck for this reference.

82. Grewal, *Transnational America*, chapter 1.

83. See Rama Rau, *The Adventuress*; Mukherjee, *Jasmine*; and Burton, "Ugly Americans."

84. Parry, "Overlapping Territories and Intertwined Histories."

85. See Robbins, "The East Is a Career." I am grateful to Nicholas Dames's essay "Trollope and the Career" for reminding me of this point.

86. Rafael, "The Culture of Area Studies in the United States," 91; see also Ludden, "Maps in the Mind and the Mobility of Asia."

87. Brennan, "Cosmopolitans and Celebrities," 2. See also his *At Home in the World*. David Hollinger, in turn, sees Brennan's book as one outcropping of many in the "flurry" of attention to cosmopolitanism as an ideological rubric in the 1990s; see his "Not Universalists, Not Pluralists: The New Cosmopolitans Find Their Way," in Vertovec and Cohen, eds., *Conceiving Cosmopolitanism*, 227.

88. I am grateful to Herman Bennett for urging me to consider this question.

89. For the term "coeval," see Fabian, *Time and the Other*. For a particularly insightful retrospective on postcolonialism in terms of its relationship to empire, see Cooppan, "The Ruins of Empire."

90. Thanks to Mrinalini Sinha for pressing this clarification on me.

91. I am grateful to one of the anonymous readers at Duke University Press for raising this question and encouraging me to deal with it.

92. See Kosambi, ed., *Pandita Ramabai's American Encounter*; and Prashad, *The Karma of Brown Folk*.

93. Booth, *May Her Likes be Multiplied*.

94. Margadant, ed., *The New Biography*.

95. Deleuze and Guattari, *Kafka*, especially p. 26.

96. Lloyd, *Nationalism and Minor Literature*.

97. Grewal and Kaplan, eds., *Scattered Hegemonies*. I am grateful to Dane Kennedy for encouraging me to clarify this point.

98. Lionnet and Shih, eds., *Minor Transnationalism*. See therein both Ali Behdad, "Postcolonial Theory and the Predicament of Minor Literature," 223–36, and Susan Koshy, "The Postmodern Subaltern: Globalization Theory and the Subject of Ethnic, Area, and Postcolonial Studies," 109–31.

99. For an example of a similar project between two different empires, see Azuma, *Between Two Empires*. Thanks to Augusto Espiritu for this reference.

100. Even Duke University Press ended up structuring the financial terms of my contract around the possibility, raised by an otherwise very sympathetic reader, that staking a monograph not just on one person but on a self-avowedly minor one like Santha Rama Rau would be a hard sell.

101. I am grateful to one of my anonymous readers at Duke University Press for pressing this question on me.

102. See his *Conscripts of Modernity: The Tragedy of Colonial Enlightenment* (Durham, N.C.: Duke University Press, 2004).

103. See Ahmad, "The Politics of Literary Post-Coloniality"; and Dirlik, "The Postcolonial Aura."

104. See Daniel Horowitz, "The Myth Weavers," *Salon*, September 17, 1999, *www.salon.com*; and Craig Offman, "Said Critic Blasts Back at Hitchens," *Salon*, September 10, 1999, which rehearses the *Commentary* debate about the memoir: *http://www.salon.com*.

105. "Liberal universalism" is Stuart Hall's term; see his "Political Belonging in a World of Multiple Identities," especially 27–31.

106. For a different exposition of this point, see van der Veer, "Colonial Cosmopolitanism."

107. Assayag and Béneï, eds., *At Home in Diaspora*.

108. See Chatterjee, "My Place in the Global Republic of Letters."

109. Chakrabarty, *Provincializing Europe*, and his *Habitations of Modernity*.

110. For engagements with this problem, see Mallon, "The Promise and Dilemma of Subaltern Studies"; and Barlow, "Eugenic Woman, Semicolonialism, and Colonial Modernity as Problems for Postcolonial Theory."

111. Schueller, "Articulations of African-Americanisms in South Asian Postcolonial Theory."

112. See, for example, Loomba, *Shakespeare, Race and Colonialism*, which has one of the more nuanced historical accounts of race and culture in the early modern world and operates out of a critically postcolonial perspective.

113. Arnold, "The Self and the Cell"; and Nair, *Lying on the Postcolonial Couch*, 173–74.

114. See Prashad, *Everybody Was Kung Fu Fighting*; Mullen, *Afro-Orientalism*; and Gomez, *Reversing Sail*. See also Kosambi, ed., *Pandita Ramabai through Her Own Words*, and Chang et al., eds., *Caste and Outcaste*.

115. See Neville Hoad, "*Welcome to our Hillbrow*." Hoad's paper examines Phaswane Mpe's 2001 novel *Welcome to Our Hillbrow* and opens with an ironic comment on the apparent contradiction inherent in the term "African cosmopolitan."

116. Cheah and Robbins, *Cosmopolitics*.

117. This is not exactly the same as the need for a "working typology" of transnationalism of the kind that sociologists have called for, but it does speak to the role of the disciplines, and especially of history, in putting pressure on narratives which romanticize the work of global capital in various "ages of empire." See Portes et al., "The Study of Transnationalism."

118. For a particularly insightful examination of this question, see Kathryn J. Oberdeck, *The Evangelist and the Impresario*.

1. *Cold War Cosmopolitanism*

1. Linda H. Peterson, ed., *The Norton Reader: An Anthology of Expository Prose* (New York: W. W. Norton and Co., 1996), 1321.

2. Rama Rau, *Gifts of Passage*.

3. Post-1945 events like the Indian "incorporation" of Goa in 1962, together with the variegated nature of Asian colonialism itself, require this kind of qualification to the term "postcolonial." I am grateful to Poshek Fu for this insight.

4. Though this transference has chiefly been understood in terms of the Middle East, à la John Foster Dulles's claim that "we must fill the vacuum of power which the British filled for a century—not merely the ability to act in an emergency but [through a] day in day out presence there." Quoted in Orde, *The Eclipse of Great Britain*, 192.

5. See Nussbaum, "Patriotism and Cosmopolitanism," 4. See also Brennan, *At Home in the World*, which dwells on the 1990s; and Vertovec and Cohen, eds., *Conceiving Cosmopolitanism: Theory, Context and Practice*, which is disposed toward historical readings but not comprehensively.

6. See Cheah and Robbins, eds., *Cosmopolitics*; Ong, *Flexible Citizenship*; and Linebaugh and Rediker, *The Many-Headed Hydra*.

7. Kumkum Sangari, "Relating Histories: Definitions of Literacy, Literature, Gender in Early Nineteenth Century Calcutta and England, " in Svati Joshi, ed., *Rethinking English: Essays in Literature, Language, History* (New Delhi: Trianka, 1993), 264.

8. See Leila Rupp, *Worlds of Women: The Making of an International Women's Movement* (Princeton, N.J.: Princeton University Press, 1997); Paisley, "Citizens of the World"; Woollacott, " 'All This is the Empire, I Told Myself,' " and her book, *To Try Her Fortune in London: Australian Women, Colonialism and Modernity* (New York: Oxford University Press, 2000); and Mrinalini Sinha, Donna J. Guy, and Angela Woollacott, eds., *Gender and History* special issue: "Feminisms and Internationalisms" 10, 3 (November 1998).

9. Sinha et al., "Introduction: Why Feminisms and Internationalisms?" *Gender and History* 10, 3 (November 1998): 345–57.

10. See for example Pheng Cheah, "The Cosmopolitical Today," and Allen W. Wood, "Kant's Project for Perpetual Peace," in Cheah and Robbins, eds., *Cosmopolitics*, 20–44 and 59–76 respectively; and Emma Rothschild, "Globalization and the Return to History," *Foreign Policy* 115 (1999): 106–16.

11. Spivak, *A Critique of Postcolonial Reason*.

12. See Susan Moller Okin, *Women in Western Political Thought* (Princeton, N.J.:

Princeton University Press, 1979); and Carole Pateman, *The Sexual Contract* (Stanford, Calif.: Stanford University Press, 1989).

13. Nussbaum, *Sex and Social Justice*; and her *Women and Human Development*.

14. See Jhabvala and Bali, eds., *My Life, My Work*; and Rose, *Where Women Are Leaders*; and Sinha, *Specters of Mother India*.

15. Nussbaum, "Patriotism and Cosmopolitanism," 4.

16. Ibid., 3–5.

17. Ibid., 5.

18. For a reading of the story and the Satyajit Ray film of the same name, see Nicholas B. Dirks, "*The Home and the World:* The Invention of Modernity in Colonial India," in Robert A Rosenstone, ed., *Revisioning History: Film and the Construction of a New Past* (Princeton, N.J.: Princeton University Press, 1995), 44–63.

19. For a critique of Nussbaum's inattention to the gender dynamics in this story, see Bruce Robbins, *Feeling Global: Internationalism in Distress* (New York: New York University Press, 1999), 161–62.

20. de Mel, *Women and the Nation's Narrative*. This is akin though not exactly equivalent to Bhabha's "vernacular cosmopolitics," especially because of its emphasis on gender as a structural location. For a stimulating reading of the worldiness of Gandhi and Ambedkar through and against Bhabha's idiomatics, see Ganguly, "Convergent Cosmopolitics in the Age of Empire."

21. For accounts of the historical trajectory of these two traditions, see Mani, *Contentious Traditions*; and Burton, *Burdens of History*.

22. For an extended discussion of the promontory, see Pratt, *Imperial Eyes*.

23. Klein, *Cold War Orientalism*.

24. See Butler, "Universality in Culture." Specifically, she argues that "to claim that the universal has not yet been articulated is to insist that the 'not yet' is proper to an understanding of the universal itself: that which remains 'unrealized' by the universal constitutes it essentially . . . the excluded, in this sense, constitutes the contingent limit of universalization" (48).

25. "Sir Benegal Rau, Indian Envoy, Dies," *New York Times,* December 14, 1969, 84.

26. Dhanvanthi Rama Rau, *An Inheritance*, 152–54. She was clearly quite pro-

gressive in a variety of ways: as she told Geraldine Forbes in an interview of her marriage to Rama Rau, "we had two marriage ceremonies—Kashmiri, and registration. I wanted to have the right to divorce. Marriage was really the only way one could lead a respectable life." Transcript courtesy of Geraldine Forbes, from interview with Dhanvanthi Rama Rau in Bombay, April 26, 1976.

27. See Rama Rau, *Home to India*, 28–29. For a discussion of the secular, the worldly, and the cosmopolitan in relationship to South Asian religions, see Aravamudan, *Guru English*.

28. Rama Rau, *An Inheritance*, 277.

29. Rama Rau, *Home to India*, 4 and 5.

30. Ibid., 1.

31. Ibid., 68–73.

32. Ibid., 14–21.

33. Ibid., 14–21.

34. This is related in the introduction to her *The Cooking of India* (New York: Time-Life Books, 1969), 6.

35. Ibid., 28–29.

36. Kwame Anthony Appiah, "Cosmopolitan Patriots," in Nussbaum et al., *For Love of Country*, 22.

37. Nehru, *India and the World*, and, later, *Glimpses of World History*.

38. Rama Rau, *Home to India*, 29.

39. Ibid., 57.

40. Ibid., 84.

41. Ibid., 65.

42. In truth, her parents did consider English universities for her but decided on an American one because of the war in Europe. The choice of Wellesley was Santha Rama Rau's. Private correspondence, Santha Rama Rau; thanks also to Barbara Ramusack for pressing this point.

43. Talking about her experience of writing *Home to India* some twenty-five years later (i.e., in 1969), Rama Rau had a very different take on it; see *The Cooking of India*, 6–7.

44. See Orville Prescott, "Books of the Times," *New York Times,* May 23, 1945, 17; Isabelle Mallet, "The Reorientation of an Anglo-Indian," *New York Times,* June 3, 1945, Book Review, 3; and Elizabeth McSherry, "East Meets West," *Hartford Courier,* June 4, 1961.

45. Rama Rau, *Gifts of Passage,* 27.

46. Romen Bose, *A Will for Freedom: Nataji and the Indian Independence Movement in Singapore and Southeast Asia, 1942–1945* (Singapore: vj Times, 1993), 30–33.

47. As Prasenjit Duara has noted, pan-Asianism has a history dating well before this; see his "The Discourse of Civilization and Pan-Asianism," *Journal of World History* 12, 1 (2001): 99–130.

48. Rama Rau, *East of Home,* 3.

49. Ibid.

50. Ibid., 265.

51. Ibid., 4–5.

52. Ibid., 16.

53. Ibid., 22.

54. See Okamoto, *The Man Who Saved Kabuki.* Okamoto links Bowers's efforts to keep kabuki alive with the article in the Japanese constitution banning censorship; see 115–16.

55. Rama Rau, *East of Home,* 42–43.

56. Phone interview with Santha Rama Rau, summer 2003. According to Samuel Leiter, who translated Shiro Okamoto's study of Bowers and the fate of kabuki, in later life Bowers was open about his homosexuality. See Okamoto, *The Man Who Saved Kabuki,* x, xi.

57. Rama Rau, *East of Home,* 6. For Santha Rama Rau's concerns about the end of her marriage as early as 1965, see Benegal Rama Rau to Santha Rama Rau, July 17, 1965, box 6, HGARC.

58. Ibid., 8.

59. Ibid., 9.

60. Ibid., 30.

61. Ibid., 24.

62. Ibid., 67.

63. Ibid., 68.

64. See Lisa Yoneyama, "Liberation under Siege: U.S. Military Occupation and Japanese Women's Enfranchisement," *American Quarterly* 57, 3 (2005): 885–910.

65. William J. Lederer and Eugene Burdick, *The Ugly American* (1958).

66. See Klein, *Cold War Orientalism*.

67. Rama Rau, *East of Home*, 75.

68. Ibid., 171.

69. Ibid., 60.

70. Ibid., 171.

71. See Klein, *Cold War Orientalism*, and, for the Euro-American scene, Christopher Endy, *Cold War Holidays: American Tourism in France* (Chapel Hill: University of North Carolina Press, 2004).

72. A. Martin Wainwright calls India a "Third Force" in post-1945 and post-1947 politics; see his *Inheritance of Empire*, especially 123ff.

73. I am grateful to Augusto Espiritu for pressing this comparison on me. For a wonderfully evocative narrative of this performative cosmopolitanism on the part of Nehru and Chou En-Lai, see Carlos P. Romulo, *The Meaning of Bandung* (Chapel Hill: University of North Carolina Press, 1956).

74. de Mel, *Women and the Nation's Narrative*. This emphasis on lateralism is also taken up by Boehmer in her *Empire, the Nation and the Postcolonial, 1890–1920*, 5ff. Thanks to Minnie Sinha for drawing my attention to this latter reference.

75. Rama Rau, *East of Home*, 56.

76. Ibid., 303.

77. The quote is from Mrinalini Sinha, private correspondence, February 2005. See also Okamoto, *The Man Who Saved Kabuki*.

78. Rama Rau, *East of Home*, 300.

79. I am grateful to Mrinalini Sinha for encouraging me to see this point.

80. Interview with Santha Rama Rau, November 2005.

81. This quote is from Rama Rau's cover story on India in the October 1953 issue

of *Holiday* (40) and hence technically predates the "New World of Asia" series. For Rama Rau on Asia, see the issues of *Holiday* listed in note 21 of the introduction. These were later collected and published in Rama Rau's *A View to the Southeast*.

82. Santha Rama Rau, "Indonesia," *Holiday*, September 1955, 106.

83. The lead-in to Michener's 1952 story on Japan read, "Just what is Japan like? And what kind of people are the Japanese?" (*Holiday*, August 1952, 27). The caption for a picture of Japan in his 1956 essay "The Great Big Wonderful World" read "Image of Asia . . . this is Japan as it exists today, but the setting would have looked the same had it been snapped a thousand winters back" (*Holiday*, March 1956, 40). American magazine readers could find more complex views of Asia—see, for example, Walter Robb's "I Weep for the Chinese," *Harper's*, September 1950, 58–63—but these were rare enough and, arguably, equally orientalist in their construction of the East as a site of abjection and pity.

84. Santha Rama Rau, "The Happy Land," *Holiday*, July 1955, color photo facing first page of article.

85. See Rama Rau, *East of Home*. A member of the Vietnamese diplomatic staff in Washington wrote to *Holiday* expressly to correct Rama Rau on a related point; see "History Rectified," letter by Nguyen Phu Duc, *Holiday*, November 1957, 5.

86. Han Suyin, "The New World of Asia: Singapore," *Holiday*, September 1954, 51. Suyin's other contributions to *Holiday* in this period were on Hong Kong (May 1955), Nepal (May 1957), and Peking (June 1957). For corroborations of this view elsewhere, see David Van Praagh, *The Greater Game: India's Race with Destiny and China* (Montreal: McGill-Queens University Press, 2003); and Chester Bowles, "The Odds on Communism in India," *Harper's* 20 (Jan. 1954): 41–48. And for the long life of India-China relations see Jairam Ramesh, *Making Sense of Chindia: Reflections on India and China* (New Delhi: India Research Press, 2005). Thanks to Shefali Chandra for this reference.

87. I am drawing here from the introduction to Chuh and Shimikawa, *Orientations*, 7–8. See also Rafael, "The Cultures of Asian Studies in the United States."

88. See Iqbal Singh, *Between Two Fires: Towards an Understanding of Jawaharlal Nehru's Foreign Policy*, vol. 1 (New Delhi: Orient Longman, 1992), 33–51.

89. Jawaharlal Nehru, "Our Foreign Policy," Indian Council of World Affairs, New Delhi, March 22, 1949; in Nehru, *Independence and After*, 24. See also

Nehru, *Glimpses of World History* and his *India and the World*. As Singh suggests, Nehru did not by any means invent this "tryst with Asia"; not only did his contemporaries (like Das) propose institutionalizing India's relationships with other states in Asia but there was a tradition of travel to and engagement with China and Japan, for example, reaching back to Tagore and before. See, for example, Hira Lal Seth, ed., *Tagore on China and Japan* (Lahore: Tagore Memorial Publications, n.d. [1940s]), and Rabindranath Tagore, *Japanayatri* (Kalikata: Bisvabharati, 1962).

90. Nehru, *Independence and After*, 250.

91. Singh, *Between Two Fires*, 268–96.

92. Keenleyside, "Nationalist Indian Attitudes towards Asia"; see also Krasa, "The Idea of Pan-Asianism and the Nationalist Movement in India." Thanks to Tony Ballantyne for these references.

93. For a particularly nuanced and astute interpretation of Mau Mau, see Lonsdale, "Mau Maus of the Mind."

94. Santha Rama Rau, "Life Goes On under Mau Mau's Shadow," *New York Times*, July 19, 1953, Sunday Magazine, 10.

95. Santha Rama Rau, "The Trial of Jomo Kenyatta," *The Reporter*, March 16, 1954, 12–23.

96. "Kenya to Fight Terrorism," *New York Times*, September 2, 1952, 12; "Native Terrorists Raid a Kenya Mission," *New York Times*, September 13, 1952, 2.

97. "Desecration Laid to Kenyan Terrorists," *New York Times*, September 17, 1952, 5; "The Mau Mau," *New York Times*, September 18, 1952, 28; C. L. Sulzberger, "Kenya Crisis Mirrors Africa's Changing Face: Mau Mau Terror is Primitive Answer to a White Man's Civilization Which Has Ousted Ancient Tribal Customs," *New York Times*, December 28, 1952, B3.

98. See James H. Merriweather, *Proudly We Can Be Africans: Black Americans and Africa, 1935–1961* (Chapel Hill: University of North Carolina Press, 2002), 124–49. Thanks to Fanon Wilkins for this citation.

99. See Elkins, *Imperial Reckoning*; and Anderson, *Histories of the Hanged*.

100. Rama Rau, "The Trial," 18.

101. Ibid., 12.

102. Horne, *Race War!* Thanks to David Roediger for this reference.

103. Author interview with Santha Rama Rau, April 2005.

104. Santha Rama Rau, "Visit to Africa," *Mademoiselle*, February 1954, 134.

105. Ibid., 162.

106. Edwards, "The Shadow of Shadows."

107. Author interview with Santha Rama Rau, April 2005.

108. Ibid.

109. See, for example, Antoinette Burton, "Tongues Untied: Lord Salisbury's 'Black Man' and the Boundaries of Imperial Democracy," *Comparative Studies in Society and History* 43, 2 (2000): 632–59; Prasad, *The Karma of Brown Folk*; and Prasad, *Everybody Was Kung Fu Fighting*.

110. Rama Rau, "Life Goes On," 11.

111. For a recent fictional account of these tensions, see Vassanji, *The In-Between World of Vikram Lall*. Thanks to Shefali Chandra for putting this in my hands.

112. For an analysis of Nehru's reception in the United States in this period, see Andrew J. Rotter, "Gender Relations, Foreign Relations: The United States and South Asia, 1947–1964," *Journal of American History* 81, 2 (September 1994): 535. See also his *Comrades at Odds: The United States and India, 1947–64* (Ithaca, N.Y.: Cornell University Press, 2000). For another instructive comparison with Nehru, see Santha Rama Rau's "Peace, Rice, Friendship and the Burma of U Nu," *The Reporter*, April 19, 1956, 18–22.

113. Santha Rama Rau, "Nehru: A Portrait," *Holiday*, November 1962, 61.

114. Author interview with Santha Rama Rau, April 2005.

115. Rama Rau, "The Trial," 15.

116. Rama Rau, "Life Goes On," 10ff.

117. Ibid., 12.

118. Rama Rau, "The Trial," 23. In an interview with Rama Rau, Pritt told her that "the biggest stumbling block in legal forms to most of the Africans" was the laws of evidence, emphasizing their incapacity to understand the difference between direct evidence and hearsay (21). Given the well-known legal training of Gandhi, this is another site of implicit contrast between Indian nationalism and African capacity.

119. Ibid., 23.

120. Indian Council on Africa, *Nehru and Africa*, 39–40. See also Nehru, *The Discovery of India*, 421. Africa appears only four times in the index of the book, with Asia registering easily five times as often.

121. Indian Council on Africa, *Nehru and Africa*, 1–25.

122. Singh, *Between Two Fires*, 289.

123. Ibid., 47–53, 26–27, and 69.

124. Ibid., 25.

125. Ibid., 23 and 55.

126. See Ferguson, "Decomposing Modernity." Quotes are from 171 and 175.

127. Rama Rau, "The Trial," 12.

128. For the Stern Gang, see Heller, *The Stern Gang;* for postwar violence against African Americans, see Anderson, *Eyes off the Prize*, 57–67. I am grateful to Matti Bunzl for the former reference and to Kristin Hoganson for the latter.

129. See, for example, "Native Terrorists," 2.

130. See von Eschen, *Race against Empire*; Plummer, *Rising Wind*; Dudziak, *Cold War Civil Rights*; and Borstelmann, *The Cold War and the Color Line.*

131. Logan, "Racism and Indian-U.S. Relations, 1947–1953."

132. See Burton, *Dwelling in the Archive.*

133. Kaplan, "Hillary Rodham Clinton's Orient," 236. For a similar reading of very different feminist subjects, see Noor, "Innocents Abroad." Thanks to Gerry Forbes for this reference.

134. Schein, "Gender and Internal Orientalism in China," 388, 401.

135. See reviews of *My Russian Journey*, clippings, box 6, HGARC.

136. Faubion Bowers, *The New Scriabin: Enigma and Answers* (New York: St. Martin's, 1973).

137. Rama Rau, *My Russian Journey*, 269.

138. Ibid., 270.

139. Ibid., 272, 273.

140. Ibid., 281–95.

141. The literature on the India-Russia connection is vast, so I will cite just a few titles here. For Tagore, see Tagore, *Letters from Russia*, which reprints his letters

from his 1930 visit, as well as essays, speeches, and variously authored accounts of his visit. For two of Rama Rau's more famous contemporaries, see Nehru, *Soviet Russia*; and K. P. S. Menon, *The Flying Troika: Extracts from a Diary by K. P. S. Menon, India's Ambassador to Russia, 1952–1961* (Oxford: Oxford University Press, 1963). For later studies, see M. A. Persits, *Revolutionaries of India in Soviet Russia* (Moscow: Progress Publishers, 1973); and Jyotsna Bakshi, *Russia and India: From Ideology to Geopolitics, 1947–1998* (Delhi: Dev Publications, 1999).

142. Elsewhere she confessed that her Russian journey had made her homesick for India. See Santha Ram Rau, "Return to India," *The Reporter*, June 9, 1960, 34–39.

143. Baldwin, *Beyond the Color Line and the Iron Curtain*; see also Erik S. Mc-Duffie's discussion of Louise Thompson in "Long Journeys: Four Black Women and the Communist Party, USA, 1930–1956" (Ph.D. diss., New York University, 2003), 93–126, and in his " 'Prefers Russia Now to Living in America': Louise Thompson's 1932 Journey through the Soviet Union and the Making of a Black Radical Internationalist Feminist" (copy of paper provided courtesy of the author).

144. Rama Rau, *My Russian Journey*, 8–9.

145. See ad for *My Russian Journey*, n.d, n.p.; clipping, box 6, HGARC.

2. *Interpreting British India in Anglo-America*

1. Vincent Canby, "The Screen: 'Passage to India,' by David Lean," *New York Times*, December 14, 1984, C10.

2. Ian Jack, " 'That's How It's Going to Be,' " (Sunday) London *Times*, April 8, 1984, 32–40. Cited in Brownlow, *David Lean*, 661–62. See also Ian Jack, "Secret Storms on A Passage to India," (Sunday) London *Times*, March 24, 1985, 13.

3. *Time*, December 31, 1984.

4. Steven Rea, "U.S. Fascinated with Images of India," *Chicago Tribune*, February 19, 1985. For *New York Times* coverage of the Festival of India, see William Borders, "India Is on Our Minds, but Whose India?" *New York Times*, February 10, 1985, 72; and Santha Rama Rau, "Growing Up with the Arts of India," *New York Times*, September 1, 1985, A1. Thanks to Jason Hansen for these references.

5. Rea, "U.S. Fascinated with Images of India"; see also Lisa Anderson, "Kipling Was Right: Past Maharajah's Riches Provide a Passage to Indian Spectacle," *Chicago Tribune*, December 11, 1985.

6. Mathur, "Living Ethnological Exhibits."

7. See Salman Rushdie, "Outside the Whale," in *Imaginary Homelands*, 87–101.

8. Canby, "The Screen: 'Passage to India,' " C10. For a slightly different rendition of this moment, see "Theater Abroad: Passage to the Stage," *Time*, February 1, 1960, 53.

9. For the most comprehensive collection of literary criticism on the novel, see Peter Childs, ed., *E. M. Forster's "A Passage to India"* (London: Routledge, 2002).

10. See, for example, Stape, ed., *E. M. Forster*, vol. 1.

11. See Harlan Kennedy, "David Lean in Interview: *A Passage to India*," *Film Comment* (January–February 1985).

12. Canby was not the only one to do this upon the debut of Lean's film. See Lago, "*A Passage to India* on Stage," where she talks in great detail about Britain and American stage productions. Lago is, together with P. N. Furbank, one of the editors of *Selected Letters of E. M. Forster*, vols. 1 and 2 (Cambridge, Mass.: Harvard University Press, 1985).

13. Manohar Malgonkar, "Stories That Make Authors Rich," *The Tribune* (India), online edition, July 8, 2001, *http://www.tribuneindia.com/2001/20010708/spectrum/time.htm*.

14. Ibid. Malgonkar was a novelist and journalist; see Moraes and Howe, eds., *John Kenneth Galbraith Introduces India*.

15. Rama Rau is not precise as to the date when she began the writing, nor have I been able to nail it down via archives or print culture sources. A letter from E. M. Forster to Crawford dated October 5, 1956, in which he gives his approval "to the production of the play based on this manuscript," suggests it might have been the summer of 1956. See Santha Rama Rau Papers, box 14, file 8, HGARC.

16. Interview with Santha Rama Rau, March 2004.

17. Ibid. See also Strauss, *A Talent for Luck*, 261–64. Strauss was Rama Rau's agent at the time she wrote *A Passage to India* (play).

18. Author interview with Santha Rama Rau, April 2005.

19. See Forster to Rama Rau, March 2, 1962, bms thr 93–14, Harvard Theatre Collection, Houghton Library, Harvard University, Cambridge, Mass. (hereafter HTC); Forster to Crawford, Santha Rama Rau Papers, box 14, file 8, HGARC.

20. "'A Passage to India' by No Means a Novelist's Play," *Times* (London), January 20, 1960, 6. This is the "absurd" review to which Canby referred in his 1984 piece on Lean's film, above. As Santha Rama Rau remarked to me in my interview with her in April 2005, "Two hundred pounds was more than anyone else had offered me for the play until that moment!"

21. Author interview with Santha Rama Rau, March 2004.

22. See reviews of BBC production 1965, box 9, HGARC.

23. Author interview with Santha Rama Rau, March 2004.

24. "Theater Abroad: A Passage to India," *Time*, February 1, 1960, 53.

25. "A Passage to India by No Means a Novelist's Play." Javed Majeed has recently suggested that *A Passage to India* can and should be read as evidence of Forster's dissatisfaction with the novel's very form. See his "Bathos, Architecture and Knowing India: E. M. Forster's *A Passage to India* and Nineteenth-Century British Ethnology and the Romance Quest," *Journal of Commonwealth Literature* 40, 1 (2005): 21–36.

26. For a very succinct account of the transition from Oxford to Broadway, including Forster's speech after the first Oxford production, see Lago, "*A Passage to India* on Stage."

27. See the review in *Time*, "Theater Abroad," 53. Langner's daughter Phyllis was living on a barge near Oxford and had gone to see the play; she wired her father immediately afterward and that is how the play came to Broadway. Interview with Santha Rama Rau, March 2004.

28. Author interview with Santha Rama Rau, April 2005.

29. Author interview with Santha Rama Rau, March 2004.

30. Santha Rama Rau, "A Passage to India; from the novel by E.M. Forster," The Theater Guild, 27 W. 53rd Street, New York, 19 NY, CO 5–6170, HTC.

31. Frank Hauser to Santha Rama Rau, February 8, 1960, HTC.

32. Ibid.

33. Santha Rama Rau to Frank Hauser, February 14, 1960, bMS Thr 93 (27), HTC. See Krishnaswamy, *Effeminism*, 147.

34. Author interview with Santha Rama Rau, April 2005. According to Rama Rau, Langner "had bought it sight unseen, on the strength of his daughter Phyllis's recommendation, and when we saw it together at Oxford he began to talk about the changes" he thought would be necessary to bring it to Broadway.

35. bMS Thr 93 (29), HTC.

36. Frank Hauser to Santha Rama Rau, April 27, 1960, box 4, HGARC.

37. As far as I know there was only one American edition of the play, copyrighted in 1960 and published in 1961; this would not have reflected the changes made specifically for the 1962 Broadway show. See *A Passage to India: A Play by Santha Rama Rau from the Novel by E. M. Forster* (New York: Harcourt, Brace and World, 1961).

38. John McCarter, "India: 1920," *The New Yorker,* February 18, 1962, 94.

39. Forster to Rama Rau, May 2, 1962, bMS Thr 93 (14), HTC. Forster said he had heard this via Natwar Singh.

40. Rama Rau to Forster, May 7, 1962, bMS Thr 93 (28), HTC.

41. "Muddle" was Forster's term for the cave drama. See Childs, ed., *E. M. Forster's "A Passage to India,"* 22.

42. Author interview with Santha Rama Rau, April 2005.

43. A notable exception was Robert Brustein in the *New Republic,* who accused Rama Rau of depoliticizing the novel so that "the conflict now is less between two nations, separated by vast cultural differences, than between stupid English bureaucrats and innocent Indian victims." *New Republic,* February 19, 1962, 21.

44. "Elusive," *Newsweek,* February 12, 1962, 52; McCarter, "India: 1920," 94.

45. Howard Taubman, "Theatre: Timely Theme," *New York Times,* February 1, 1962, 23.

46. K. Natwar Singh, "E. M. Forster's 'Passage to Broadway,' " *Illustrated Weekly of India,* March 25, 1962, 42.

47. "Bridge party," *Time,* February 9, 1962, 61.

48. "Elusive," 52.

49. Taubman, "Theatre," 23.

50. Howard Taubman, "Worth Adapting: Much of Quality of Forster Novel in Santha Rama Rau's Play," *New York Times*, February 11, 1962, 109.

51. Edward Said, *Orientalism* (New York: Vintage Books, 1978); and Sinha, *Colonial Masculinity*.

52. "Elusive," 52.

53. Taubman, "Theatre," 23.

54. Andrew J. Rotter, "Gender Relations, Foreign Relations: The United States and South Asia, 1947–1964," *Journal of American History* 81, 2 (September 1994): 535. See also his *Comrades at Odds: The United States and India, 1947–64* (Ithaca, N.Y.: Cornell University Press, 2000).

55. Rotter, "Gender Relations," 539.

56. Ibid.

57. Ibid., 538.

58. Here I am making a similar argument to the one Steven Caton makes in his analysis of how 1960s audiences would have heard certain passages of dialogue in David Lean's film *Lawrence of Arabia* through the prism of the Suez Crisis and its aftermath. See Caton, *Lawrence of Arabia*, 176–78. I am grateful to Durba Ghosh for this reference.

59. John Keating, "Meet Mohyeddin: Co-Star of 'A Passage to India' Dispels a Few Misconceptions," *New York Times* March 4, 1962, 107.

60. Ibid.

61. Ibid.

62. See Sara Suleri, "Forster's Imperial Erotic," in Jeremy Tambling, ed., *E. M. Forster* (New York: St. Martin's Press, 1995), 151–70 (taken originally from her *The Rhetoric of English India*).

63. "Bridge Party," 61.

64. See Stape, ed., *E. M. Forster*.

65. Taubman, "Worth Adapting," 109.

66. Ibid.

67. Ibid.

68. See also Harold Clurman's review in *The Nation*, February 17, 1962, 155,

which was equally oblique in its connections between the Forster drama and its relevance "to other people and other places."

69. Poppy Cannon Whittier, no title, no date, clipping from *Amsterdam News*, box 4, HGARC.

70. See von Eschen, *Race against Empire*; Mary L. Dudziak, *Cold War Civil Rights: Race and the Image of American Democracy* (Princeton, N.J.: Princeton University Press, 2000); Borstelmann, *The Cold War and the Color Line*; Plummer, ed., *Window on Freedom*.

71. She was an occasional "feature" herself. See "Never the Twain," *The New Yorker*, January 6, 1951, 26–27. For some of Rama Rau's own writing for the magazine, see "By Any Other Name," March 17, 1951, 26–28; "Letter from Bombay," May 3, 1952, 81–94; and "The Laughing Dutchman and the Devil Dancers," November 2, 1957, 119–40.

72. Santha Rama Rau, "Songs of India Badly Out of Tune," *New York Times*, July 31, 1960, Book Review, 1.

73. Lewis Funke, "News and Gossip of the Rialto," *New York Times*, February 7, 1960, XI.

74. The "smart set" refers to a magazine of that name which ran from 1900 to 1935; more generically it refers to *The New Yorker* and similar New York–based "highbrow" periodicals. See Carl R. Dolmetsch, *The Smart Set* (New York: Dial Press, 1966), ix–xii.

75. Orville Prescott, "Books of the Times," *New York Times*, May 23, 1945, 17. See also Isabelle Mallett, "The Reorientation of an Anglo-Indian," *New York Times*, June 3, 1945, Book Review, 3.

76. For the photo of the family's arrival, see *New York Times*, August 10, 1948, 5; for Harper's contract see "Books—Authors," *New York Times*, January 31, 1950, 18.

77. In fact, she did a lecture tour in April 1961 to promote her autobiography, *Gifts of Passage;* see box 3, HGARC.

78. Quote from review of *Remember the House* (1956) from the *New York Herald Tribune*, typescript list of reviewer quotes, box 3, HGARC.

79. "Coming of Age," *Time*, April 16, 1956, 117.

80. List of review excerpts, box 3, HGARC.

81. Santha Rama Rau, "Independent India, a Republic Restless and Harassed," *New York Times*, July 1, 1951, 131.

82. Santha Rama Rau, "A Conflict of Loyalties," *New York Times*, January 15, 1956, Book Review, 3–4; "Death Rode the Train," *New York Times*, February 19, 1956, Book Review, 3.

83. Ibid.

84. Orville Prescott, "Books of the Times," *New York Times*, November 1, 1950, 33. See also John J. Espey, "An Asiatic in Asia," *New York Times*, November 5, 1950, 223.

85. Prescott, "Books," 33.

86. Ibid.

87. Douglas, *The Smart Magazines*.

88. Ibid., 172; see also Cohen, *A Consumers' Republic*. For a more detailed discussion of the Wolfe brouhaha, see Mehta, *Remembering Mr. Shawn's New Yorker*, 221ff. The ramifications of this contretemps for foreign policy were directly articulated by Arthur Schlesinger Jr., who linked excessive consumerism with feminine weakness and vulnerability to communism. See Robert D. Dean, "Masculinity as Ideology: JFK and the Domestic Politics of Foreign Policy," *Diplomatic History* 22, 1 (1998): 36ff., and K. A. Courdileone, " 'Politics in an Age of Anxiety': Cold War Political Culture and the Crisis in American Masculinity, 1949–1960," *Journal of American History* 87, 2 (September 2000): 515–45.

89. Santha Rama Rau, "These Things I Learned," *New York Times*, April 8 1956, Book Review, 3. She also reviewed Chester Bowles's *Ambassador's Report*. See "Understanding Free India," *The Nation*, June 30, 1954, 95–96.

90. To give just one example, the young aspiring director Ismail Merchant started out in New York as a kind of pageboy at the United Nations, taking care of Indian delegates. He used the UN delegates' lounge to seek investors for his early films. The Indian premiere of his film *The Householder* occurred at Galbraith's ambassadorial residence in New Delhi and was attended by Nehru and his family. See Merchant, *My Passage from India*, 26, 31, 33, 51–52. For a very different look at the intersection of diplomacy foreign policy and celebrity, see

Mike Marqusee, *Redemption Song: Mohammed Ali and the Spirit of the Sixties* (London: Verso 1999).

91. See "India and Pakistan to Hail Queen," *New York Times*, January 16, 1961, 3; "New Delhi in Gala Array," January 21, 1961, 2; Paul Grimes, "India Hails Queen in Huge Welcome," January 22, 1961, 3; "Queen in India Rides Elephant," January 23, 1961, 25; "Queen Goes on Hunt but Tigers are Shy," January 24, 1961, 10; "Marchers Halted in Bombay," February 24, 1961, 4.

92. Grimes, "India Hails," 3.

93. "Mrs. Kennedy Plans India-Pakistan Trip," *New York Times*, November 4, 1961, 1. This is somewhat at odds with Galbraith's own account, which suggests that he first approached President Kennedy in Washington in September of 1961 about a visit by Mrs. Kennedy to India; no mention was made of Pakistan in the initial discussion, at least as Galbraith recorded it. See Galbraith, *Ambassador's Journal*, 207.

94. "India Waits in Curiosity," *New York Times*, March 11, 1962, 43.

95. "Mrs Kennedy Celebrates Hindu Festival on Her Last Day in India," *New York Times*, March 22, 1962, 3.

96. Paul Grimes, "First Lady Given Horse in Pakistan," *New York Times*, March 23, 1962, 8.

97. Galbraith, *Ambassador's Report*, 332.

98. "Mrs. Kennedy Guest of Queen at Lunch," *New York Times*, March 29, 1962, 1.

99. "Playwright of 'A Passage to India,'" (London) *Times*, April 6, 1960, 15.

100. Santha Rama Rau, "Indian Entries from a Dairy: Introduction," *Harper's Magazine*, February 1962, 46–47.

101. Ibid., 45.

102. Santha Rama Rau, "A Passage to Broadway," *Theatre Arts* 46, 2 (February 1962): 66.

103. Ibid.

104. Ibid.

105. Nirad C. Chaudhuri, "Passage to and From India," *Encounter* 2 (1954): 19–

24. Reprinted in Rutherford, ed., *Twentieth Century Interpretations of "A Passage to India,"* 68–77.

106. Santha Rama Rau to E. M. Forster, n.d., box 6, HGARC. According to this letter, Rama Rau and Natwar Singh proposed Satyajit Ray a second time as director and promised that Mohyeddin would play Aziz. She also recalled the first time Ray had asked her about this: "I said (quoting you and trying, as I remember, to imitate your voice), 'I think the simplest answer is to say "No."' "

107. Rama Rau, "A Passage to Broadway," 66.

108. Forster to Rama Rau, May 2, 1962, bMS Thr 93 15, HTC.

109. Forster to Rama Rau, November 2, 1960, bMS Thr 93 (7), HTC.

110. Clipping from *Show,* February 1962, 42, box 4, HGARC.

111. Ibid.

112. See Singh, *Profiles and Letters,* especially 37–45, which deals with *A Passage to India* in America and his Forster commemorative volume; and his *Curtain Raisers,* 45–58, which also reminisces about Forster.

113. See Santha Rama Rau to Michael Bessie at Atheneum, May 3, 1963; to Barnie Rosset at Grove Press, May 2, 1963; and to Elizabeth Lawrence at *Harper's,* April 29, 1963. Julian P. Miller of Harcourt, Brace and World—which eventually published the volume—cautioned that "there is a fairly limited market for such a volume," not because of Forster per se but because other such collections on famous authors (Walter Lippman, Carl Sandburg) had not done well. Box 3, HGARC.

114. Santha Rama Rau, chapter 5 (no title), in Singh, *E. M. Forster,* 56.

115. Ibid., 57.

116. Ibid., 62.

117. "Coming of Age," review of her first novel *Remember the House, Time,* April 16, 1956, 117.

118. See, for example, her essay "That Much-Abused Word: Friendship," *McCall's,* November 1965, 54, 56, 182, where she quotes Forster's line about loyalty to friends over loyalty to country in times of war as the exemplar of her own position (182).

119. Rama Rau, chapter 5, in Singh, *E. M. Forster,* 63.

120. Santha Rama Rau, "Home Thoughts from England," *The Reporter*, July 7, 1960, 53–54.

121. Nanda, *Jawaharlal Nehru*, 263.

122. See Lord Beloff, "The End of the British Empire and the Assumption of World-Wide Commitment by the U.S.," in William Roger Louis and Hedley Bull, eds., *The "Special relationship": Anglo-American Relations since 1945* (Oxford: Clarendon Press, 1986), 250.

123. "Coming of Age," *Time*, April 16, 1956, 117.

124. Santha Rama Rau, "Oranges, Birds and Crystals" [review of Wilfred Stone, *The Cave and the Mountain: A Study of E. M. Forster*], *The Reporter*, March 24, 1966, 56.

125. See Walkowitz, *Cosmopolitan Style*. I am grateful to the author for sharing her pre-publication work with me and for engaging me in very stimulating and provocative conversations on the subject of cosmopolitan style.

126. Kusum Nair, "Galbraith in India," *Harper's Magazine*, December 1961, 50. See also Vijay Lakshmi Pandit, "India to America," *The Atlantic*, October 1953, 107–9. This was part of a special *Atlantic* supplement called "India Today," which mixed high politics and the arts with an introduction to the languages and cartography of the subcontinent. Pandita also appeared in venues like *Reader's Digest*: see "The Best Advice I Ever Had," *Reader's Digest*, January 1956, 153–55.

127. Author interview with Santha Rama Rau, March 2004.

128. Ibid.

129. Ibid.

130. Ibid.

131. Guinness, *Blessings in Disguise*, 216. Guinness denied any tension between himself and Lean, remarking, "I owe him my film career," largely because of his role in *The Bridge over the River Kwai* (ibid.).

132. Ibid.

133. Brownlow, *David Lean*, 645.

134. Ibid., 655.

135. Ibid.

136. Author interview with Santha Rama Rau, March 2004.

137. Brownlow, *David Lean*, 672.

138. Santha Rama Rau, "Introduction to Indian Entries from a Diary by E. M. Forster," *Harper's Magazine*, February 1962, 47.

139. E. M. Forster to Santha Rama Rau, May 21, 1960, bMS Thr 93 (4), HTC.

140. Forster wrote to Rama Rau, "I do hope they will let Frank Hauser produce, and as for Zia Mohyeddin—they are *mad* if they don't let him. He *is* the part— please tell them for me, with all the eloquence at your disposal." Forster to Rama Rau, May 21, 1960, bMS Thr 93 (4), HTC (emphasis in original). Forster later wrote, "Zia—we all respect—is important and must remain so even if poisoned by some aspiring Porto Rican." Forster to Rama Rau, October 23, 1961, bMS 93 (10), HTC. This is the same letter in which he insists that the "nude beautiful punkah wallah" was "MOST IMPORTANT OF ALL."

141. Author interview with Santha Rama Rau, April 2005.

142. Author interview with Santha Rama Rau, August 2003. When I made allusion to the discussion of Bowers's homosexuality as referenced in Okamoto, *The Man Who Saved Kabuki*, she said, "We were married for fifteen years—ten years of bliss, and five years of hell."

143. See Boone, "Vacation Cruises."

144. Author interview, 2005. See also Krishnaswamy, *Effeminism*, 159.

145. Brownlow, *David Lean*, 647–48.

146. Santha Rama Rau, "Remembering E. M. Forster," *Grand Street* 5, 4 (Summer 1986): 114.

147. Rama Rau is quoting from Forster's letter to her, March 2, 1962, which ends with "so I am not bluffing when I tell Miss Strauss [Rama Rau's agent] that, as far as I am concerned, the play can come off at once." bMS Thr 93 (13), HTC.

148. Ibid., 119. Writing at about the same time, Forster quipped to Rama Rau, "My main trouble is with untidiness; where, where for instance at this very moment is my pen?" Forster to Rama Rau, May 14, 1962, box 4, HGARC.

149. I am exceedingly grateful to Jed Esty for encouraging me to consider this point.

150. Krishnaswamy, *Effeminism*, 162–63.

151. Nor did she invoke him only in the context of *A Passage to India*. Her account "The Ubiquitous Spoon," for the August 1963 *House and Garden*, for example, embedded Forster's ideas about the "human predicament" (118) almost effortlessly into a discussion otherwise devoted to culinary implements.

152. For a discussion of the foreign policy aspects of this reversal of power, see Orde, *The Eclipse of Britain*, especially chapter 6. For an attempt at a cultural, almost psychological, reading of the process, see Dumbrell, *A Special Relationship*.

153. Dean, *Imperial Brotherhood*.

154. Author interview with Santha Rama Rau, April 2005.

155. For the long history of this, see Moser, *Twisting the Lion's Tail*; for the special relationship as a cultural phenomenon, see Dumbrell, *Special Relationship*.

156. Mollie Panter-Downes, "Profiles: Kingsman," *The New Yorker*, September 19, 1959, 51–86.

157. Cronin, *Imagining India*, 177.

158. Though we await the history of Forster's career in America, see V. S. Pritchett, "A Private Voice in Public Places Gave Two Cheers for Democracy, One for Humanity," *New York Times*, December 29, 1968, Book Review, 1 (the occasion was Forster's ninetieth birthday); and Glenay Escott, "A Dinner, a Talk, a Walk with Forster," *New York Times*, October 10, 1971, Book Review, 2, for a sense of his place in the American literary imagination by the end of the 1960s.

159. Cronin, *Imagining India*, 177–78. As Jed Esty's work on an earlier Forster demonstrates, this is merely a late-twentieth-century incarnation of modernism's work of "cultural repair" with respect to postimperial Englishness. See Esty, *A Shrinking Island*.

3. Home to India

1. Santha Rama Rau, *The Cooking of India*, 24–26. She was not the only one to demystify curry; see "Indian Party," *Ladies' Home Journal*, July 1961, 91.

2. See for example, Ruth P. Collins, "The Right Way to Make a Real Curry,"

House and Garden, September 1954, 106 (whence the quote); "Exotic Curry," *Life*, April 19, 1954, 78–82; and Virginia T. Habeeb, "Curry on a Cart," *American Home*, June 1967, 99.

3. Appadurai, "How to Make a National Cuisine," 3.

4. Roy, "Reading Communities and Culinary Communities," 480.

5. See Susan J. Leonardi, "Recipes for Reading: Summer Pasta, Lobster à la Riseholme, and Key Lime Pie," *PMLA* 104.3 (May 1989): 340–47; Appadurai, "How to Make," 3–24. In fact, some textualization of culinary knowledge did occur in Bengal in the nineteenth century, with publication of some of these texts coming out of Rabindranath Tagore's household. See Pragyasundari Devi, *Amis O Niramis Ahaar* (Calcutta, 1900), which translates as "Vegetarian and Non-Vegetarian Cooking / Food" (*Ahaar* means food, but it can refer to cooking as well). Devi was from the Tagore clan and married an Assamese writer. Rama Rau, private correspondence with the author. I am grateful to Srirupa Prasad for the Pragyasundari Devi citation and the translation as well.

6. Appadurai, "Gastro-poetics in Hindu Asia."

7. Appadurai, "How to Make," 3.

8. Ibid., 5, 7, 11.

9. McKim Marriott, "Caste Ranking and Food Transaction"; Khare, *Culture and Reality*; Khare and Rao, eds., *Food, Society and Culture*; and Khare, ed., *The Eternal Food*.

10. See Katherine Fisher, "Curries They'll Like," *Good Housekeeping*, February 1946, 87–89; Jane Nickerson, "Curries to Add Zest," *New York Times Magazine*, September 29, 1946, 42–43; Ruth Mils Teague, "Conversation Piece," *Ladies' Home Journal*, November 1946, 144–48; "Exotic Curry," *Life*, April 19, 1954, 78–82; "'Let's Have Dinner in India Tonight,'" *Sunset*, October 8, 1954, 164–68; "Dishes of India," *Life*, November 18, 1957, 11–17; "The Fabled Food of India," *McCall's*, August 1961, 98–99; "Indian Party," *Ladies' Home Journal*, July 1965, 74–77; "This Curry Is Actually Easier Here than in India," *Sunset*, November 1965, 204–8; "A Taste of India," *Ladies' Home Journal*, November 1969, 112ff.

11. See, for example, June Owen, "News of Food: Indian Curry," *New York Times*, July 19, 1955, 24; Jane Nickerson, "'Spicy' Cookbook Sheds Light on

Indian Dishes," *New York Times*, October 11, 1956, 60; and Nickerson, "Indian Kebabs Spice Outdoor Menus," *New York Times*, September 7, 1957, 146.

12. Roy, "Reading Communities," 471–502.

13. Attia Hosain and Sita Pasricha, *Cooking the Indian Way* (London: Spring Books, 1962). This was part of a series that included *Cooking the French Way* and *Cooking the Chinese Way*, which included eleven "uniform" titles in all, according to the frontispiece of the 1962 edition.

14. Jaffrey, *Invitation to Indian Cooking*. See also her *Madhur Jaffrey's Indian Cookery*, *Taste of India*, and *Quick and Easy Indian Cooking* (San Francisco: Chronicle Books, 1996); and Ismail Merchant, *Ismail Merchant's Indian Cuisine* (New York: St. Martin's Press, 1986), *Ismail Merchant's Passionate Meals* (Columbia, Mo.: South Asia Books, 2000), and his inimitably gastro-poetic autobiography, *My Passage to India*.

15. Rama Rau, *Cooking of India*, 6.

16. Ibid.

17. This is the title of chapter 1, pp. 8–34. I am grateful to Barbara Ramusack for her emphasis on the senior Rama Rau's mixed marriage as itself a species of cosmopolitanism.

18. Rama Rau, *The Cooking of India*, 7.

19. See chapter 1, above.

20. Rama Rau, *The Cooking of India*, 7.

21. M. F. K. Fisher, *The Cooking of Provincial France* (New York: Time-Life Books, 1968). See also Helen and George Papashvily, *Russian Cooking* (New York: Time-Life Books, 1969), which closely approximates Fisher's in rhetorical style. I am grateful to George Robb for sharing this, which is part of his personal collection. For a full list of all the books and authors in the series see Nika Hazelton, "Because All Men Eat," *New York Times*, June 6, 1971, Book Review, 40. Hazelton praised Rama Rau's cookbook as one of the best and singled out Fisher (among several others) for criticism. Emily Hahn was the author of the Chinese volume, based on the strength of her popularity as a commentator on Asia and the world from the 1940s onward. See Ken Cuthbertson, *Nobody Said Not to Go: The Life, Loves and Adventures of Emily Hahn* (New York: Faber and Faber, 1998).

22. The Bengal famine of 1943–44 occurred in regions where U.S. troops were stationed (as support for the airlift of supplies to China, which was one political avenue through which such images were channeled). See Robert Trumbull, "India's Food Presents a Long-Range Problem," *New York Times*, February 19, 1951, 127; A. M. Rosenthal, "India's Food Loan from U.S. Brings Long-Term Benefit," *New York Times*, September 2, 1956, E5 (with sketch of emaciated Indian man holding out "India's Bread Basket"); Thomas F. Brady, "Indian Food Shortages Are Posing a Major Political Issue," *New York Times*, August 30, 1964, E8; and Chester E. Bowles, "Not Enough Food for Too Many People," *New York Times*, September 6, 1964, Sunday Magazine, 7. See also Merrill, *Bread and the Ballot*.

23. Isaacs, *Scratches on Our Minds*, 37.

24. For a series of arresting images, see Chester Bowles, "Asia Challenges us Through India," *New York Times*, March 23, 1952, Sunday Magazine, 7; John Sherman Cooper, "India: Crucial test of Foreign Aid, *New York Times*, March 16, 1958, Sunday Magazine, 12; and Bowles, "Not Enough Food," Sunday Magazine, 7.

25. Markandaya, *Nectar in a Sieve*.

26. R. K. Narayan, "Ghee Is for 'Good,'" *New York Times*, March 6, 1955, Sunday Magazine, 78.

27. Nathan Glazer recounts a story about when he first met the Indian intellectual and Gandhian Nirmal Kumar Bose in 1966. Bose is alleged to have said, "You give us a great deal of aid. It makes us feel like beggars. How does it make you feel?" Quoted in Glazer and Glazer, eds., *Conflicting Images*, 18.

28. Bowles, "Not Enough Food," Sunday Magazine, 7. There were of course serious hunger problems in the United States as well; see Robert Coles, *Still Hungry in America* (New York: World Publishing Company, 1969), which had amazing, and chilling, photos of Americans of all colors struggling at and below the poverty line.

29. Rama Rau, *The Cooking of India*, 11.

30. Ibid., 10.

31. Ibid., 8.

32. Ibid.

33. Ibid., 73, 102, 72.

34. Ibid., 13.

35. Fisher, *The Cooking of Provincial France*, 12.

36. Rama Rau, *The Cooking of India*, 26–27.

37. Appadurai, "How to Make," 7.

38. Ibid., 113.

39. Conlon, "Dining Out in Bombay."

40. Thomas Hansen, *Wages of Violence: Naming and Identity in Postcolonial Bombay* (Princeton, N.J.: Princeton University Press, 2001).

41. Rama Rau, *The Cooking of India*, 113–14.

42. Appadurai, "How to Make."

43. Rama Rau, *The Cooking of India*, 24.

44. Ibid., 19, 169, and 126.

45. Hosain and Parischa, *Cooking the Indian Way*, 6.

46. Rama Rau, *The Cooking of India*, 67.

47. Ibid., 48.

48. Ibid., 23.

49. Nehru, *Glimpses of World History* (New York: John Day Company, 1942); and Nehru, *India and the World*, 2–11.

50. Rama Rau, *The Cooking of India*, 24.

51. Arnold Erlich (of *Venture* magazine) to Santha Rama Rau, June 26, 1967, box 13, HGARC. All letters cited refer to this collection unless specified otherwise.

52. See Santha Rama Rau, "India's Spice of Life," *Venture: The Traveler's World*, December / January 1968, 60–68. I am inestimably grateful to Danielle Kinsey, who alone knows how hard it was to track down this source.

53. Appadurai, "How to Make," 3. For a history of restaurant culture in Bombay, see Conlon, "Dining Out in Bombay," and Khare, *Culture and Reality*, 65.

54. "Restaurant Guide," *New York Times*, April 8, 1958, 39; Craig Claiborne, "A Directory to Dining in City," *New York Times*, September 20, 1968, 50; and "Dining on Tandoori Chicken under Colorful Indian Tent," *New York Times*, December 10, 1971, 48. East of Suez was run by a Carl Henderson (Jane Dicker-

son, "The Rice Table, a Touch of Indonesia, Appears at East of Suez," *New York Times*, May 24, 1955, 28), but it's not clear how the others are related to the restaurants started by six Bangladeshi brothers in the 1960s as discussed by Denker, *World on a Plate*, 122–23. Denker lists a 1975 edition of Rama Rau's *The Cooking of India* in his footnotes on p. 179. Thanks to Kristin Hoganson for this reference. Contrast this with the "Little Indias" that grew up in Jackson Heights, Queens, in the 1970s; see Shukla, *Indians Abroad*, 108ff. Khandelwal also gives a very short account of the 1960s restaurant scene in her *Becoming American, Being Indian*, 13.

55. Owen Lassiter to Santha Rama Rau, December 6, 1968, box 13, HGARC.

56. Craig Claiborne, "Debut for a Series of International Cookbooks," *New York Times*, February 19, 1968, 46. Claiborne had written on Indian food himself; see "The Flavor of India," *New York Times Magazine*, January 15, 1961, 60.

57. In fact, as she later told me, it was at this moment that she was going through the divorce from Faubion Bowers. Author interview with Santha Rama Rau, April 2005. "I was pretty distracted," she said. "There were gaps."

58. "Notes on Food," box 14, file 1, HGARC.

59. Dickerson, "The Rice Table," 28.

60. "Notes on Food." For George Lang, see typed sheet "Second tasting" and Irene Saint to Santha Rama Rau, April 14, 1967.

61. Santha Rama Rau (Bombay) to Bill Goolrick, October 17, 1968.

62. Bill Goolrick to Santha Rama Rau, May 29, 1968.

63. Ibid.

64. Dick Williams, Office Memo to Santha Rama Rau, June 2, 1967.

65. Irene Saint to Santha Rama Rau, April 14, 1967.

66. Bill Goolrick to Santha Rama Rau, January 10, 1969.

67. See Neuhaus, *Manly Meals and Mom's Home Cooking*, 163–90 and 249–53. Thanks to Kristin Hoganson for this reference.

68. Fisher, *The Cooking of Provincial France*, 86.

69. Santha Rama Rau, "To be Used and Read" (review of Dharam Jit Singh's *Classic Cooking from India*), *New York Times*, December 2, 1956, Book Reviews, 20.

70. Bill Goolrick to Santha Rama Rau, August 12, 1968.

71. See Santha Rama Rau's notes on books consulted, box 14, HGARC.

72. Ibid.

73. Indira Talyarkham was a niece of Janaki Agnes Penelope Majumdar and a granddaughter of W. C. Bonnerjee, the first president of the Indian National Congress. Sally Singh (Majumdar's daughter-in-law), correspondence with the author, April 14, 2005. For an account of Majumdar's life, see Burton, ed., *Family History*.

74. Thangam Philip to Santha Rama Rau, n.d., and Rama Rau's notes of interviews, both in box 14, HGARC.

75. Appadurai, "How to Make," 11; and Goody (also citing Khare), *Cooking, Cuisine and Class*, 121.

76. Santha Rama Rau to Bill Goolrick, October 17, 1968.

77. Ganguly, *States of Exception*, 127ff.

78. Claiborne's review of Fisher's book indicates that some testing of the "provincial" dishes occurred in a New York restaurant; whether this was the case for the recipes in Rama Rau's book I do not know. See Claiborne, "Debut for a Series of International Cookbooks," 46.

79. Devika Teja to Santha Rama Rau, August 6, 1968.

80. Devika Teja to Santha Rama Rau, November 1, 1967.

81. Ibid. She may have been referring to Mrs. Balbir Singh, *Indian Cookery* (New York: Weathervane Books, 1973), which seems to be a second edition of an earlier work. The book was expressly aimed at an English-speaking audience and opens with a brief overview of the variety of Indian cookbooks "available in the market." (v); her goal was to create recipes that "suit the tastes of readers all over the globe" (vi).

82. Barbara Leach to Santha Rama Rau, September 25, 1968.

83. Thangam E. Philip, *Modern Cooking for the Teaching and the Trade*, vol. 1 (4th ed., Bombay: Orient Longman, 1997).

84. Thangam Philip to Santha Rama Rau, n.d.

85. Thangam Philip to Santha Rama Rau, December 13, 1968.

86. Grace Brynolson to Santha Rama Rau, July 25, 1968.

87. Invoice (n.d.), file 3, HGARC.

88. Rama Rau, *The Cooking of India*, 208.

89. Bill Goolrick to Santha Rama Rau, October 28, 1968.

90. Santha Rama Rau to Bill Goolrick, October 29, 1968.

91. For reference to Indo-Pakistani relations in the United States a few years after the publication of Rama Rau's cookbook, see Khalid H. Shah and Linda Shah, "Indians in New York," *Illustrated Weekly of India*, April 22, 1973, 22.

92. See, for example, Craig Claiborne, "Yoghurt à la Pakistani," *New York Times Magazine*, February 16, 1958, 60–61, complete with a picture of "Pakistani specialities."

93. See, for example, Hosain and Pasricha, *Cooking the Indian Way*, 6.

94. Santha Rama Rau to Bill Goolrick, October 29, 1968.

95. Ibid.

96. Rama Rau, *The Cooking of India*, 137.

97. Santha Rama Rau to Bill Goolrick, October 29, 1968.

98. For Aftab's official bio, see Rama Rau, *The Cooking of India*, inside cover; for his chapter, see 183–85.

99. Rama Rau, *The Cooking of India*, 183–85.

100. Ibid., 184.

101. Ibid., 22.

102. There is also a chapter on "North Indian" lamb (156–81), but this is as much about lamb as about the region per se.

103. Rama Rau, *The Cooking of India*, 145.

104. Ibid., 152.

105. Pearl S. Buck, *Oriental Cookbook* (New York: Simon and Schuster, 1972). Thanks to George Robb, who shared this with me from his personal collection.

106. Indian food (as opposed to reviews of cookbooks per se) was also covered in magazines like *Better Homes and Gardens* ("A Classic from India—Curried Lamb Dinner," October 1967, 86–110) and *House and Garden* ("Indian Cook Book," September 1964, 197–206).

107. Santha Rama Rau, "To be Used—and Read," *New York Times*, December 2,

1956, Book Review, 20. Singh got a lot of attention; see also Jane Nickerson, "Hot Puddings for a Change," *New York Times Magazine*, November 13, 1955, 52–53, and Dharam Jit Singh, "Curry and Cook Book," *House and Garden*, August 1957, 89–95, and "Dishes of India," *Life*, November 18, 1957, 116–17.

108. See note 9, above.

109. Craig Claiborne, "Indian Actress is a Star in the Kitchen, Too," *New York Times*, July 7, 1966, 57; and Merchant, *My Passage to India*, 64.

110. Claiborne, "Debut for a Series of International Cookbooks," 46.

111. Within two years he had written a Time-Life book of his own, *Classic French Cooking* (New York: Time-Life Books, 1970).

112. See Goody, *Cooking, Cuisine and Class*, 25 and 30–31. For Lévi-Strauss, see "Le triangle culinaire," *L'Arc* 26 (1965): 19–29; translated by Peter Brooks for *Partisan Review* 33 (1966): 586–95; and his *L'Origine des manières de table* (Paris, 1968). For Mary Douglas, see "Deciphering a Meal," in Clifford Geertz, ed., *Myth, Symbol and Culture* (New York: Norton, 1971).

113. Rama Rau, *The Cooking of India*, chapter 4 (91–111).

114. Ibid., 91.

115. For a broader discussion of the differentials of foodways in a global context, see Goody, *Cooking, Cuisine and Class*.

116. Rama Rau, *The Cooking of India*, 35.

117. Ibid., 40.

118. Goody, *Cooking, Cuisine, and Class*, 101, 115.

119. See George on Beeton and Steel in *The Politics of Home*, and Judith E. Walsh, *Domesticity in Colonial India: What Women Learned When Men Gave Them Advice* (Lanham, Md.: Rowman and Littlefield, 2004).

120. W. G. Rodgers called it "not her best." See "Like Becky Sharp Kay was Fast on her Feet," *New York Times*, October 18, 1970, Book Review, 26. For one serialized installment of the novel, see Santha Rama Rau, "The Countess," *Ladies' Home Journal*, December 1963, 102–4. For another, see "Softly," *Saturday Evening Post*, December 7, 1963, 51–87. Santha Rama Rau confessed to me that she didn't think the book was "particularly successful" as a novel. She had written the four sections as short stories but she remembered her publishers

thinking that they worked better as a whole. Author interview April 2005. See also Burton, "Ugly Americans."

121. See Jaya Thadani, *Illustrated Weekly of India*, April 22, 1973, 22.

122. Box 14, file 3, HGARC; see correspondence with draft criticism from Gene (Genevieve) Young for *The Adventuress*.

123. Her correspondence from the late 1960s suggests that she did this journalistic work for the income it brought, and in order to support her fiction writing. See Santha Rama Rau to Lois [?], October 29, 1968, box 14, HGARC.

124. Ira Raja, "Ageing Subjects, Agentic Bodies: Appetite, Modernity and the Middle Class in Two Indian Short Stories in English," *Journal of Commonwealth Literature* 40, 1 (2005): 73–89.

Epilogue

1. I am grateful to William Reddy for this insight.

2. Mohanram and Rajan, eds., *English Postcoloniality*.

3. I am grateful to Adam Geary for enabling me to see and to appreciate this point.

4. See Alex Tickell, "The God of Small Things: Arundhati Roy's Postcolonial Cosmopolitanism," *Journal of Commonwealth Literature* 38 (2003): 73–76.

5. My reference is to Roberts, *Disruptive Acts*. "Sighted in circulation" is an appreciative play on Bishnupriya Ghosh's chapter title "Sighting Circulation," in her book *When Borne Across*. Hers may in turn be a riff on Niranjana's *Siting Translation*.

6. See Amireh, "Framing Nawal El Saadawi"; Brennan, *At Home in the World*; and Huggan, *The Postcolonial Exotic*.

7. See Casanova, *The World Republic of Letters*.

8. Peter Gowan, "The New Liberal Cosmopolitanism," in Daniele Archibugi, ed., *Debating Cosmopolitics* (London: Verso, 2003), 50–66.

9. See, for example, Boehmer, *Empire, the National, and the Postcolonial, 1890–1920*; and Mullen, *Afro-Orientalism*.

10. Ibid. See also Espiritu, *Five Faces of Exile*.

11. See Butler, "Merely Cultural."

12. Arnold and Blackburn, eds., *Telling Lives in India*.

13. See Parama Roy's review of Purnima Bose, *Organizing Empire*, in *American Historical Review* 110, 5 (December 2005): 1151.

14. Quoted in Nair, *Lying on the Postcolonial Couch*, 227.

15. See Huggan, *The Postcolonial Exotic*, 12.

16. See Boehmer, *Empire*; Ghosh, *When Borne Across*; and Tickell, "Arundhati Roy's Postcolonial Cosmopolitanism," 73–89.

17. For the fate of some of those—Amit Chaudhuri among them—see Anis Shivani, "Indo-Anglian Fiction: The New Orientalism," *Race and Class* 47, 4 (2006): 1–25. Thanks to Debbie Hughes for this reference.

18. See Kwame Anthony Appiah, "The Case for Contamination," *New York Times Magazine*, January 1, 2006, 30–37, 52.

19. See Robbins, "Celeb-Reliance." The quote is from Ganguly, *States of Exception*, 5.

20. Antoinette Burton, "The Ugly Americans," 5–19.

21. See Dhanvanthi Rama Rau, *An Inheritance*; and Devi and Rama Rau, *A Princess Remembers*. Manuscripts of both of these are in the Howard Gotlieb Archive Collection, Boston University. For a review of the latter, see Caroline Seebohm, "Fairy Tale with a Dark Ending," *New York Times*, March 13, 1977, 256.

22. El Saadawi is cited in Amireh, "Framing," 215.

23. http://www.quotemountain.com.

24. Santha Rama Rau, "By Any Other Name," *The New Yorker*, March 17, 1951, 26–28.

25. Author interview with Santha Rama Rau, April 2005.

26. See, for example, *http://www.sauguscenturions.com/tolisano/engspring/nonfiction.htm*: Tenth English and Modern Civilizations Team English Spring Semester—Nonfiction Unit, which is accompanied by these study questions: "Why did the girls leave the school permanently? How does Santha feel after the headmistress changes her name? Why does Premila want to wear a cotton dress and take sandwiches to school?" See also *http://www.faculty.fairfield.edu/rjregan/rr11su03.htm*.

27. See *http://research.soe.purdue.edu/challenge/* (accessed June 2003).

Materials and Resources: "The following pieces of literature were chosen for their content related to the subject and their availability. They are intended as a springboard for creative thought and further exposure to different types of literature. Other stories or poems may be substituted, or this aspect of the assignment may be considered optional for the teacher. These selections may be found in McDougal Littel's *Literature and Language, English and World Literature*, Purple Level 1994."

28. See Taylor et al., *Multiculturalism and "The Politics of Recognition."*

29. Rama Rau told me in my April 2005 interview with her that it is *Gifts of Passage* that still generates the biggest annual revenue checks for her (i.e., the first place where "By Any Other Name" was reprinted).

Ahmad, Aijaz. "The Politics of Literary Post-Coloniality." *Race and Class* 36, 3 (1995): 1–20.

Amireh, Amal. "Framing Nawal El Saadawi: Arab Feminism in a Transnational World." *Signs* 26, 1 (2000): 214–49.

Anderson, Amanda. *The Powers of Distance: Cosmopolitanism and the Cultivation of Detachment*. Princeton, N.J.: Princeton University Press, 2001.

Anderson, Carol. *Eyes Off the Prize: The United Nations and the African American Struggle for Human Rights, 1944–1955*. Cambridge: Cambridge University Press, 2003.

Anderson, David. *Histories of the Hanged: The Dirty War in Kenya and the End of Empire*. New York: W.W. Norton, 2005.

Appadurai, Arjun. "Gastro-Poetics in Hindu Asia." *American Ethnologist* 8, 3 (August 1981): 495–511.

———. "How to Make a National Cuisine: Cookbooks in Contemporary India." *Comparative Studies in Society and History* 30, 1 (January 1988): 3–24.

Appy, Christian G., ed. *Cold War Constructions: The Political Culture of United States Imperialism, 1945–1966*. Amherst: University of Massachusetts Press, 2000.

Aravamudan, Srinivas. *Guru English: South Asian Religion in a Cosmopolitan Language*. Princeton, N.J.: Princeton University Press, 2006.

Arnold, David. "The Self and the Cell: Indian Prison Narratives as Life Histories." In David Arnold and Stuart Blackburn, eds., *Telling Lives in India:*

Biography, Autobiography and Life History, 29–53. Delhi: Permanent Black / Indiana University Press, 2004.

Assayag, Jackie, and Véronique Bénéï, eds. *At Home in Diaspora: South Asian Scholars in the West*. Delhi: Permanent Black, 2003.

Azuma, Eiichero. *Between Two Empires: Race, History and Transnationalism in Japanese America*. New York: Oxford University Press, 2005.

Baldwin, Kate. *Beyond the Color Line and the Iron Curtain: Reading Encounters between Black and Red, 1922–1962*. Durham, N.C.: Duke University Press, 2002.

Barlow, Tani E. "Eugenic Woman, Semicolonialism, and Colonial Modernity as Problems for Postcolonial Theory." In Loomba et al., eds., *Postcolonial Studies and Beyond*, 359–84.

Basham, A. L. *The Wonder That Was India*. New York: Hawthorn Books, 1963.

Berlanstein, Lenard R. "Historicizing and Gendering Celebrity Culture: Famous Women in Nineteenth Century France." *Journal of Women's History* 16, 4 (2004): 65–91.

Bhattacharya, Nandini. *Reading the Splendid Body: Gender and Consumerism in Eighteenth Century Writing about British India*. Newark: University of Delaware Press, 1998.

Boehmer Elleke. "East Is East and South Is South: The Cases of Sarojini Naidu and Arundhati Roy." *Women: A Cultural Review* 11, 1 / 2 (2000): 65–70.

——. *Empire, the National, and the Postcolonial, 1890–1920*. New York: Oxford University Press, 2002.

Boone, Joseph. "Vacation Cruises: The Homoerotics of Orientalism." In John C. Hawley, ed., *Postcolonial, Queer: Theoretical Intersections*, 43–78. Albany: SUNY Press, 2001.

Booth, Marilyn. *May Her Likes Be Multiplied: Biography and Gender Politics in Egypt*. Berkeley: University of California Press, 2001.

Borstelmann, Thomas. *The Cold War and the Color Line: American Race Relations in the Global Arena*. Cambridge, Mass.: Harvard University Press, 2001.

Bose, Arun Coomer. "Indian Nationalist Agitations in the U.S.A. and Canada until the Arrival of Har Dayal in 1911." *Journal of Indian History* 43, 1 (April 1965): 227–39.

Bowers, Faubion. *The Dance in India*. New York: Columbia University Press, 1953.

——. *Theatre in the East: A Survey of Asian Dance and Drama*. New York: Grove Press, 1956.

Brands, H. W. *India and the United States: The Cold Peace*. Boston: Twayne, 1990.

Brennan, Timothy. *At Home in the World: Cosmopolitanism Now*. Cambridge, Mass: Harvard University Press, 1997.

——. "Cosmopolitans and Celebrities." *Race and Class* 31 (July–September 1989): 1–19.

Brownlow, Kevin. *David Lean: A Biography*. New York: St. Martin's Press, 1996.

Buck, Pearl S. *Mandala: A Novel of India*. New York: John Day Company, 1970.

Burton, Antoinette. *Burdens of History: British Feminists, Indian Women, and Imperial Culture, 1865–1915*. Chapel Hill: University of North Carolina Press, 1994.

——. *Dwelling in the Archive: Women Writing House, Home and History in Late Colonial India*. New York: Oxford University Press, 2003.

——. "The Ugly Americans: Gender, Geopolitics and the Career of Postcolonial Cosmopolitanism in the Novels of Santha Rama Rau." *Journal of Commonwealth Literature* 41, 2 (2006): 5–19.

——, ed. *Family History: Janaki Agnes Penelope Majumdar*. Delhi: Oxford University Press, 2003.

Buruma, Ian, and Avishai Margalit. *Occidentalism: The West in the Eyes of its Enemies*. New York: Penguin, 2004.

Butler, Judith. "Merely Cultural." *New Left Review* 227 (1998): 33–44.

——. "Universality in Culture." In Cohen, ed., *For Love of Country*, 45–52.

Calhoun, Craig. "The Class Consciousness of Frequent Travellers: Towards a Critique of Actually Existing Cosmopolitanism." In Vertovec and Cohen, eds., *Conceiving Cosmopolitanism*, 86–109.

Casanova, Pascale. *The World Republic of Letters*. Cambridge, Mass.: Harvard University Press, 2004.

Caton, Stephen C. *Lawrence of Arabia: A Film's Anthropology*. Berkeley: University of California Press, 1999.

Chakrabarty, Dipesh. *Habitations of Modernity: Essays in the Wake of Subaltern Studies*. Chicago: University of Chicago Press, 2002.

——. *Provincializing Europe: Postcolonial Thought and Historical Difference*. Princeton, N.J.: Princeton University Press, 2000.

Chakravarty, Amya, ed. *A Tagore Reader*. Boston: Beacon Press, 1961.

Chang, Gordon H., Purnima Mankekar, and Akhil Gupta, eds. *Caste and Outcaste: Dhan Gopal Mukerji*. Stanford, Calif.: Stanford University Press, 2001.

Chatterjee, Partha. "My Place in the Global Republic of Letters." In Assayag and Bénëi, eds., *At Home in Diaspora*. 44–51.

Cheah, Pheng, and Bruce Robbins, eds. *Cosmopolitics: Thinking and Feeling beyond the Nation*. Minneapolis: University of Minnesota Press, 1998.

Childs, Peter, ed. *E. M. Forster's A Passage to India*. London: Routledge, 2002.

Chiu, Fred Yen Liang. "Suborientalism and the Subimperialist Predicament: Aboriginal Discourse and the Poverty of State-Nation Imagery." *positions* 8, 1 (2000): 101–49.

Chuh, Kandice, and Karen Shimikawa, eds., *Orientations: Mapping Studies in the Asian Diaspora*. Durham, N.C.: Duke University Press, 2001.

Clymer, Kenton J. "Jawaharlal Nehru and the United States: The Preindependence Years." *Diplomatic History* 14, 2 (spring 1990): 143–61.

Cohen, Lizbeth. *A Consumers' Republic: The Practice of Mass Consumption in Postwar America*. New York: Vintage, 2003.

Conlon, Frank. "Dining Out in Bombay." In Carol A. Breckenridge, ed., *Consuming Modernity: Public Culture in a South Asian World*, 90–127. Minneapolis: University of Minnesota Press, 1995.

Cooppan, Vilashini. "The Ruins of Empire: The National and Global Politics of America's Return to Rome." In Loomba et al., eds., *Postcolonial Studies and Beyond*, 80–99. Durham: Duke University Press, 2005.

Cronin, Richard. *Imagining India*. New York: St. Martin's Press, 1989.

Dames, Nicholas. "Trollope and the Career: Vocational Trajectories and the Management of Ambition." *Victorian Studies* 45, 2 (winter 2003): 247–78.

Das, Taraknath. "The Struggle of Indians to Attain Equal Rights in the United States of America." *Modern Review* 80 (1946): 263–66.

Dean, Robert D. *Imperial Brotherhood: Gender and the Making of Cold War Foreign Policy*. Amherst: University of Massachusetts Press, 2001.

Deleuze, Gille, and Félix Guattari. *Kafka: Toward a Minor Literature*. Minneapolis: University of Minnesota Press, 1986. [1975].

de Mel, Neloufer. *Women and the Nation's Narrative: Gender and Nationalism in Twentieth Century Sri Lanka*. New Delhi: Kali for Women, 2001.

Denker, Joel. *World on a Plate: A Tour through a History of America's Ethnic Cuisines*. Boulder, Colo.: Westview Press, 2003.

Desai, S. K. *Santha Rama Rau*. New Delhi: Arnold-Heinemann Publishers, 1976.

Devi, Gayatri, and Santha Rama Rau. *A Princess Remembers: The Memories of the Maharani of Jaipur*. New Delhi: Tarang Paperbacks, 1976.

Dirlik, Arif. "The Postcolonial Aura: Third World Criticism in the Age of Global Capitalism." In Dirlik, ed., *The Postcolonial Aura: Third World Criticism in the Age of Global Capitalism*, 52–83. Boulder, Colo: Westview Press, 1997.

Douglas, George H. *The Smart Magazines: Fifty Years of Literary Revelry and High Jinks at "Vanity Fair," "The New Yorker," "Life," "Esquire," and "The Smart Set."* Hamden, Conn.: Shoestring Press, 1991.

Dudziak, Mary L. *Cold War Civil Rights: Race and the Image of American Democracy*. Princeton, N.J.: Princeton University Press, 2002.

Dumbrell, John. *A Special Relationship: Anglo-American Relations in the Cold War and After*. New York: St. Martin's Press, 2001.

Edwards, Brent Hayes. "The Shadow of Shadows." *positions* 11, 1 (2003): 11–49.

Elkins, Caroline. *Imperial Reckoning: The Untold Story of Britain's Gulag in Kenya*. New York: Henry Holt, 2005.

Espiritu, Augusto. *Five Faces of Exile: The Nation and Filipino American Intellectuals*. Stanford, Calif.: Stanford University Press, 2005.

Esty, Jed. *A Shrinking Island: Modernism and National Culture in England*. Princeton, N.J.: Princeton: University Press, 2004.

Fabian, Johannes. *Time and the Other: How Anthropology Makes Its Object*. New York: Columbia University Press, 1983.

Ferguson, James. "Decomposing Modernity: History and Hierarchy after Development." In Loomba et al., *Postcolonial Studies and Beyond*, 66–81.

Fisher, M. F. K. *The Cooking of Provincial France*. New York: Time-Life Books, 1968.

Fisher, Maxine P. *The Immigrants of New York City: A Study of Immigrants from India*. New Delhi: Heritage Publishers, 1980.

Galbraith, John Kenneth. *Ambassador's Journal: A Personal Account of the Kennedy Years*. Boston: Houghton Mifflin, 1969.

Ganguly, Debanji. "Convergent Cosmopolitics in the Age of Empire: Gandhi and Ambedkar in World History." *borderlands* (e-journal) 4, 3 (2005).

Ganguly, Keya. *States of Exception: Everyday Life and Postcolonial Identity*. Minneapolis: University of Minnesota Press, 2001.

George, Rosemary Marangoly. *The Politics of Home: Postcolonial Relocations and Twentieth Century Fiction*. New York: Cambridge University Press, 1996.

Ghosh, Bhishnupriya. *When Borne Across: Literary Cosmopolitics in the Contemporary Indian Novel*. New Brunswick, N.J.: Rutgers University Press, 2004.

Glazer, Sulochana Raghavan, and Nathan Glazer, eds. *Conflicting Images: India and the United States*. Glenn Dale, Md.: Riverdale Company, 1990.

Gomez, Michael A. *Reversing Sail: A History of the African Diaspora*. New York: Cambridge University Press, 2005.

Goody, Jack. *Cooking, Cuisine and Class: A Study in Comparative Sociology*. New York: Cambridge University Press, 1982.

Greet, Annie, Syd Harrex, and Susan Hosking, eds. *Raj Nostalgia: Some Literary and Critical Implications*. Bedford Park, Mass.: Centre for Research in the New Literatures in English, 1992.

Grewal, Inderpal. *Transnational America: Feminisms, Diasporas, Neoliberalisms*. Durham, N.C.: Duke University Press, 2005.

Grewal, Inderpal, and Caren Kaplan, eds. *Scattered Hegemonies: Postmodernity and Transnational Feminist Practices*. Minneapolis: University of Minnesota Press, 1994.

Guinness, Alec. *Blessings in Disguise*. New York: Alfred A. Knopf, 1986.

Hall, Stuart. "Political Belonging in a World of Multiple Identities." In Vertovec and Cohen, eds., *Concerning Cosmopolitanism*, 27–31.

Heller, J. *The Stern Gang: Ideology, Politics and Terror, 1940–1949*. London: Frank Cass, 1995.

Hoad, Neville. "*Welcome to Our Hillbrow:* An Elegy for African Cosmopolitanism." Paper, University of Illinois, Urbana-Champaign, spring 2005, in conjunction with the Illinois Program for Research in the Humanities reading group, Comparative Queer Studies.

Horne, Gerald. *Race War! White Supremacy and the Japanese attack on the British Empire*. New York: New York University Press, 2004.

Huggan, Graham. *The Postcolonial Exotic: Marketing the Margins*. London: Routledge, 2001.

Indian Council on Africa. *Nehru and Africa: Extracts from Jawaharlal Nehru's Speeches on Africa, 1946–1963*. New Delhi, 1964.

Isaacs, Harold. *Scratches on Our Minds: American Views of China and India*. Armonk, N.Y.: M. E. Sharpe, 1980 [1958].

Jaffrey, Madhur. *Invitation to Indian Cooking*. New York: Alfred A. Knopf, 1973.

———. *Madhur Jaffrey's Indian Cookery*. Woodbury, N.Y.: Barron's, 1983.

———. *Taste of India*. London: Pavilion Books, 1985.

Jensen, Joan M. *Passage from India: Asian Indian Immigrants in North America*. New Haven, Conn.: Yale University Press, 1988.

Jhabvala, Renana, and Namrata Bali, eds. *My Life, My Work: A Sociological Study of SEWA's Urban Members.* Ahmedabad: SEWA Academy, n.d.

Jones, Dorothy B. *The Portrayal of China and India on the American Screen, 1896–1955.* Cambridge: MIT Center for International Studies, 1955.

Kaplan, Caren. "Hillary Rodham Clinton's Orient: Cosmopolitan Travel and Global Feminist Subjects." *Meridians* 2, 1 (2001): 219–40.

Kaufman, Eric P. *The Rise and Fall of Anglo-America.* Cambridge, Mass.: Harvard University Press, 2004.

Keenleyside, T. A. "Nationalist Indian Attitudes towards Asia: A Troublesome Legacy for Post-Independence Indian Foreign Policy." *Pacific Affairs* 55, 2 (1982): 210–30.

Khandelwal, Madhulika S. *Becoming American, Being Indian: An Immigrant Community in New York City.* Ithaca, N.Y.: Cornell University Press, 2002.

Khare, R. S. *Culture and Reality: Essays on the Hindu System of Managing Foods.* Simla: Indian Institute of Advanced Study, 1976.

———, ed. *The Eternal Food: Gastronomic Ideas and Experiences of Hindus and Buddhists.* Albany: State University of New York Press, 1992.

Khare, R. S., and M. S. Rao, eds. *Food, Society and Culture: Aspects in South Asian Food Systems.* Durham, N.C.: Carolina Academic Press, 1986.

Klein, Christina. *Cold War Orientalism: Asia in the Middlebrow Imagination, 1945–1961.* Berkeley: University of California Press, 2003.

Kosambi, Meena, ed. *Pandita Ramabai's American Encounter.* Bloomington: Indiana University Press, 2003.

———. *Pandita Ramabai through Her Own Words: Selected Works.* Delhi: Oxford University Press, 2000.

Krasa, Molislav. "The Idea of Pan-Asianism and the Nationalist Movement in India." *Archiv Orientalni* 40 (1972): 238–60.

Krishnaswamy, Revathi. *Effeminism: The Economy of Colonial Desire.* Ann Arbor: University of Michigan Press, 1998.

Lago, Mary. "*A Passage to India* on Stage." *Times Literary Supplement,* February 22, 1985, 200.

Leong, Karen J. *The China Mystique: Pearl S. Buck, Anna May Wong, Mayling Soong, and the Transformation of American Orientalism.* Berkeley: University of California Press, 2005.

Linebaugh, Peter, and Marcus Rediker. *The Many-Headed Hydra: Sailors, Slaves,*

Commoners, and the Hidden History of the Revolutionary Atlantic. Boston: Beacon Press, 2000.

Lionnet, Françoise, and Shu-mei Shih, eds. *Minor Transnationalism*. Durham, N.C.: Duke University Press, 2005.

Lipsitz, George. *The Possessive Investment in Whiteness: How White People Profit from Identity Politics*. Philadelphia: Temple University Press, 1998.

Lloyd, David. *Nationalism and Minor Literature: James Clarence Mangan and the Emergence of Irish Cultural Nationalism*. Berkeley: University of California Press, 1987.

Logan, Frenise A. "Racism and Indian-U.S. Relations, 1947–1953: Views in the Indian Press." *Pacific Historical Review* 54, 1 (February 1985): 71–79.

Lonsdale, John. "Mau Maus of the Mind: Making Mau Mau and Remaking Kenya." *Journal of African History* 31 (1990): 393–421.

Loomba, Ania. *Shakespeare, Race and Colonialism*. New York: Oxford University Press, 2002.

Loomba, Ania, Suvir Kaul, Matti Bunzl, Antoinette Burton, and Jed Esty, eds. *Postcolonial Studies and Beyond*. Durham, N.C.: Duke University Press, 2005.

Louis, William Roger, and Hedley Bull, eds. *The "Special Relationship": Anglo-American Relations since 1945*. Oxford: Clarendon Press, 1986.

Ludden, David. "Maps in the Mind and the Mobility of Asia." *Journal of Asian Studies* 62, 4 (2003): 1057–78.

Mallon, Florencia. "The Promise and Dilemma of Subaltern Studies: Perspectives from Latin American History." *America Historical Review* 99, 5 (1994): 1491–1515.

Mani, Lata. *Contentious Traditions: The Debate on Sati in Colonial India*. Berkeley: University of California Press, 1998.

Margadant, Jo Burr, ed. *The New Biography: Performing Femininity in Nineteenth Century France*. Berkeley: University of California Press, 2000.

Markandaya, Kamala. *Nectar in a Sieve*. New York: John Day Company, 1954.

Marriott, McKim. "Caste Ranking and Food Transaction: A Matrix Analysis." In Milton Singer and Bernard S. Cohn, eds., *Structure and Change in Indian Society*, 133–172. Chicago: Aldine Publishing, 1968.

Mathur, Saloni. "Living Ethnological Exhibits: The Case of 1886." *Cultural Anthropology* 15, 4 (November 2000): 492–524.

Mehta, Ved. *Remembering Mr. Shawn's New Yorker*. Woodstock, N.Y.: Overlook Press, 1998.

Merchant, Ismail. *My Passage from India: A Filmmaker's Journey from Bombay to Hollywood and Beyond*. New York: Viking Studio, 2002.

Merrill, Dennis. *Bread and the Ballot: The United States and India's Economic Development*. Chapel Hill: University of North Carolina Press, 1990.

Merriweather, James H. *Proudly We Can Be Africans: Black Americans and Africa, 1935–1961*. Chapel Hill: University of North Carolina Press, 2002.

Mohanram, Radhika, and Gita Rajan, eds. *English Postcoloniality: Literatures from around the World*. Westport, Conn.: Greenwood Press, 1996.

Moraes, Frank, and Edward Howe, eds. *John Kenneth Galbraith Introduces India*. London: Andre Deutsch, 1974.

Moser, John E. *Twisting the Lion's Tail: American Anglophobia between the Wars*. New York: New York University Press, 1999.

Mukherjee, Bharati. *Jasmine*. New York: Grove Weidenfeld, 1989.

Mullen, Bill V. *Afro-Orientalism*. Minneapolis: University of Minnesota Press, 2004.

Nair, Rukmini Bhaya. *Lying on the Postcolonial Couch: The Idea of Indifference*. Minneapolis: University of Minnesota Press, 2002.

Nanda, B. R. *Jawaharlal Nehru: Rebel and Statesman*. New Delhi: Oxford University Press, 1998.

Nehru, Jawaharlal. *The Discovery of India*. Calcutta: Signet Press, 1946.

———. *Glimpses of World History*. New York: John Day Company, 1942.

———. *Independence and After: A Collection of Speeches, 1946–1949*. New York: John Day Company, 1950.

———. *India and the World*. London: George Allen Unwin, 1936.

———. *Soviet Russia: Some Random Sketches and Impressions*. Bombay: Chetna, 1949.

Neuhaus, Jessamyn. *Manly Meals and Mom's Home Cooking: Cookbooks and Gender in Modern America*. Baltimore: Johns Hopkins University Press, 2003.

Niranjana, Tejaswini. *Siting Translation: History, Post-Structuralism, and the Colonial Context*. Berkeley: University of California Press, 1992.

Noor, Farish. "Innocents Abroad: The Erasure of the Question of Race and Power in Contemporary Feminist and 'Nostalgic' Travelogues." *South East Asia Research* 5, 1 (1997): 57–88.

Nussbaum, Martha C. "Patriotism and Cosmopolitanism." In Nussbaum et al., *For Love of Country*, 2–17.

———. *Sex and Social Justice*. New York: Oxford University Press, 1999.

———. *Women and Human Development: The Capabilities Approach*. Cambridge: Cambridge University Press, 2000.

Nussbaum, Martha C., et al. *For Love of Country: Debating the Limits of Patriotism*. Edited by Joshua Cohen. Boston: Beacon Press, 1996.

Oberdeck, Kathryn J. *The Evangelist and the Impresario: Religion, Entertainment and Cultural Politics in America, 1884–1914*. Baltimore: Johns Hopkins University Press, 1999.

Okamoto, Shiro. *The Man Who Saved Kabuki: Faubion Bowers and Theatre Censorship in Occupied Japan*. Translated and adapted by Samuel L. T. Leiter. Honolulu: University of Hawaii Press, 2001.

Ong, Aiwha. *Flexible Citizenship: The Cultural Logics of Transnationality*. Durham, N.C.: Duke University Press, 1999.

Orde, Anne. *The Eclipse of Great Britain: The United States and British Imperial Decline, 1895–1956*. New York: St. Martin's Press, 1996.

Paisley, Fiona. "Citizens of the World: Australian Feminism and Indigenous Rights in the International Context, 1920s and 1930s." *Feminist Review* 58 (1998): 66–84.

Parry, Benita. "Overlapping Territories and Intertwined Histories: Edward Said's Postcolonial Cosmopolitanism." In Michael Sprinker, ed., *Edward Said: A Critical Reader*, 19–47. Oxford: Blackwell, 1992.

Plummer, Brenda Gayle. *Rising Wind: Black Americans and U.S. Foreign Affairs, 1935–1960*. Chapel Hill: University of North Carolina Press, 1996.

———, ed. *Window on Freedom: Race, Civil Rights and Foreign Affairs*. Chapel Hill: University of North Carolina Press, 2003.

Portes, Alejandro, Luis E. Guarnizo, and Patricia Landbolt. "The Study of Transnationalism: Pitfalls and Promise of an Emergent Research Field." *Ethnic and Racial Studies* 22, 2 (March 1999): 217–37.

Prashad, Vijay. *Everybody was Kung Fu Fighting: Afro-Asian Connections and the Myth of Cultural Purity*. Boston: Beacon Press, 2001.

———. *The Karma of Brown Folk*. Minneapolis: University of Minnesota Press, 2000.

Pratt, Mary Louise. *Imperial Eyes: Travel Writing and Transculturation*. New York: Routledge, 1992.

Radhakrishnan, R. "Toward an Eccentric Cosmopolitanism." *positions* 3, 3 (1995): 814–21.

Rafael, Vincente. "The Culture of Area Studies in the United States." *Social Text* 41 (winter 1994): 91–111.

Ralhan, O. P. *Jawaharlal Nehru Abroad.* Delhi: S.S. Publishers, 1983.

Rama Rau, Dhanvanthi. *An Inheritance.* New York: Harper and Row, 1977.

Rama Rau, Santha. *The Adventuress.* New York: Dell, 1970.

———. *The Cooking of India.* New York: Time-Life Books, 1969.

———. *East of Home.* New York: Harper, 1950.

———. *Gifts of Passage.* New York: Harper and Row, 1961.

———. *Home to India.* New York: Harper, 1945.

———. *My Russian Journey.* New York: Harper, 1959.

———. *A Passage to India: A Play by Santha Rama Rau from the Novel by E. M. Forster.* 1st American ed. New York: Harcourt, Brace and World, 1961.

———. *This Is India.* New York: Harper, 1954.

———. *A View to the Southeast.* New York: Harper Brothers 1957.

Rangaswamy, Padma. *Namasté America: Indian Immigrants in an American Metropolis.* University Park.: Penn State University Press, 2000.

Raucher, Alan. "American Anti-Imperialists and the Pro-Indian Movement, 1900–1932." *Pacific Historical Review* 43, 1 (1974): 83–110.

Robbins, Bruce. "Celeb-Reliance: Intellectuals, Celebrity, and Upward Mobility." *Radical History Review* 76 (2000): 3–14.

———. "The East Is a Career: Edward Said and the Logics of Professionalism." In Michael Sprinker, ed., *Edward Said: A Critical Reader,* 48–73. Oxford: Blackwell, 1992.

Roberts, Mary Louise. *Disruptive Acts: The New Woman in Fin-de-Siècle France.* Chicago: University of Chicago Press, 2002.

Rose, Kalima. *Where Women Are Leaders: The SEWA Movement in India.* New Delhi: Vistaar Publications, 1992.

Rotter, Andrew. *Comrades at Odds: The United States and India, 1947–64.* Ithaca, N.Y.: Cornell University Press, 2000.

Roy, Parama. "Reading Communities and Culinary Communities: The Gastropoetics of the South Asian Diaspora." *positions* 10, 2 (2002): 473–502.

Rushdie, Salman. *Imaginary Homelands: Essays and Criticism, 1981–1991.* London: Penguin, 1991.

Rustomji-Kerns, Roshni. "Expatriates, Immigrants and Literature: Three South Asian Women Writers." *Massachusetts Review* 29, 4 (winter 1988): 855–65.

Rutherford, Andrew, ed. *Twentieth Century Interpretations of "A Passage to India":
A Collection of Critical Essays.* New Jersey: Prentice Hall, 1970.

Ryan, Alan, "The Magic of 'I.'" Review of Kwame Anthony Appiah's *The Ethics
of Identity. New York Review of Books*, April 28, 2005, 35.

Sahgal, Nayantara. *Prison and Chocolate Cake.* New York: Alfred A. Knopf, 1954.

Schein, Louisa. "Gender and Internal Orientalism in China." In Susan Brownell
and Jeffery N. Wasserstrom, eds., *Chinese Femininities / Chinese Masculinities:
A Reader*, 385–411. Berkeley: University of California Press, 2002.

Schueller, Malini Johar. "Articulations of African-Americanisms in South Asian
Postcolonial Theory: Globalism, Localism and the Question of Race." *Cultural Critique* 55 (fall 2003): 35–62.

Shukla, Sandhya. *Indians Abroad: Diasporic Cultures of Postwar America and
England.* Princeton, N.J.: Princeton University Press, 2003.

Singh, K. Natwar. *Curtain Raisers: Essays, Reviews, Letters.* New Delhi: Vikas,
1984.

———. *E. M. Forster: A Tribute.* New York: Harcourt Brace, 1964.

———. *Profiles and Letters.* New Delhi: Rupa and Co., 2003.

Singham, A. W., and Shirley Hune. *Non-Alignment in an Age of Alignments.*
London: Zed Books, 1986.

Sinha, Mrinalini. *Colonial Masculinity: The "Manly Englishman" and the "Effeminate Bengali" in the Late Nineteenth Century.* Manchester: Manchester University Press, 1995.

———. *Specters of Mother India: The Global Restructuring of an Empire.* Durham,
N.C.: Duke University Press, 2006.

Spivak, Gayatri Chakravorty. *A Critique of Postcolonial Reason: Toward a History
of the Vanishing Present.* Cambridge, Mass.: Harvard University Press, 1999.

Stape, J. H., ed. *E. M. Forster: Critical Assessments.* Volume 1. East Sussex: Helm
Information, 1997.

Strauss, Helen M. *A Talent for Luck: An Autobiography.* New York: Random
House, 1979.

Tagore, Rabindranath. *The Diary of a Westward Voyage.* London: Asia Publishing House, 1962.

———. *Letters from Russia.* Calcutta: Visva-Bharati, 1960.

———. *A Visit to Japan.* New York: East West Institute, 1961.

Taylor, Charles, et al. *Multiculturalism and "The Politics of Recognition."* Princeton, N.J.: Princeton: University Press, 1992.

Trilling, Lionel. *E. M. Forster.* Norfolk, Conn.: New Directions Books, 1943.

van der Veer, Peter. "Colonial Cosmopolitanism." In Vertovec and Cohen, eds., *Conceiving Cosmopolitanism,* 165–79.

Vassanji, M. G. *The In-Between World of Vikram Lall.* New York: Alfred A. Knopf, 2004.

Vertovec, Steven, and Robin Cohen, eds. *Conceiving Cosmopolitanism: Theory, Context and Practice.* New York: Oxford University Press, 2002.

von Eschen, Penny. *Race against Empire: Black Americans and Anti-Colonialism, 1937–1957.* Ithaca, N.Y.: Cornell University Press, 1997.

——. *Satchmo Blows Up the World: Jazz Ambassadors Play the Cold War.* Cambridge, Mass.: Harvard University Press, 2004.

Wainwright, Martin. *Inheritance of Empire: Britain, India, and the Balance of Power in Asia, 1938–55.* Westport, Conn.: Praeger, 1994.

Walkowitz, Rebecca L. *Cosmopolitan Style: Modernism beyond the Nation.* New York: Columbia University Press, 2006.

Woollacott, Angela. "'All This is the Empire, I Told Myself': Australian Women's Voyages 'Home' and the Articulation of Colonial Whiteness." *American Historical Review* 102, 4 (October 1997): 1003–1029.

——. *To Try Her Fortune in London: Australian Women, Colonialism and Modernity.* New York: Oxford University Press, 2000.

Zimmer, Heinrich. *The Art of Indian Asia.* Completed and edited by Joseph Campbell. Princeton, N.J.: Princeton University Press, 1955.

——. *Myths and Symbols in Indian Art and Civilization.* New York: Harper Torch Books, 1946.

Elizabeth II, 92, 94
Erlich, Arnold, 123

Famine in India, 115–116, 120, 122
Flair (magazine), 6
Food: socio-cultural analysis and,
111–112, 140–142, 144; women
and, 142
Forster, E. M., 13–15, 74, 77, 78, 80–
81, 101, 103–104, 108. See also *Passage to India*; Rama Rau, Santha
Fox, Gardner, 5

Gender: in Africa, 64–65; Cold War
politics and, 54, 57, 83–84; cosmopolitanism and, 19–20, 34–35, 53–
54, 113–114, 116, 123, 164 n. 19;
food and, 142; postcoloniality and,
6. See also Domesticity
Gifts of Passage (1961), 4, 144, 145,
151–152. See also *Cooking of India*:
as autobiography
Goolrick, Bill, 124–130, 133–137, 141.
See also Time-Life
Guinness, Alec, 102

Han Suyin, 6, 57
Harper (publisher), 6, 8, 50, 70, 128
Hauser, Frank, 77, 79–81. See also
Passage to India (play)
Holiday (magazine), 1, 5, 6, 55–57
Home to India (1945), 8, 32, 47, 90;
Americanism and, 39–42, 99;
domesticity and, 39–44, 113;
locality and, 42–44; orientalist cosmopolitanism of, 39–44, 113; pop-

ularity of, 4, 6, 7, 61, 88; postcoloniality and, 61; as translation of
"East to West," 6, 7, 10, 39–44
Hybridity, 117, 119, 121, 133, 139. See
also *Cooking of India*

Imperialism, U.S., 45–46, 48, 107–108
India: at exhibition, 72–73; national
cuisine and, 116, 119; partition, 90,
135; as urban, 120, 137. *See also*
Cold War: politics; *Cooking of
India*; Cosmopolitanism: Indian;
Home to India
India-Japan relations, 44–45
India-Soviet Union relations, 69. *See
also* Nehru, Jawaharlal
India-United States relations, 13, 67–
68, 83, 93–94, 135. *See also* American audiences; Kennedy, John F.;
Nehru, Jawaharlal
Indonesia, 124–126

Jaffrey, Madhur, 111–113, 122, 139,
142
Jaffrey, Sayeed, 77
*JANA: The News Magazine of Resurgent
Asia and Africa*, 9
Japan, 44–57. See also *East of Home*
Jones, Dorothy B., 5

Kashmir, 102, 116–117
Kennedy, Jacqueline, 5, 179 n. 93;
tour of India and Pakistan, 93–94
Kennedy, John F., 74, 83, 93, 107
Kenya, 15, 59–67, 170 n. 118. *See also*
Mau Mau Rebellion

Ross, Harold, 3, 152
Round Table Conference, 2, 38, 42
Roy, Arundhati, 2, 149–150
Roy, Parama, 112
Rushdie, Salman, 149

Said, Edward, 4, 21, 23 27, 82
Saint, Irene, 127. *See also* Time-Life
Schueller, Malini Johar, 28–29
Sexuality, 47, 104

Tagore, Rabindranath, 35, 36, 69
Teja, Devika, 131
This Is India (1954), 4, 154 n. 13, 154 n. 19
Time-Life, 122–130, 133–137, 141
Transnationalism: minor, 9; history and, 148
Travel writing, 32, 33, 39, 44, 47, 50, 56, 62, 68, 91–94, 114–115, 118, 147

United States audiences. *See* American audiences

United States civil rights movement, 15–16, 67–68, 87, 96, 147
United States imperialism, 45–46, 48, 107–108
United States-India relations. *See* India-United States relations

Visual culture, 55–57, 121, 128

Wellesley College, 3, 43, 114, 165 n. 42
Whiteness, 13. *See also* Anglo-American relations; Race and racial difference
William Morris (talent agency), 8, 76, 123–124
Williams, Dick, 124, 126–127. *See also* Time-Life
Woman of Kali, 5
Women: cosmopolitanism and, 35–37; food and, 142; informants, 47–48; politics and, 91
Wong, Anna May, 6
World literature, 22–23

Antoinette Burton is the Catherine C. and Bruce A. Bastian Professor of Global and Transnational Studies at the University of Illinois, Urbana-Champaign. She is the author of *Dwelling in the Archive: Women Writing House, Home, and History in Colonial India* (2003), *At the Heart of the Empire: Indians and the Colonial Encounter in Late-Victorian Britain* (1998), and *Burdens of History: British Feminists, Indian Women, and Imperial Culture, 1865–1915* (1994). She has edited *Archive Stories: Facts, Fiction, and the Writing of History* (Duke University Press, 2005), *After the Imperial Turn: Thinking with and through the Nation* (Duke University Press, 2003), *Family History: Janaki Agnes Penelope Majumdar, 1886–1963* (2003), *Politics and Empire in Victorian Britain: A Reader* (2001), and *Gender, Sexuality, and Colonial Modernities* (1999). She is the coeditor of *Bodies in Contact: Rethinking Colonial Encounters in World History* (with Tony Ballantyne, Duke University Press, 2005), and of *Postcolonial Studies and Beyond* (with Ania Loomba, Suvir Kaul, Matti Bunzl, and Jed Esty, Duke University Press, 2005). With Jean Allman, she edits the *Journal of Women's History*.

Library of Congress Cataloging-in-Publication Data

Burton, Antoinette M.

The postcolonial careers of Santha Rama Rau / Antoinette Burton.

p. cm. — (Next wave: new directions in women's studies)

Includes bibliographical references and index.

ISBN-13: 978-0-8223-4050-8 (cloth : acid-free paper)

ISBN-13: 978-0-8223-4071-3 (pbk. : acid-free paper)

1. Rama Rau, Santha, 1923–

2. Women authors, Indic—20th century—Biography.

3. East Indian Americans—United States—Biography.

4. India—In literature.

I. Title. PR9499.3.R327Z6 2007

828'.5209—dc22

2007014063

ANT-9814